CW00607096

CHARMING
SMALL HOTEL
GUIDES

Britain

CHARMING SMALL HOTEL GUIDES

Britain

Edited by Chris Gill

DUNCAN PETERSEN

HUNTER
PUBLISHING INC

300 Raritan Center Parkway,
CN 94, Edison, N.J. 08818

Conceived, designed and produced by
Duncan Petersen Publishing Ltd,
Edited by Fox and Partners, The Old Forge,
Norton St Philip, Bath, U.K.

Editor	Chris Gill
Assistant editors	Amanda Crook, Ian Stratford
Proof reader	Edward Hunt
Production editor	Nicola Davies
Art director	Mel Petersen

This edition published in the UK and Commonwealth 1994 by
Duncan Petersen Publishing Ltd,
54 Milson Road, London W14 OLB,
and distributed by
Automobile Association Publishing,
c/o Exel Logistics MS,
Invicta Warehouse, Sir Thomas Langley Road,
Medway City Estate, Rochester, Kent

ISBN 1 872576 28 1

A CIP catalogue record for this book is available
from the British Library

AND

Published in the USA 1994 by
Hunter Publishing Inc.,
300 Raritan Center Parkway, CN 94, Edison, N.J. 08818.
Tel (908) 225 1900 Fax (908) 417 0482

ISBN 1-55650-634-1

Typeset by Fox and Partners, Bath and PCS TYpesetting, Frome
Originated by Reprocolor International S.R.I., Milan
Printed by G. Canale & Co SpA, Turin

Contents

Readers' reports

Reports from readers are of enormous help to us in keeping up to date with the hotels in the guide – and other hotels that should be in it. The most helpful reporters are invited to join our Travellers' Panel, and to stay in listed hotels at little or no cost. More information on p216.

Introduction

This guide to hotels in Britain and Ireland – completely revised for 1994 – is part of a series also covering France, Italy, Spain, Germany, Austria and Switzerland.

The *Charming Small Hotel Guides* are different from other accommodation guides. The most fundamental difference is suggested by the title: we aim to include only those hotels and guest-houses which are in some way captivating, and which offer truly personal service, usually from the owner. In this volume, most of our recommendations have fewer than 15 rooms.

The guides are different in other ways, too. Our entries employ, above all, words: they contain not one symbol. They are written by people with something to say, not a bureaucracy which has long since lost the ability to distinguish the praiseworthy from the mediocre. Every entry aims to give a definite feel of what it is actually like to stay in that place. The editorial team is small and highly experienced at assessing hotels, at noticing all-important details. Although we place great emphasis on consistency, we make use of reports from readers, and would welcome more of them (see page 216).

These are features which will reveal their worth as you use your *Charming Small Hotel Guide*. Its other advantages are more obvious: it contains colour photographs of about one-third of the entries – usually the more attractive ones; the entries are presented in clear geographical groups; and each entry is categorized by the type of accommodation (for example, country inn).

Our ideal hotel has a peaceful, pretty setting; the building itself is either handsome or historic, or at least has a distinct character. The rooms are spacious, but on a human scale – not grand or intimidating. The decorations and furnishings are harmonious, comfortable and impeccably maintained, and include antique pieces that are meant to be used, not revered. The proprietors and staff are dedicated, thoughtful and sensitive in their pursuit of their guests' happiness – friendly and welcoming without being intrusive. Last but not least, the food, whether simple or ambitious, is fresh, interesting and carefully prepared. Elaborate facilities such as trouser-presses count for little.

Despite its title, this guide does not confine itself to places called hotels, or places that behave like hotels. On the contrary, we actively look for places that offer a home-from-home. We include pubs, guest-houses and bed-and-breakfast establishments; and we include quite a number of places that operate on 'house-party' lines, where you are introduced to other guests and take meals at a communal table. Many such places are part of a marketing group called Wolsey Lodges.

Introduction

Small hotels in Britain and Ireland
No one who has observed the changes that have taken
place on the British hotel scene over the last 20 years can
fail to be impressed by the improvement in the style and
quality of what is available – particularly on the culinary
front, where the progress has been little short of
spectacular. Small hotels of the kind that are our
stock-in-trade are in the forefront of this revolution.
Some of the most comfortable hotel rooms in the land
are in 'our' hotels, and some of the best food is served in
dining-rooms of domestic size, in establishments that
have no pretensions to restaurant status. Naturally, we are
delighted to be part of this trend, and to encourage its
continuation.

But small hotels are not automatically wonderful
hotels; and the very individuality of small, owner-run
hotels makes them prone to peculiarities that the
mass-produced hotel experience avoids. For the benefit
of those who run the small hotels of Britain – and those
contemplating the plunge – we have looked back over
the past year of hotel-going to identify some pet hates.

The Hushed Dining-room This commonly results when
an establishment falls between the two stools of a really
small place, where the owner makes sure the ice is
broken, and the not-so-small hotel, where there are
enough people to create a bit of a hubbub.

The Ordinary Breakfast Even hotels that go to great
lengths to prepare special dinners are capable of serving
prefabricated orange juice and sliced bread at breakfast.

The Schoolteacher Mentality People tempted to set up
small hotels should perhaps undergo psychometric
testing to determine whether they are sufficiently flexible
and accommodating to deal with the whims of travellers;
some of them certainly are not.

The Excess of Informality At one not-cheap London
address this year (one which did not find its way into the
guide) we were shown around by a young man in jeans
(which might be acceptable) and socks (which is not).

The Inexperienced Waiter Or waitress. Running a small
operation does not excuse the imposition on the paying
public of completely untrained (and sometime ill-suited)
staff who can spoil the most beautifully cooked meal.

The Imposing Name An unimportant one, this, but an
irritant nonetheless. A charmingly cosy whitewashed
cottage in the Lake District does not, in our view,
constitute a 'country house hotel'.

The Lumpy Old Bed Surely, every hotel proprietor knows
that they should occasionally sleep in each of the beds in
each of their rooms? Otherwise, it's the easiest thing in
the world to fail to spot the gradual decay of a mattress.

Introduction

How to find an entry
In this guide, the entries are arranged in convenient
geographical groups, and these groups are arranged in a
sequence starting in the extreme south-west (Cornwall)
and working west to east and south to north. Ireland
comes last in the sequence.

To find a hotel in a particular area, simply browse
through headings at the top of the pages until you find
that area – or use the maps following this introduction to
locate the appropriate pages. To locate a specific hotel or
a hotel in a specific place, use the indexes at the back,
which list the entries alphabetically, first by name and
then by place-name.

How to read an entry
At the top of each entry is a coloured bar highlighting
the name of the town or village where the establishment
is located, along with a categorization which gives some
clue to its character. These categories are as, far as
possible, self-explanatory. 'Country house hotel' needs,
perhaps, some qualification: it is reserved for places
whose style is appropriately gracious.

Fact boxes
The fact box given for each hotel follows a standard
pattern which requires little explanation; but:

Under **Tel** we give the telephone number starting with
the area code used within the United Kingdom; when
dialling from another country, omit the initial zero.

Under **Location** we give information on the setting of the
hotel and on its parking arrangements, as well as pointers
to help you find it.

Under **Food & drink** we list the meals available. A 'full'
breakfast is a traditional British hot meal of bacon, eggs
and so on; such a breakfast may be available at extra cost,
even in hotels where we have not mentioned it.

We also say what licence the hotel possesses for the sale
of alcoholic drinks. A restaurant licence permits the sale
of drinks with meals, a residential licence permits the sale
of drinks to those staying in the hotel, and a full licence
permits the sale of drinks to anyone over the age of 18
during certain prescribed hours.

All the **Prices** in this volume – unlike those on France,
Italy, Spain, Germany and Austria – are **per person**.

Normally, a range of prices is given, representing the
smallest and largest amounts you might pay in different

Introduction

circumstances – typically, the minimum is half the cost of the cheapest double room in low season, while the maximum is the cost of the dearest single in high season.

We give prices for bed and breakfast unless dinner is inescapable. After the B&B price, we give either the price for dinner, bed and breakfast (DB&B), or for full board (FB – that is, all meals included) or, instead, an indication of the cost of individual meals. After all this basic information comes, where space allows, a summary of reductions available for long stays or for children.

Rates include tax and service. Wherever possible we have given prices for 1994, but for many hotels these were not available; actual prices may therefore be higher than those quoted, simply because of inflation. But bear in mind also that the proprietors of hotels and guest-houses may change their prices from one year to another by much more than the rate of inflation. Always check when making a booking.

Our lists of facilities in **Rooms** cover only mechanical gadgets, and not ornaments such as flowers or consumables such as toiletries or free drinks.

Under **Facilities** we list public rooms and then outdoor and sporting facilities which are either part of the hotel or immediately on hand; facilities in the vicinity of the hotel, but not directly connected with it (for example, a nearby golf-course) are not listed, though they sometimes feature at the end of the main description in the **Nearby** section, which presents a selection of interesting things to see or do in the locality.

We use the following abbreviations for **Credit cards**:

AE	American Express
DC	Diners Club
MC	MasterCard (Access/Eurocard)
V	Visa (Barclaycard/Bank Americard/Carte Bleue etc)

The final entry in a fact box is normally the name of the **Proprietor(s)**; but where the hotel is run by a manager we give his or her name instead.

Unfamiliar terms
'Self-catering' means that cooking facilities such as a kitchenette or small kitchen are provided for making your own meals, as in a rental apartment. 'Bargain breaks' or 'breaks' of any kind mean off-season price reductions are available, usually for a stay of a specific or minimum period.

Hotel location maps

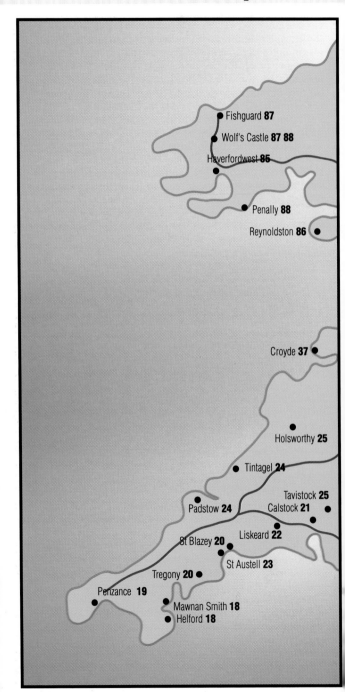

Fishguard **87**

Wolf's Castle **87 88**

Haverfordwest **85**

Penally **88**

Reynoldston **86**

Croyde **37**

Holsworthy **25**

Tintagel **24**

Tavistock **25**

Calstock **21**

Padstow **24**

Liskeard **22**

St Blazey **20**

St Austell **23**

Tregony **20**

Penzance **19**

Mawnan Smith **18**

Helford **18**

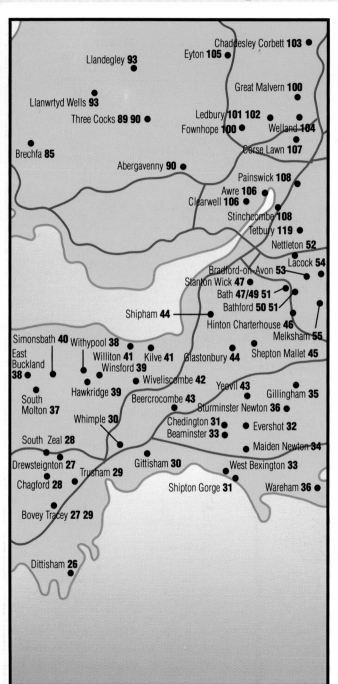

Chaddesley Corbett **103**
Eyton **105**
Llandegley **93**
Great Malvern **100**
Llanwrtyd Wells **93**
Three Cocks **89 90**
Ledbury **101 102**
Fownhope **100**
Welland **104**
Brechfa **85**
Corse Lawn **107**
Abergavenny **90**
Painswick **108**
Awre **106**
Clearwell **106**
Stinchcombe **108**
Tetbury **119**
Nettleton **52**
Lacock **54**
Bradford-on-Avon **53**
Stanton Wick **47**
Bath **47/49 51**
Shipham **44**
Bathford **50 51**
Hinton Charterhouse **46**
Melksham **55**
Simonsbath **40** Withypool **38**
East
Buckland
38
Williton **41** Kilve **41** Glastonbury **44** Shepton Mallet **45**
Winsford **39**
Wiveliscombe **42**
Hawkridge **39**
Yeovil **43**
Gillingham **35**
South
Molton **37**
Beercrocombe **43**
Whimple **30**
Sturminster Newton **36**
Chedington **31** Evershot **32**
Beaminster **33**
South Zeal **28**
Maiden Newton **34**
Drewsteignton **27**
Gittisham **30**
West Bexington **33**
Trusham **29**
Chagford **28**
Shipton Gorge **31**
Wareham **36**
Bovey Tracey **27 29**
Dittisham **26**

11

Hotel location maps

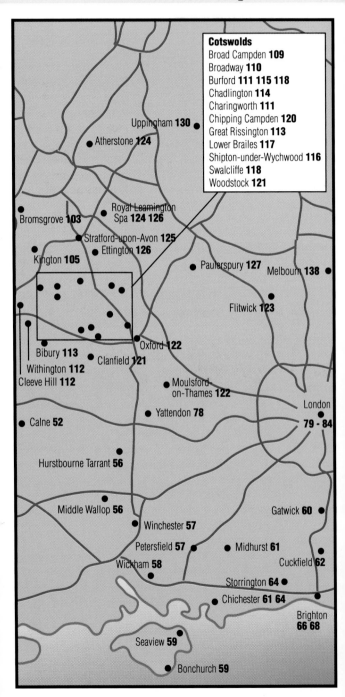

Cotswolds
Broad Campden **109**
Broadway **110**
Burford **111 115 118**
Chadlington **114**
Charingworth **111**
Chipping Campden **120**
Great Rissington **113**
Lower Brailes **117**
Shipton-under-Wychwood **116**
Swalcliffe **118**
Woodstock **121**

Uppingham **130**
Atherstone **124**

Bromsgrove **103**
Royal Leamington
Spa **124 126**
Stratford-upon-Avon **125**
Kington **105**
Ettington **126**
Paulerspury **127**
Melbourn **138**
Flitwick **123**
Bibury **113**
Oxford **122**
Withington **112**
Clanfield **121**
Cleeve Hill **112**
Moulsford-
on-Thames **122**
London
79 - 84
Yattendon **78**
Calne **52**
Hurstbourne Tarrant **56**
Middle Wallop **56**
Gatwick **60**
Winchester **57**
Petersfield **57**
Midhurst **61**
Cuckfield **62**
Wickham **58**
Storrington **64**
Chichester **61 64**
Brighton
66 68
Seaview **59**
Bonchurch **59**

Hotel location maps

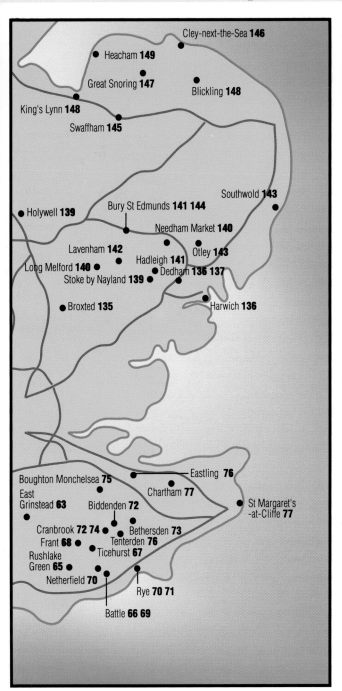

Cley-next-the-Sea **146**

Heacham **149**

Great Snoring **147**

Blickling **148**

King's Lynn **148**

Swaffham **145**

Southwold **143**

Holywell **139**

Bury St Edmunds **141 144**

Needham Market **140**

Lavenham **142**

Otley **143**

Hadleigh **141**

Long Melford **140**

Dedham **135 137**

Stoke by Nayland **139**

Broxted **135**

Harwich **136**

Boughton Monchelsea **75**

Eastling **76**

East
Grinstead **63**

Chartham **77**

Biddenden **72**

St Margaret's
-at-Cliffe **77**

Cranbrook **72 74**

Bethersden **73**

Frant **68**

Tenterden **76**

Rushlake
Green **65**

Ticehurst **67**

Netherfield **70**

Rye **70 71**

Battle **66 69**

Hotel location maps

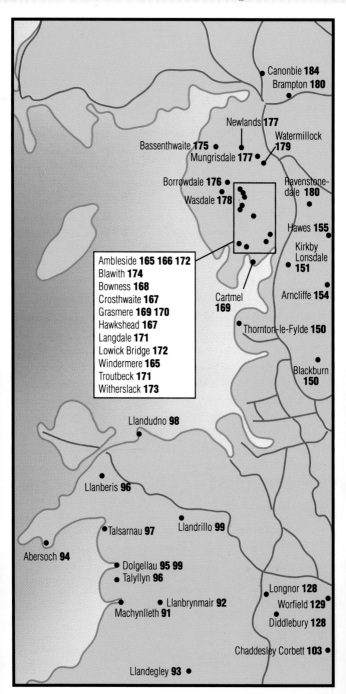

Canonbie **184**
Brampton **180**

Newlands **177**

Bassenthwaite **175** •
Watermillock **179**

Mungrisdale **177**

Borrowdale **176** •
Ravenstone-dale **180**

Wasdale **178**

Hawes **155**

Kirkby Lonsdale **151**

Ambleside **165 166 172**
Blawith **174**
Bowness **168**
Crosthwaite **167**
Grasmere **169 170**
Hawkshead **167**
Langdale **171**
Lowick Bridge **172**
Windermere **165**
Troutbeck **171**
Witherslack **173**

Arncliffe **154**

Cartmel **169**

Thornton-le-Fylde **150**

Blackburn **150**

Llandudno **98**

Llanberis **96**

Talsarnau **97**
Llandrillo **99**

Abersoch **94**

Dolgellau **95 99**
Talyllyn **96**

Longnor **128**
Worfield **129**

Llanbrynmair **92**
Machynlleth **91**
Diddlebury **128**

Chaddesley Corbett **103** •

Llandegley **93** •

14

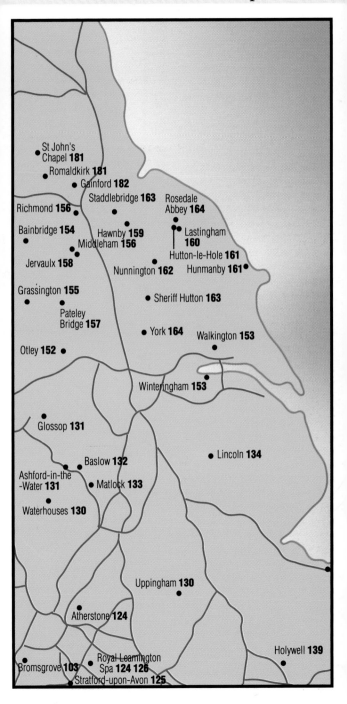

St John's
Chapel **181**
Romaldkirk **181**
Gainford **182**
Staddlebridge **163**
Rosedale
Abbey **164**
Richmond **156**
Bainbridge **154**
Hawnby **159**
Lastingham
160
Middleham **156**
Hutton-le-Hole **161**
Jervaulx **158**
Nunnington **162**
Hunmanby **161**
Grassington **155**
Sheriff Hutton **163**
Pateley
Bridge **157**
York **164**
Walkington **153**
Otley **152**
Winteringham **153**
Glossop **131**
Lincoln **134**
Baslow **132**
Ashford-in-the
-Water **131**
Matlock **133**
Waterhouses **130**
Uppingham **130**
Atherstone **124**
Holywell **139**
Royal Leamington
Spa **124 126**
Bromsgrove **103**
Stratford-upon-Avon **125**

Hotel location maps

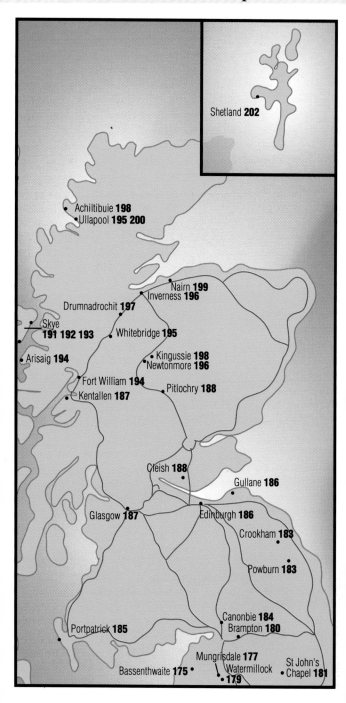

Shetland **202**

Achiltibuie **198**
Ullapool **195 200**

Nairn **199**
Inverness **196**
Drumnadrochit **197**
Skye
191 192 193   Whitebridge **195**
Arisaig **194**
Kingussie **198**
Newtonmore **196**
Fort William **194**
Kentallen **187**   Pitlochry **188**

Cleish **188**
Gullane **186**
Glasgow **187**   Edinburgh **186**
Crookham **183**

Powburn **183**

Canonbie **184**
Brampton **180**
Portpatrick **185**
Mungrisdale **177**   St John's
Bassenthwaite **175**   Watermillock   Chapel **181**
179

16

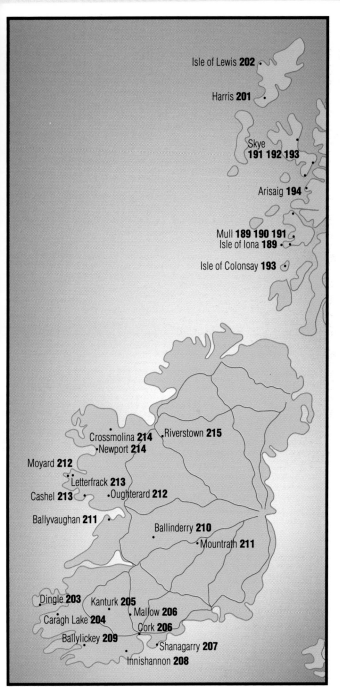

Isle of Lewis **202**

Harris **201**

Skye
191 192 193

Arisaig **194**

Mull **189 190 191**
Isle of Iona **189**

Isle of Colonsay **193**

Crossmolina **214**   Riverstown **215**
Newport **214**

Moyard **212**
Letterfrack **213**
Cashel **213**   Oughterard **212**

Ballyvaughan **211**

Ballinderry **210**

Mountrath **211**

Dingle **203**   Kanturk **205**
Caragh Lake **204**   Mallow **206**
Cork **206**
Ballylickey **209**
Shanagarry **207**
Innishannon **208**

West Cornwall

Riverside

This row of charming whitewashed cottages in a seductive spot beside a tidal creek has strong echoes of the French country restaurant with rooms, with its flowery terraces, beamed dining-room and simple, pretty and adequately spacious bedrooms. An inspector was deeply impressed by the tasteful decoration and furnishing, the 'outstanding' food, making excellent use of local fresh fish and organic vegetables, and the excellent wine list. Service approaches perfection – attentive but relaxed and unobtrusive. Breakfast features home-made croissants and marmalade.
Nearby Glendurgan Garden, one mile (1.5 km); Lizard Peninsula.

Helford, near Helston, Cornwall TR12 6JU
Tel (0326) 231443 **Fax** 231103
Location 12 miles (19 km) E of Helston in village; with garden and ample car parking
Food & drink breakfast, dinner; light lunch, picnic by arrangement; restaurant licence
Prices B&B £37.50-£47.50; dinner £18-£28
Rooms 7 double, all with bath; all rooms have central heating, TV, tea/coffee kit, minibar
Facilities sitting-room, dining-room
Credit cards not accepted
Children welcome; camp beds, cots and high tea provided – under 10 not allowed at dinner
Disabled access possible but difficult
Pets not accepted
Closed late Nov to early Feb
Proprietor Susie Darrell

Nansidwell

This turn-of-the-century house was long since converted to a hotel but only since 1988 has it been in the hands of Jamie and Felicity Robertson – he an ex-London restaurateur, she an ex-banker. The stone-mullioned house has a glorious setting, in large sub-tropical gardens with the Cornwall Coast Path only a stroll away. To this sound basis the Robertsons have added cosy but tasteful traditional decoration, home-like trimmings (magazines, fresh flowers, open fires) and ambitious, original cooking, including home-smoked salmon. More reports welcome.
Nearby Glendurgan and Trebah gardens, both one mile (1.5 km).

Mawnan Smith, Falmouth, Cornwall TR11 5HU
Tel (0326) 250340
Fax (0326) 250440
Location 0.5 mile (0.8 km) SW of village, SW of Falmouth; in gardens, with ample car parking
Food & drink breakfast, lunch, dinner, residential and restaurant licence
Prices DB&B £65-£93
Rooms 12 double, all with bath; all rooms have central heating, colour TV, phone
Facilities 2 sitting-rooms, dining-room; tennis
Credit cards MC, V
Children accepted
Disabled access possible – 2 ground-floor bedrooms
Pets accepted by arrangement
Closed Jan
Proprietors Jamie and Felicity Robertson

West Cornwall

Town guest-house, Penzance

The Abbey

Jean and Michael Cox have taken a characterful house in the heart of old Penzance (it was built in the mid-17th century and given a Gothic façade in Regency times); they have decorated and furnished it with unstinting care, great flair and a considerable budget; and they have called it a hotel. But they run it much more as a private house, and visitors who expect to find hosts eager to satisfy their every whim are liable to be disappointed. If you poke your head into the kitchen in search of (say) a sandwich, you may or may not find someone able and willing to provide it – though your chances have improved with the arrival of chef/manager Glyn Green.

For its fans, the absence of hovering flunkies is of course a key part of the appeal of The Abbey. But there are other attractions – the confident and original decor, with abundant antiques and bric-a-brac, the spacious, individual bedrooms (one with an enormous pine-panelled bathroom); the welcoming, flowery drawing-room and elegant dining-room (both with log fires burning 'year-round'); the delightful walled garden behind the house; and not least, the satisfying dinners. Front rooms overlook the harbour and the somewhat noisy dry dock.

Nearby Tregwainton Garden, 1.5 miles (2.5 km), St Michael's Mount, 3.5 miles (5.5 km); Land's End, 10 miles (16 km).

Abbey Street, Penzance,
Cornwall TR18 4AR
Tel (0736) 66906
Location in middle of town, overlooking harbour; with private parking for 6 cars in courtyard
Food & drink breakfast, dinner; residential and restaurant licence
Prices B&B £40-£65; dinner £22.50
Rooms 6 double, 3 with bath, 3 with shower; one suite with bath; all rooms have central heating, tea/coffee kit, colour TV
Facilities sitting-room, dining-room
Credit cards AE, MC
Children welcome if well behaved
Disabled access difficult
Pets dogs allowed in bedrooms
Closed never
Proprietors Jean and Michael Cox

South Cornwall

Country guest-house, St Blazey

Nanscawen House

A respected Bath hotelier first drew our attention to this relaxing retreat, having been repeatedly impressed by Janet Martin's 'first-class' dinners (four set courses, not available in July or August) and warmth of welcome. An inspection confirms the attractions of the carefully extended old house, in beautiful mature gardens. There are only three rooms, all comfortable with good bathrooms; the vast Rashleigh is worth its extra £10. There is a welcoming sitting-room; you normally eat in the cane-furnished conservatory. The pool is pleasantly secluded and sunny, with a fine view. No smoking is permitted.

Nearby beaches, coast path; Lanhydrock House, 6 miles (10 km).

Prideaux Road, St Blazey, nr Par, Cornwall PL24 2SR **Tel** and **Fax** (0726) 814488 **Location** in countryside, 0.5 mile (1 km) off A390, NW of St Blazey, 3 miles (5 km) NE of St Austell; in 5-acre grounds, with car parking **Food & drink** breakfast, dinner (not in Jul, Aug); residential licence **Prices** B&B £30-£50; dinner £22.50; DB&B Nov to Feb £40	**Rooms** 3 double (one twin), all with spa bath; all have TV, phone, central heating, radio, hairdrier; video on request **Facilities** sitting-room, conservatory dining-room; heated outdoor swimming-pool **Credit cards** MC, V **Children** not accepted under 12 **Disabled** access difficult **Pets** not accepted **Closed** Christmas, 2 days **Proprietors** Janet and Keith Martin

---

Village guest-house, Tregony

Tregony House

We get a steady trickle of favourable reports from visitors to this friendly guest-house which fronts on to the main street of Tregony, as it has since the seventeenth century – when this was an important river port, and not a neglected backwater. Barry Sullivan tends the rooms, the guests and the wine-list, while his wife Judith cooks imaginative meals based on local produce, including herbs from the flowery walled garden (where guests can relax and take tea). The rooms are comfortably and individually furnished, all having some antique pieces from the Sullivans' collection.

Nearby Trelissick Garden, 6 miles (10 km).

Tregony, Truro, Cornwall TR2 5RN **Tel** (087253) 671 **Location** 7 miles (11 km) E of Truro on A3078; with gardens and private parking for 5 cars **Food & drink** breakfast, dinner; residential and restaurant licence **Prices** DB&B £28.75-£31.75; reductions for 7 nights or more	**Rooms** 5 double, one with bath, one with shower; one single; tea/coffee kit **Facilities** dining-room, sitting-room, bar **Credit cards** not accepted **Children** welcome over 7 **Disabled** access difficult **Pets** guide-dogs only **Closed** Nov to Feb **Proprietors** Barry and Judith Sullivan

South Cornwall

Country hotel, Calstock

Danescombe Valley Hotel

This colonial-style house, a hotel since 1860, was once owned by the National Trust, whose Cotehele House is just 15 minutes' walk up through the woods. Every room in the hotel has a stunning view over a picturesque meander in the River Tamar. The antique furniture, traditional furnishings, abundance of original paintings and natural light lend an airy and relaxed atmosphere. The Smiths have been resident since 1985; in the intervening years, Anna's cooking (using mainly fresh local produce including Tamar salmon) has firmly established the restaurant as one of the best in the south-west. Dinner is a set four courses with no choice, but you are consulted as to your dislikes on booking.

Nearby Cotehele House; Morwelham Quay, 4 miles (6 km).

Lower Kelly, Calstock, Cornwall PL18 9RY
Tel and fax (0822) 832414
Location 0.5 mile (0.8 km) W of Calstock; with private parking for 3 cars and further parking in quiet lane
Food & drink breakfast, dinner; residential and restaurant licence
Prices DB&B £92.50 (single room by arrangement)
Rooms 5 double, all with bath and shower; all rooms have central heating
Facilities sitting-room, bar, dining-room
Credit cards DC, MC, V
Children welcome over 12
Disabled access difficult
Pets not accepted
Closed Nov to Mar (open Christmas); Wed, Thu
Proprietors Martin and Anna Smith.

South Cornwall

Country hotel, Liskeard

Well House

'We'll do anything for our guests,' said Nicholas Wainford; at the time he was providing a cream tea at short notice, but the same philosophy applies throughout his operation. Everything here has been carefully chosen to create an atmosphere of calm and stylish luxury – up to country-house standard, but on a smaller scale (and at lower cost). The house itself was built by an ex-tea-planter in 1894, obviously with no expense spared – the beautifully tiled entrance hall, the staircase and all the woodwork are as new. The dining-room, the terrace and most of the richly decorated bedrooms look out over wooded grounds which sweep away down to the Looe valley, barely another building in sight.

The contemporary decoration and paintings on the walls are in no way at odds with the atmosphere of the old stone house. Nor is the modern style of the dishes on the daily changing menu. This is one of the best places to eat in Cornwall – and one of the most attractive too, with its calm, pink-and-grey colour scheme. The wine list is extensive and largely French, with a heavy slant towards prestigious clarets. The lunch and dinner menus change daily.

Nearby Looe, Plymouth; Bodmin Moor.

St Keyne, Liskeard, Cornwall
PL14 4RN
Tel (0579) 342001
Location in countryside just outside village of St Keyne, 2 miles (3 km) S of Liskeard, off B3254; in 3.5-acre gardens with ample car parking
Food & drink breakfast, lunch, dinner; restaurant and residential licence
Prices B&B £34-£70; lunch £21, dinner £25; 15% reduction for 4 nights or more
Rooms 6 double, one family

room, all with bath; all have central heating, phone, radio, hairdrier, TV, trouser-press
Facilities dining-room, sitting-room, bar; tennis, heated swimming-pool, croquet
Credit cards MC, V
Children welcome; only over-8s in restaurant (high tea available for younger ones)
Disabled no special facilities
Pets welcome by arrangement
Closed never
Proprietor Nicholas Wainford

South Cornwall

Boscundle Manor

It is well over a decade now since the Flints swapped their metropolitan existence for the different challenge of running this largely 18thC house, but they still exude enthusiasm, still attend as carefully as ever to the needs of guests, and still find time to tend the large terraced garden themselves. Mary is the chef and her daily changing menu of simple but imaginative dishes (with the emphasis on fish) is an important ingredient in the Boscundle recipe. The wine list is long and interesting, too.

The delight of the place is its happy informality – the house is the Flints' home, with assorted furniture (some luxurious modern, some stripped pine, some elegant antiques) rather than a consistently applied formula. There are pictures, flowers, books and postcards everywhere. A couple of years ago the Flints made further improvements to the bedrooms; all now have spa baths and some have separate 'power showers'.

Nearby Fowey, 5 miles (8 km); Restormel Castle, 6 miles (10km)

Tregrehan, St Austell, Cornwall PL25 3RL
Tel (0726) 813557 **Fax** 814997
Location 2.5 miles (4 km) E of St Austell, close to A390; in 10-acre woodland gardens; ample car parking
Food & drink full breakfast, light lunches and snacks, dinner; residential licence
Prices B&B £45-£75; DB&B £65-£95; reductions for more than one night
Rooms 8 double, all with spa bath; 2 single, both with shower; all rooms have central heating, phone, colour TV with Teletext, radio/alarm, minibar, tea/coffee kit
Facilities 2 sitting-rooms, bar, 2 dining-rooms, conservatory/breakfast room, exercise room, heated outdoor swimming-pool, croquet, 2 practice golf holes
Credit cards MC, V
Children welcome
Disabled access difficult to house, but access easy to bungalow in grounds
Pets accepted by arrangement but not allowed in public rooms
Closed Nov to Easter
Proprietors Andrew and Mary Flint

North Cornwall

Seafood Restaurant

The rooms above this first-rate restaurant are excellent – attractive, spacious and more than adequately comfortable, especially numbers five and six, which have wonderful estuary views. The real reason to stay here, though, is the superb seafood produced by Rick and Jill Stein – straight from the fishing boats to the kitchen door, cooked using herbs from the garden, and served by efficient, friendly staff in a lively dining-room. What the place lacks in public rooms and grounds, it makes up for in laid-back atmosphere and its prime position on the quay.

Nearby Surfing beaches, Trevose Head.

Riverside, Padstow, Cornwall PL28 8BY **Tel** (0841) 532485 **Fax** 533344 **Location** on quay in village, 4 miles (6 km) NW off A39 between Wadebridge and St Columb; car park opposite **Food & drink** full breakfast, lunch, dinner; restaurant and residential licence **Prices** B&B £30-£85; dinner £27; reductions for 2 nights out of season, and for children	**Rooms** 10 double, all with bath; all rooms have central heating, phone, TV, minibar, radio, tea/coffee kit **Facilities** conservatory **Credit cards** AE, MC, V **Children** welcome **Disabled** access difficult **Pets** dogs accepted **Closed** mid-Dec to 1 Feb; restaurant only, Sun **Proprietors** Richard and Jill Stein

Old Millfloor

A steep path is the only access to this converted mill, situated (as you might expect) by a stream amid gardens, orchards and paddocks. It has been in Janice Waddon-Martyn's family since the early 1960s, and her home since the 1970s. Janice runs the house with the help of her daughter, and succeeds admirably in giving her guests a relaxing 'away from it all' stay. She adores cooking for her guests, and likes nothing better than to be told of their preferences so that she can be sure her creations will be enjoyed. You are welcome – indeed, exhorted – to take your own wine. Bedrooms are neat and pretty, with high beamed ceilings. Families are welcome, but not smokers.

Nearby Tintagel Castle, 2 miles (3 km); Bodmin Moor.

Trebarwith Strand, Tintagel, Cornwall PL34 0HA **Tel**(0840) 770234 **Location** 2 miles (3 km) S of Tintagel on B3263; in 10-acre grounds with ample car parking **Food & drink** full breakfast, tea, dinner; no licence **Prices** B&B £16; dinner £11; reductions for more than one night and for children	**Rooms** 3 double; all rooms have TV, hairdrier **Facilities** sitting-room, dining-room **Credit cards** not accepted **Children** welcome **Disabled** access difficult **Pets** not accepted **Closed** Dec to Feb **Proprietor** Janice Waddon-Martyn

West Devon

Country house hotel, Holsworthy

Court Barn

'Eclectic' best sums up the decorative style of Court Barn, a four-square Victorian house where antiques, souvenirs, books and games jostle with sometimes unusual furnishings in a carefree medley of patterns. The result is oddly reassuring; this home-like environment spells comfort far beyond the meretricious harmony of hotels colour-matched by interior designers. Several acres of beautifully kept mature grounds surround the house; croquet hoops, putting holes and badminton and tennis nets suggest plenty to do outside.

Nearby Bude, 7 miles (11 km); Dartmoor within reach.

Clawton, Holsworthy, Devon EX22 6PS
Tel (040927) 219
Location 3 miles (5 km) S of Holsworthy, close to A388; with ample car parking
Food & drink full breakfast, lunch, tea, dinner; residential and restaurant licence
Prices B&B £35-45; dinner £19; reductions for children; bargain breaks
Rooms 7 double, 5 with bath, 2 with shower; one single with shower; all rooms have central heating, TV, phone, radio, tea/coffee kit, hairdrier
Facilities 2 sitting-rooms, bar, 2 dining-rooms, TV room; croquet, putting, badminton, tennis **Credit cards** AE, DC, MC, V **Children** welcome
Disabled no special facilities
Pets accepted in bedrooms
Closed 2 weeks Jan
Proprietors Susan and Robert Wood

Restaurant with rooms, Tavistock

The Horn of Plenty

Since they arrived here in 1990, Ian and Elaine Gatehouse have enhanced the already high reputation of the place by close attention to detail, a natural talent for hospitality and sheer hard work. The secluded creeper-covered 1830s house overlooks sloping lawns and pasture-land, a view shared by all seven of the spacious bedooms in the converted coach-house, fifty yards from the main house. Dinner is the main event, skilfully prepared by chef Peter Gorton in the modern style, and served at neat tables in front of the picture windows of the two-part dining room.

Nearby Cotehele House, 3 miles (5 km); Dartmoor.

Gulworthy, Tavistock, Devon PL19 8JD
Tel (0822) 832528
Location 3 miles (2 km) W of Tavistock on A390; with ample car parking
Food & drink breakfast, lunch, dinner; residential licence
Prices B&B £35.50-45; meals £14.50-£25.50
Rooms 7 double, 5 with bath, 2 with shower; all have central heating, phone, hairdrier, TV, minibar, radio
Facilities 2 dining-rooms, sitting-room
Children not accepted under 13 years **Disabled** one suitable bedroom **Pets** accepted in bedrooms **Closed** Christmas; restaurant only, Mon lunch
Proprietors Ian and Elaine Gatehouse

South Devon

Manor house hotel, Dittisham

Fingals

Richard Johnston was already running a successful restaurant called Fingals (in London's Fulham Road) when he took on the restoration of this manor farm house in a secluded valley, close to the River Dart. He calls it a 'hotel and restaurant', but anyone expecting a conventional example of either would be in for a surprise. In practice, Fingals comes much closer to the 'country house party' type of guest-house, where it is normal (though not necessary) for guests to share a big table at dinner, with any social ice melted by house wine.

The house – 17thC with Queen Anne front additions – has plenty of charm, and has been stylishly done out with a successful blend of new and old furniture, pine and oak. In 1989 it was sympathetically extended, adding 5 bedrooms. It is an exceptionally relaxed place – you pour your own drinks, eat breakfast whenever you like – and those who insist on everything being just so are likely to be disappointed. The four-course dinners chosen from a short menu are modern in style, competent in execution, and ample in quantity.

Nearby Dartmouth Castle, 3 miles (5 km).

Old Coombe Manor Farm, Dittisham, near Dartmouth, Devon TQ6 0JA
Tel (080422) 398 **Fax** 401
Location 4 miles (6 km) N of Dartmouth, one mile (1.5 km) from village; with garden and ample car parking
Food & drink breakfast, snack lunch, dinner; residential and restaurant licence
Prices B&B £32.50-£60; dinner £25; reductions for 3 nights or more **Rooms** 10 double, 9 with bath, one with shower; one family room, with bath; all rooms have central heating, phone, radio/alarm, tea/coffee kit; TV on request
Facilities dining-room, bar, library, TV room; swimming-pool, jacuzzi, sauna, snooker, croquet, tennis, wind-surfing
Credit cards AE, DC, MC, V
Children welcome if well behaved
Disabled access difficult
Pets accepted if well behaved, but not allowed in public rooms
Closed New Year to Easter
Proprietor Richard Johnston

Dartmoor

Hunts Tor

Hunts Tor is a compact 17thC house with Regency additions next to an ancient pub on the square of an unspoiled village. The Harrisons quit the rat race to set up here, opening their doors in 1985. They have restored the house carefully, and furnished it in a distinctive style, indulging their affection for art deco. Bedrooms are simple but tasteful and comfortable; over the years, beds have been sacrificed to make space for baths. One room has a sitting area – probably worth the extra £10. A key attraction is Sue's food: four courses with no choice, but 'well balanced and beautifully cooked and presented,' according to a recent report.
Nearby Castle Drogo; Dartmoor.

Drewsteignton, Devon EX6 6QW
Tel (0647) 21228
Location on village square, 12 miles (19 km) W of Exeter; with private parking for 2 cars and parking on the square
Food & drink breakfast, dinner; restaurant licence
Prices £20-£30; dinner £17
Rooms 4 double (2 twin), all with bath; all rooms have central heating, hairdrier
Facilities 2 dining-rooms (one with bar), sitting-room
Credit cards not accepted
Children accepted over 14
Disabled access difficult
Pets well behaved dogs accepted in bedrooms
Closed Dec, Jan
Proprietors Sue and Chris Harrison

Bel Alp House

Peacefully set in 8 lush acres, this fine Edwardian house set high above Haytor enjoys magnificent panoramic views. It is immaculately kept, as you might expect with a retired army captain at the helm. One sitting room echoes the formality of the elegantly furnished dining-room, while the other is more relaxed, with deep armchairs. Bedrooms and bathrooms are generally large and comfortable, with every extra; muted, restful colour schemes. The Curnocks are charming, attentive hosts; Sarah cooks dinners in dinner party style, but with a choice at each of the five courses.
Nearby Haytor Rocks, Lustleigh, Dartmoor.

Haytor, nr Bovey Travey, Devon, TQ13 9XX
Tel (0364) 661217 **Fax** 661292
Location in countryside, E of Haytor, 2.5 miles (4 km) W of Bovey Tracey off B3187; in 8-acre grounds with private car parking
Food & drink full breakfast, light lunch, dinner; restaurant licence
Prices B&B £60-84, lunch £10-20, dinner £33
Rooms 9 double (5 twin), all with bath or shower; all have central heating, phone, radio, hairdrier, TV, tea/coffee kit
Facilities 2 sitting-rooms, dining-room, billiard room.
Credit cards AE, MC, V
Children very welcome; baby-listening, games room
Disabled easy access; lift/elevator, 2 ground-floor rooms **Pets** welcome
Closed Dec to Feb
Proprietors Roger & Sarah Curnock

Dartmoor

Country house hotel, Chagford

Gidleigh Park

The Hendersons, Americans with no previous hotel experience before taking on Gidleigh in 1977, aim to provide nothing but the best; and over the years they have polished the interior of this Edwardian mock-Tudor house, in a privileged wooded setting, to the point where its combination of comfort and informal elegance is more or less unmatched. Service is meant to be 'always friendly and enthusiastic, sometimes efficient', and it works. The eclectic food is wonderful – even the cheeses are remarkable – while wines run to 400 bins plus 250 bin-ends.

Nearby Castle Drogo, 4 miles (6.5 km); Dartmoor.

Chagford, Devon TQ13 8HH
Tel (0647) 432367 **Fax** 432574
Location 2 miles (3 km) W of Chagford; in 40 acre grounds with ample car parking
Food & drink breakfast, lunch, dinner; restaurant and residential licence
Prices DB&B £130-£175
Rooms 14 double, all with bath, 10 also with shower; all rooms have central heating,
TV, radio, hairdrier
Facilities sitting-room, bar, loggia, 2 dining-rooms; croquet, fishing, tennis, bowls
Credit cards AE, DC, MC, V
Children welcome only if adult in behaviour
Disabled no special facilities
Pets welcome
Closed never
Proprietors Paul and Kay Henderson

Inn, South Zeal

Oxenham Arms

This creeper-covered granite inn has been serving the needs of the visitor since at least the 15th century. The building is the great attraction: plumbing and wiring apart, it has changed little since Tudor times, with its wealth of mullions, flagstones, dark panelling and oak beams, and the furniture is in keeping. It is more of a hotel than a pub – the bar is small (though cosy), and there is a pleasant sitting-room. Bedrooms are appropriately simple. Food is plain, too, but good value. There is a pretty half-acre garden at the back.

Nearby Okehampton Castle, Castle Drogo; Dartmoor.

South Zeal, near Okehampton, Devon EX20 2JT
Tel (0837) 840244 **Fax** 840791
Location 4 miles (6 km) E of Okehampton, just off A30, in middle of village; with garden at rear, and adequate car parking in forecourt
Food & drink breakfast, lunch, tea, dinner; full licence
Prices B&B £25-£45; dinner from £15.50
Rooms 8 double with bath, 4
also with shower; all rooms have colour TV, telephone, tea/coffee kit
Facilities bar with family room, dining-room, sitting-room
Credit cards AE, DC, MC, V
Children welcome
Disabled access difficult
Pets welcome
Closed never
Proprietors Mr and Mrs James H Henry

Dartmoor

Bed and breakfast guest-house, Bovey Tracey

Willmead Farm

You might expect to see rabbits wearing aprons outside this idyllic thatched stone farmhouse, set in a quiet green valley on the eastern fringes of Dartmoor. But the human welcome is warm enough from Hilary Roberts, who has been running Willmead as a far-above-average B&B place since the mid-1970s. The 14thC building has been beautifully restored, to reveal a wealth of oak beams and vast open fireplaces, and there is antique furniture to match. A 'scrumptious' farmhouse breakfast (including several home-made jams) is served in the splendidly olde-worlde dining-room, and for dinner there is a reasonable choice of local inns and restaurants. Smoking is not allowed anywhere in the house. We have a chorus of approving reports.

Nearby Lustleigh; Newton Abbot, 5 miles (8 km); Dartmoor.

Bovey Tracey, near Newton Abbot, Devon TQ13 9NP	have central heating
Tel (06477) 214	**Facilities** sitting-room, dining-room
Location 2 miles (3 km) NW of Bovey Tracey, off A382	**Credit cards** not accepted
Food & drink full breakfast	**Children** accepted over 10
Prices B&B £21-£30	**Disabled** not suitable
Rooms 3 double, one with bath, 2 with shower; all rooms	**Pets** must sleep in cars
	Closed Christmas, New Year
	Proprietor Mrs H Roberts

Country inn, Trusham

Cridford Inn

The oldest house in Devon has become one of its newest inns, lovingly restored and refurbished over the past year or two by its enthusiastic and friendly new owners. Unlike many inns, it has a pleasant sitting area, ideal for morning newspapers or afternoon tea, complete with ticking grandfather clock and other period pieces. Ye olde oak dining-room has an impressive fireplace plus a floor 'window' revealing a unique Saxon mosaic (circa 800). The cosy bar has suitably antique wooden seats, a stone floor and stained glass. There are no open fires – because of the thatched roof, the insurers said no! Bedrooms were still being refurbished when we visited. They vary in size and shape. David's food is regionally based, but interestingly adventurous.

Nearby Bradley Manor, Stover Park, Bovey Tracey, Dartmoor.

Trusham, Newton Abbot, Devon TQ13 0NR	have central heating, TV, tea/coffee kit
Tel (0626) 853694	**Facilities** dining room with sitting-room attached, bar
Location 3 miles (5 km) off A38, along B3193, 3 miles (5 km) NE of Bovey Tracey	**Credit cards** not accepted
Food & drink full breakfast, lunch, dinner; full licence	**Children** not suitable
Prices B&B £25-35, dinner from £11.50	**Disabled** not suitable
Rooms 4 double (2 twin), 2 with bath, 2 with shower; all	**Pets** welcome, though not in bedrooms or dining room
	Closed 3 weeks in January
	Proprietors David and Sally Hesmondhalgh

East Devon

Combe House

When they came here in 1970, John Boswell (direct descendant of 'the' Boswell) and his wife Thérèse faced the massive task of refurbishing the imposing Elizabethan manor from scratch. They have made it an exceptionally comfortable, quiet and spacious hotel in the grand manner, with moulded ceilings, panelled walls and Chippendale furniture. Mark, their eldest son, oversees the young and enthusiastic chefs with a trained eye – and Thérèse is responsible for the murals which grace some of the public rooms.

Nearby Cadhay House, 4 miles (6 km); south Devon coast.

Gittisham, near Honiton, Devon EX14 0AD
Tel (0404) 42756 **Fax** 46004
Location one mile (1.5 km) SW of Honiton off A30; ample car parking
Food & drink full breakfast, tea, dinner; restaurant & residential licence
Prices B&B £48.50-£100; dinner from £21; reductions for children sharing room; winter breaks
Rooms 15 double, all with bath; all rooms have central heating, colour TV, phone, hairdrier
Facilities bar, sitting-rooms, 2 dining-rooms; fishing, croquet
Credit cards AE, DC, MC, V
Children welcome; special supper facilities
Disabled access easy to ground floor only
Pets welcome, but not allowed in public rooms
Closed Sun and Mon in Jan and Feb
Proprietors John and Thérèse Boswell

Woodhayes

Antiques, oil paintings, prints and fabrics of high quality characterize the public rooms of this gracious Georgian house, while the bedrooms (some of them exceptionally large) are individually and harmoniously decorated, and equipped with every conceivable extra. Since their arrival the Rendles have converted a stone-floored kitchen to create a cosy bar. Katherine's meals follow a satisfying dinner-party style but offer some choice, and are properly served at well-spaced tables in the elegant dining-room. All the public rooms have open fires in winter.

Nearby Cadhay House, 3 miles (5 km); Exe valley.

Whimple, near Exeter, Devon EX5 2TD
Tel (0404) 822237
Location 9 miles (14.5km) E of Exeter, close to A30; in 3-acre grounds with parking for 20 cars
Food & drink full breakfast, dinner; lunch by arrangement; residential and restaurant licence
Prices B&B £40-£60; DB&B £80-£120
Rooms 7 double, all with bath; all rooms have central heating, TV, phone, radio
Facilities 2 sitting-rooms, dining-room, bar; croquet, tennis court
Credit cards AE, DC, MC, V
Children welcome over 12
Disabled access difficult
Pets not accepted
Closed never
Proprietors Katherine and Frank Rendle

West Dorset

Innsacre

The basic formula of Innsacre is rather unusual: a restaurant with rooms in a converted 17thC farmhouse and barns, set in 10 acres of orchards and hillsides which guests share with an assortment of animals – goats, donkeys, Muscovy ducks. Inside are six comfortable bedrooms with carved darkwood French beds and a small first-floor sitting-room; and there is a secluded south-facing terrace which catches the evening sunshine. Cooking is increasingly serious under Tim Emberley, and the wine list is equally serious and instructive. A great place for families with impedimenta (children or animals).

Nearby coast, 3 miles (5 km); Abbotsbury, 7 miles (12.5 km).

Shipton Gorge, Bridport,
Dorset DT6 4LJ
Tel (0308) 56137
Location in quiet countryside,
2 miles E of Bridport, S of
A35; with ample car parking
Food & drink breakfast,
dinner; residential and
restaurant licence
Prices B&B £33-£45 (children
under 3 free, 50% reduction
for children sharing); lunch
£13.50, dinner £17.50-£23.50

Rooms 5 double, one family
room, all with bath; all have
TV, radio **Facilities** bar,
dining-room, sitting-room
Credit cards MC, V
Children welcome; high-chairs
and baby-listening devices
Disabled no special facilities
Pets welcome **Closed** 2 weeks
mid-Nov, Dec 25; restaurant
only, Mon, Sun dinner
Proprietors Sydney and Lesley
Davies

Chedington Court

We've called it a manor, and it looks like a Jacobean one, but Chedington Court was built 'only' 150 years ago. The house (in a secluded and panoramic setting) is full of character, deeply comfortable and entirely relaxing – and the grounds add another dimension, whether for lazing or exploring. The Chapmans were well established restaurateurs before they became hoteliers, so it is no surprise to find excellent food. Dinners (from a short menu) are of very high quality – seafood especially.

Nearby Mapperton Gardens, Parnham House, 6 miles (10 km).

Chedington, Beaminster,
Dorset DT8 3HY
Tel (0935) 891265 **Fax** 891442
Location in countryside just
off A356, 4.5 miles (7 km) SE
of Crewkerne at Winyard's
Gap; in 10-acre gardens, with
ample private parking
Food & drink breakfast,
dinner; restaurant licence
Prices B&B £43.50-£61.50;
dinner £26.50
Rooms 9 double (4 twin), one
family room, all with bath; all

rooms have central heating,
phone, TV, radio, hairdrier,
baby-listening
Facilities sitting-room, dining-
room, library, billiard room;
putting, croquet, 9-hole golf
course (par 74)
Credit cards AE, MC, V
Children accepted; high tea
for under 10s **Disabled** no
special facilities **Pets** accepted
Closed most of Jan
Proprietors Hilary and Philip
Chapman

West Dorset

Country house hotel, Evershot

Summer Lodge

The Corbetts are the living evidence that not all 'professional' hoteliers are mediocre; we don't know what contribution they made to guests' happiness when they were at the Savoy, but the dedication and talent they have applied to that cause since they escaped to Dorset is remarkable indeed.

For many visitors, Summer Lodge is all that a country house hotel should be. The Georgian/Victorian building is on just the right scale to give a sense of slight extravagance without being intimidating, and the Corbetts are masters at making guests feel instantly at home in it. French windows lead from the public rooms (William Morris fabrics, open fires) to the beautiful flowery garden – and Margaret's professional flower arrangements are a special feature of the charming bedrooms, which range from the merely delightful to the quite grand.

The excellent cooking – 'not mean, but not heavy' – is now offered as a monthly changing *carte* with daily specials.

Nearby Minterne Gardens, Maperton Gardens, Parnham House, 6 miles (10 km); Montacute House.

Summer Lane, Evershot,
Dorset DT2 0JR
Tel (0935) 83424 **Fax** 83005
Location 15 miles (24 km)
NW of Dorchester, off A37 on
edge of village; ample car
parking
Food & drink full breakfast,
lunch, dinner; residential and
restaurant licence
Prices B&B £62.50-£100;
DB&B £92-£135; reductions
for children sharing; bargain
breaks
Rooms 8 double, 3 single, one
family room, 6 suites, all with

bath; all rooms have central
heating, phone, tea/coffee
kit, hairdrier; TV, radio
Facilities dining-room,
sitting-room, bar, reading-
room; croquet, outdoor
heated swimming-pool, tennis
Credit cards AE, MC, V
Children welcome by
arrangement
Disabled access good to
ground-floor bedrooms
Pets dogs welcome by
arrangement
Closed never **Proprietors**
Nigel and Margaret Corbett

West Dorset

Country house hotel, Beaminster

Hams Plot

Hams Plot, a Regency villa with a strong French influence in its architecture, is Giles Dearlove's family home, to which he and Judy moved back in 1980. The house has large secluded grounds with a swimming-pool – and a sunny veranda, for tea or pre-dinner drinks in summer. Inside, the comfortable library and airy sitting-room are dotted with antiques and water-colours – 'all beautifully furnished and warm' notes a recent winter visitor.
Nearby Parnham House, Mapperton Gardens, 1.5 miles (2.5 km); Kingcombe Meadows, 3 miles (5 km).

Beaminster, Dorset DT8 3LU
Tel (0308) 862979
Location on S edge of Beaminster just off A3066; ample car parking
Food & drink full breakfast, dinner; residential licence
Prices B&B £26-£36; dinner £10-£25 at restaurant opposite hotel
Rooms 3 double, 2 with bath, one with shower; all rooms have central heating, tea/coffee kit
Facilities sitting-room, library, bar; swimming- pool tennis, croquet
Credit cards not accepted
Children welcome over 10
Disabled access not easy
Pets not accepted
Closed Nov to Mar
Proprietors J and G Dearlove

Country hotel, West Bexington

The Manor Hotel

Richard and Jayne Childs have not striven for elegance or richness in the decoration of their 'manor'; in character with the farmhouse-style of this inn-cum-hotel-cum-restaurant (which dates from the 15th and 16th centuries but is partly Victorian) they have aimed for the warmth of a private home. Bedrooms vary widely in size (though not price); they are neat, bright and decorated in Laura Ashley style. The dining-room retains its stone-flagged floor. The 'cellar' bar opens on to the big garden (via a new 'Victorian' conservatory) with a children's play area.
Nearby Abbotsbury Gardens 2.5 miles (4 km).

West Bexington, Dorchester Dorset DT2 9DF
Tel (0308) 897616
Location 5.5 miles (9 km) SE of Bridport, close to B3157; in 3.5-acre grounds with ample car parking
Food & drink breakfast, lunch, dinner, bar snacks; full licence
Prices B&B £35-£46; DB&B £55-£66; dinner £16-£19
Rooms 12 double, one single, 9 with bath, 4 with shower; all rooms have central heating colour TV, tea/coffee kit, phone
Facilities 2 sitting-rooms, bar, dining-room, skittle alley, conference room, function room
Credit cards AE, DC, MC, V
Children welcome
Disabled access difficult
Pets not accepted
Closed Christmas
Proprietors Richard and Jayne Childs

West Dorset

Country house hotel, Maiden Newton

Maiden Newton House

'Breakfast served when you are ready' is the rule here, summing up the approach that Bryan and Elizabeth Ferriss take to their guests – which is to attend personally and carefully to their every need. They opened their doors only in 1985, but settled immediately into their stride.

Maiden Newton House is very firmly a non-hotel. You are entertained as friends visiting a private house: guests are encouraged to foregather in the drawing room for pre-prandial drinks, and proceed to enjoy 'good food and good conversation' at one elegant table presided over by the Ferrisses on the stroke of 8pm. Elizabeth's eclectic menus offer no choice, but you get advance warning of the day's fare and adjustments can be made if necessary.

The house is a Victorian reconstruction of a much older dwelling, and has a distinctly medieval look. It is richly and tastefully furnished, with abundant antiques, and each of the inviting bedrooms is decorated in an individual style. The only distractions are the sounds of agriculture and worship – the village church is next door.

Nearby Cerne Abbas, 5 miles (8 km); Mapperton Gardens, 6 miles (10 km); Minterne Gardens, 6 miles (10 km); Dorchester, 7 miles (11 km).

Maiden Newton, near Dorchester, Dorset DT2 0AA
Tel (0300) 20336
Location 7 miles (11 km) NW of Dorchester, close to A356; in 2-acre garden and 9 acres of parkland, with ample car parking
Food & drink full breakfast, tea, dinner; full licence
Prices B&B £42-£83; dinner £25
Rooms 6 double, all with bath; all rooms have central heating, TV, hairdrier, trouser-press
Facilities library with TV/video, sitting-room, dining-room; fishing, croquet
Credit cards MC, V
Children accepted, but those under 12 not allowed at dinner
Disabled access easy to ground floor, but no ground-floor bedrooms
Pets accepted, but not allowed in public rooms
Closed Dec
Proprietors Bryan and Elizabeth Ferriss

East Dorset

Country house hotel, Gillingham

Stock Hill House

This restored Victorian manor house, reached up a long drive through wooded grounds, has been beautifully furnished and decorated, with many of the Hausers' personal possessions in evidence. Sanderson and Baker designs abound, although each of the luxurious bedrooms is individual in style. The public rooms, too, are full of character and charm.

But your lasting memory of Stock Hill House is more likely to be of the Hausers' boundless enthusiasm and obvious delight in their work. Peter does all the cooking and produces superb results. His Austrian roots are reflected in the menu, which changes daily. Fruit and vegetables come from Peter's own immaculate walled kitchen garden. While he works away in the kitchen, guests pop in for a chat or to see what he is planning for dinner that evening. Before the evening meal, Chef Hauser draws his guests together before the grand fireplace in the entrance hall by playing his zither: thus begins an evening of good food and wine, hosted by a charming couple. Ties must be worn at dinner.

Nearby Shaftesbury, 5 miles (8 km); Stourhead House and Gardens, 6 miles (10 km); Salisbury and Longleat within reach.

Wyke, Gillingham, Dorset SP8 5NR
Tel (0747) 823626
Location 5 miles (8 km) NW of Shaftesbury on B3081; in 10-acre grounds with ample car parking
Food & drink breakfast, lunch, dinner; restaurant licence
Prices DB&B £80-£105; reductions for 3 nights or more
Rooms 6 double, 4 with bath (2 also with shower), one with shower; 2 singles, one with bath, one with shower; one suite with bath and shower; all rooms have central heating, radio, colour TV, phone, alarm clock, hairdrier, trouser-press
Facilities sitting-room, dining-room, breakfast room; tennis court, croquet (Easter to Oct)
Children welcome over 7 if well behaved
Disabled access difficult, except to ground-floor suite
Pets not accepted
Closed never
Proprietors Peter and Nita Hauser

East Dorset

Plumber Manor

This Jacobean manor house, 'modernized' earlier this century, has been in the Prideaux-Brune family for well over 300 years. Since 1973 they have been running it as an elegant but relaxed restaurant with comfortable bedrooms; in 1982 they converted a stone barn to provide a further 6, even more spacious rooms; and another conversion increased the number again. The owner's brother Brian produces highly regarded food, and the dining-room attracts many non-residents.
Nearby Purse Caundle Manor, 6 miles (10 km).

Hazelbury Bryan Road, Sturminster Newton, Dorset DT10 2AF
Tel (0258) 472507 **Fax** 473370
Location 2 miles (3 km) SW of Sturminster Newton; private car parking
Food & drink full breakfast, dinner; full licence
Prices B&B £40-£60; dinner £20-£25; reductions for 4 nights or more
Rooms 14 double, all with bath and shower; 2 small doubles, with bath and shower; all rooms have central heating, TV, phone, tea/coffee kit
Facilities dining-room, sitting-room, bar; croquet, tennis
Credit cards AE, DC, MC, V
Children welcome over 12
Disabled easy access to stable-block bedrooms and dining-room **Pets** not accepted
Closed Feb **Proprietor** Richard Prideaux-Brune

Priory Hotel

After 800 years of mixed history, both ecclesiastical and secular, the old Priory of St Mary has settled comfortably into its present-day role of luxurious hotel, expertly managed by John of the brothers Turner. The peaceful, manicured gardens lead down to the river Frome, specimen trees screening guests from occasionally intrusive boating cries. Housed under the Priory's gabled roofs is a myriad of rooms expensively decorated in chintz and swags, interspersed with family antiques. The cooking is an elaborate interpretation of traditional English 'fayre'.
Nearby Blue Pool 3 miles (5 km); Brownsea Island 5 miles (8 km).

Church Green, Wareham, Dorset BH20 4ND
Tel(0929) 552772 **Fax** 554519
Location on edge of river in small town on A351; in grounds with parking for cars
Food & drink breakfast, lunch, dinner, snacks; residential licence
Prices B&B £35-£95; lunch £11.50, dinner from £22.50; winter breaks
Rooms 16 double (4 twin), 14 with bath, 2 with shower; 3 single with bath; all rooms have central heating, phone, hairdryer, TV, minibar, radio
Facilities 2 sitting-rooms, 2 dining-rooms, bar; fishing, sailing, croquet
Credit cards AE, DC, MC, V
Children not accepted
Pets not accepted
Disabled 4 bedrooms on ground floor
Closed never
Proprietors Stuart and John Turner

North Devon

Whitechapel Manor

Before they moved to Whitechapel in 1984, the Shaplands had been taking guests in their farmhouse at nearby Kerscott. They brought to this much grander Elizabethan manor house the qualities of the British guest-house at its best – the emphasis is on comfort and hospitality, not on appearances and ceremony. This is not to say that the house lacks visual style – on the contrary, it is richly furnished with great taste (and at great expense). Food is a highlight – 'modern French' using local ingredients, professionally prepared by a French chef, to the applause of the gourmet guides.

Nearby Exmoor.

South Molton, Devon EX36 3EG
Tel (0769) 573377 **Fax** 573797
Location 3 miles (5 km) E of South Molton, one mile from A361; with car parking
Food & drink full breakfast, lunch, dinner; restaurant licence
Prices B&B £49-£80; dinner from £26; special breaks
Rooms 8 double, 2 single; all with bath and shower; all rooms have central heating, colour TV, radio, hairdrier
Facilities sitting-room, bar, dining-room; croquet
Credit cards AE, DC, MC, V
Children accepted
Disabled access difficult
Pets not accepted
Closed never
Proprietors John and Patricia Shapland

The Whiteleaf

The Wallingtons built a high reputation for themselves at the Rhydspence Inn, which they left in 1986 to revamp this small, unremarkable but pleasant 1930s guest-house. What it lacks in visual appeal is more than balanced by the high standard of comfort and hospitality. The garden is a peaceful retreat from the lively seaside village of Croyde, which has an excellent beach. What's more, David's cooking goes from strength to strength – English/Continental, some original dishes, regularly changing menus – 'superb' was one visitor's verdict.

Nearby Exmoor, Lundy Island, North Devon Coast Path.

Croyde, Nr Braunton, Devon EX33 1PN
Tel (0271) 890266
Location quarter of a mile (400m) SW of village, on B3231; with car parking
Food & drink breakfast, dinner; restaurant and residential licence
Prices B&B £27-£34.50; DB&B £44-£51.50
Rooms 2 double, both with bath and shower; one family room with bath and shower; all rooms have central heating, TV, radio, alarm, hairdrier, tea/coffee kit, minibar
Facilities sitting-room, dining-room
Credit cards MC, V
Children welcome but no special meals
Disabled not suitable
Pets welcome
Closed occasionally
Proprietors David and Flo Wallington

North Devon/Exmoor

Lower Pitt Restaurant

As the name suggests, the emphasis here is firmly on food. Word is spreading fast about the Lyons' small restaurant in this quiet Exmoor hamlet. The house is a pretty one: a long, low white cottage with plants clambering around the porch. The rear gardens also indicate green fingers – conifers have to be restrained from bursting in on the diners in the airy conservatory. Guests perch for drinks in the small bar or sitting-room before dinner. The three comfortable bedrooms are small and cottagey, tastefully decorated but by no means luxurious. A relaxed and informal atmosphere prevails.

Nearby Exmoor, coast – about 15 miles (24km).

East Buckland, Barnstaple, North Devon EX32 0TD **Tel & Fax** (0598) 760243 **Location** in village, 5 miles (8km) NW of South Molton; with garden and car parking **Food & drink** breakfast, dinner; restaurant licence **Prices** DB&B £55; reduction for 2 nights or more; dinner about £20 **Rooms** 3 double, one with bath, 2 with shower; all have central heating, hairdrier **Facilities** bar, sitting-room, two dining-rooms **Credit cards** MC, V **Children** accepted over 10 **Disabled** access difficult **Pets** not accepted **Closed** Christmas; restaurant only, Sun and Mon in winter **Proprietors** Jerome and Suzanne Lyons

Royal Oak

Not to be confused with the other Royal Oak at nearby Winsford (see page 39), this popular Exmoor inn has much to recommend it besides its Lorna Doone associations (Blackmore stayed here while writing the novel in 1866). The two bars are similarly kitted out with a variety of antlers, fox's masks and hunting scenes – even the candlesticks are fashioned from staghorn. Bar menus offer a satisfying assortment of steaks and sandwiches, with more interesting additions such as venison sausages or local trout. More formal dining takes place in the strikingly colour-schemed restaurant, firelit on chilly days. The quaint bedrooms vary considerably in size, but are well coordinated in cottagey prints.

Nearby Exmoor; walking, riding, fishing, shooting.

Withypool, Somerset TA24 7QP **Tel** (064383) 506 **Fax** 659 **Location** in middle of village, just off B3223, 15 miles SW of Minehead; with ample car parking **Food & drink** breakfast, lunch, dinner; full licence **Prices** B&B £28-£46; meals £10.50-£20 **Rooms** 7 double, 6 with bath, 1 with shower; one family room with bath; all rooms have central heating, phone, hairdrier, TV, radio **Facilities** dining-room, sitting-room, 2 bars **Credit cards** AE, DC, MC, V **Children** welcome over 10 **Disabled** access difficult **Pets** welcome in bedrooms **Closed** Christmas **Proprietor** Mike Bradley

Exmoor

Country house hotel, Hawkridge

Tarr Steps Hotel

This long, low whitewashed building, originally a Georgian rectory, has had just enough of the surrounding woods cleared to give most rooms a delectable view. Desmond Keane has taken great care to keep the character of a private house, with fine antiques in the relaxed, comfortable public rooms, and menus which emphasize fresh ingredients and home cooking.

Nearby Tarr Steps bridge; Exmoor.

Hawkridge, near Dulverton, Somerset TA22 9PY
Tel (064385) 293
Location 7 miles (11 km) NW of Dulverton, W of B3223, in countryside; in 8-acre park with parking for 20 cars
Food & drink full breakfast, lunch, tea, dinner; residential and restaurant licence
Prices DB&B £59.50; reductions mid-week, for more than one night and for children sharing parents' room
Rooms 11 double with bath; 3 single; all rooms have central heating
Facilities bar, sitting-room, 2 dining-rooms; stables; clay pigeon shooting, rough shooting, fishing
Credit cards MC, V
Children welcome if well behaved **Disabled** access good to all public rooms and one ground-floor bedroom
Pets dogs accepted if well behaved, but not in public rooms; kennels available
Closed Feb **Proprietors** Mr and Mrs Desmond Keane

Inn, Winsford

Royal Oak

An ancient, remarkably picturesque inn, thatched and cream-painted. Inside, the cosy and well-furnished part-panelled lounge bar, with its huge stone hearth, does not disappoint. The Stevenses, who have been here since the early 1970s, have a firm eye on standards, which are as well maintained in the food – both bar and restaurant – as in the surroundings. Roughly half the bedrooms are in the relatively new courtyard annexe. Those in the old part have more character.

Nearby Winsford Hill; Exmoor, Brendon Hills.

Winsford, Exmoor National Park, Somerset TA24 7JE
Tel (064385) 455 **Fax** 388
Location 10 miles (16 km) SW of Minehead, 1.5 miles (2.5 km) W of A396; in middle of village, with ample car parking
Food & drink full breakfast, lunch, bar meals, dinner; full licence
Prices B&B £35-£45; dinner £22.50; off-season breaks
Rooms 14 double, 12 with bath; one family room, with bath; all rooms have central heating, TV, phone; radio/alarm, hairdrier
Facilities 3 sitting-rooms, 2 bars, dining-room; fishing
Credit cards AE, DC, MC, V
Children welcome
Disabled access easy to public rooms and annex bedrooms
Pets welcome
Closed never
Proprietors Charles and Sheila Steven

Exmoor

Country house hotel, Simonsbath

Simonsbath House

The first house on Exmoor when it was built in 1654, this long, low whitewashed stone building still presides over an isolated stretch of the moor, well placed for exploring (either by car or on foot) all the corners of the splendidly varied National Park. But the hotel itself is anything but desolate: Mike and Sue Burns, who arrived some years ago, inherited a tradition of providing unstinting comfort, generous and interesting food and a warm welcome in almost wickedly luxurious surroundings – and they carry on that tradition with vigour. Original features abound – wood panelling and large open fires in the sitting-room and bar/library, four-posters in some of the bedrooms – and great efforts have been made to keep the furnishings and decorations in harmony with the antiquity of the building. There is a modest but relaxing lawned garden, and beyond it the expanse of the moor.

The view of one of our most widely travelled reporters sums up Simonsbath: 'Very suave and comfortable; I'd love to go again, but it would have to be at someone else's expense.'

Nearby Lynton, 10 miles (16 km); Exmoor.

Simonsbath, Exmoor,
Somerset TA24 7SH
Tel (064383) 259
Location 10 miles (16 km) S
of Lynton, on B3223, in
village; in one-acre grounds,
ample car parking
Food & drink breakfast,
lunch, dinner; residential and
restaurant licence
Prices B&B £39-£60; DB&B
£57-£78; reductions for 2
nights or more
Rooms 7 double, all with bath,
5 also with shower; all rooms
have central heating, colour
TV, phone, radio, hairdrier
Facilities library with bar,
sitting-room, dining-room
Credit cards AE, DC, MC, V
Children welcome over 10
Disabled access difficult –
steps to entrance
Pets not allowed in house
Closed Dec to Jan
Proprietors Mike and Sue
Burns

West Somerset

Meadow House

This former Georgian rectory with 16thC origins has a beautifully peaceful setting between the Quantocks and the sea. It is furnished with real taste, and immaculately cared for; the bedrooms (and bathrooms) are large, the public rooms warm and inviting (with hundreds of books for guests' use). Cooking is based on local and seasonal produce – much of which comes from the hotel's kitchen gardens.

Nearby Dunster Castle, 10 miles (16 km); Quantock Hills.

Sea Lane, Kilve, Somerset TA5 1EG
Tel (0278) 741546 **Fax** 741663
Location N of village of Kilve, on A39 5 miles (8 km) E of Williton; in 8-acre grounds with ample car parking
Food & drink full breakfast, dinner; retail, residential and restaurant licence
Prices B&B from £55; DB&B from £76; dinner £21; reductions for 2 nights or more
Rooms 10 double, all with bath; cottage suites available; all rooms have TV, central heating, radio/alarm, tea/coffee kit, hairdrier, phone
Facilities dining-room, sitting-room, study, bar, conservatory; croquet
Credit cards AE, DC, MC, V
Children welcome
Disabled access difficult
Pets by arrangement
Closed never
Proprietors Howard and Judith Wyer-Roberts

White House

Dick and Kay Smith, who have been at Williton for more than 25 years now, continue to go from strength to strength. The mostly Georgian house remains immaculately and stylishly decorated, with pretty co-ordinated fabrics in the comfortable bedrooms. The Smiths' passionate interest in food and wine ensures that the daily changing menus are appetizing, and the wine cellar is one of the best in the west.

Nearby Cleeve Abbey, 1.5 miles (2.5 km); Quantock Hills.

ll Long Street, Williton, Somerset TA4 4QW
Tel (0984) 632306
Location 9 miles (14.5 km) SE of Minehead, in middle of village set back from A39; ample car parking
Food & drink full breakfast, dinner; residential and restaurant licence
Prices B&B £28-£45; DB&B £51-£68; reductions for 2 nights or more
Rooms 11 double, 9 with bath, 3 also with shower; two family rooms, with bath; all rooms have phone, radio, TV; 8 rooms have central heating, hairdrier, tea/coffee kit
Facilities sitting-room, bar, dining-room
Credit cards not accepted
Children welcome if well behaved; cots and highchairs available **Disabled** access good; ground-floor bedrooms
Pets dogs accepted if well behaved, but not in dining-room
Closed Nov to mid-May
Proprietors Dick and Kay Smith

West Somerset

Country house hotel, Wiveliscombe

Langley House

This is the first hotel the Wilsons can call their own, but they are hardly beginners in the business: Peter, who cooks, came to it via the Lygon Arms at Broadway and then Ston Easton Park (in different ways, both excellent hotels, and excluded from this guide only because they fall outside our price and size limits); while Anne, who fronts, used to run the British Tourist Authority's Commendation Scheme – gamekeeper turned poacher, as it were. Between them, they ought to know what they are about.

The house is a modest building with a rambling garden in delectable, rolling Somerset countryside which is neglected by most visitors to the West Country. (Anne Wilson is happy to advise guests on where to go touring during the day and provides them with maps.) It is not ideally furnished – less elegance, more informality would be our prescription, both for the sitting-rooms and some of the bedrooms – but the Wilsons' warmth of welcome overcomes such reservations. Peter's five-course dinners help too. They are entirely fixed until the dessert, when there is an explosion of choice. His food is light and unconventional, lovingly presented, in the best modern British manner, and elicits plenty of praise from his guests.

Nearby Gaulden Manor, 2.5 miles (4 km); Exmoor; Quantock Hills; Taunton within reach.

Langley Marsh, Wiveliscombe, Somerset TA4 2UF
Tel (0984) 623318 **Fax** 624573
Location one mile (1.5 km) NW of Wiveliscombe, off B3227; in 4-acre gardens with ample car parking
Food & drink breakfast, dinner; residential and restaurant licence
Prices B&B £37.50-£68.50; dinner £22.50-£26.50; reductions for 2 nights or more
Rooms 7 double, 6 with bath, one with shower; 2 single, both with bath; one family room, with bath; all rooms have central heating, TV, phone, radio, hairdrier
Facilities bar, 2 sitting-rooms, restaurant; croquet
Credit cards AE, MC, V
Children welcome over 7, under 7 only by arrangement
Disabled access to ground floor easy but no lift to bedrooms
Pets accepted
Closed Feb
Proprietors Peter and Anne Wilson

South Somerset

Farm guest-house, Beercrocombe

Frog Street Farm

Veronica Cole's flower-bedecked Somerset 'longhouse' is hidden deep in the countryside. When you eventually find Frog Street Farm, you can be sure of a warm welcome from Mrs Cole and her two daughters, who have been looking after guests with care and generosity since 1981. Inside, the house has great character and warmth, with a handsome oak-beamed inglenook in one sitting-room and some very antique panelling. The guests now have separate tables at dinner – a carefully prepared set meal of English food, employing vegetables and dairy produce fresh from the farm, with a choice of delicious puddings. Mrs Cole is pleased to cater for special diets, and you are welcome to take your own wine.

Nearby Barrington Court, 5 miles (8 km); Vale of Taunton.

Beercrocombe, Taunton, Somerset TA3 6AF
Tel (0823) 480430
Location 6 miles (10 km) SE of Taunton, one mile (1.5 km) from A358; car parking
Food & drink full breakfast, dinner; no licence
Prices B&B £25; dinner £15; reductions for 4 days or more
Rooms 3 double, 2 with bath, one with shower; all rooms have central heating, tea/coffee kit
Facilities 2 sitting-rooms; outdoor heated swimming-pool
Credit cards not accepted
Children welcome over 11
Disabled access difficult
Pets not accepted
Closed Christmas/New Year
Proprietor Veronica Cole

Restaurant with rooms, Yeovil

Little Barwick House

The great appeal of this listed white-painted Georgian dower house is its friendly informality – it is first and foremost the family home of the Colleys, with no sign of hotel rules or regulations. The bedrooms are comfortable, but simply furnished – don't expect four-star luxury – and the public rooms are lived-in, not smart. Veronica has gained an enviable reputation for her cooking, with local game a speciality. Christopher looks after the restaurant and cellar sitting-room – the latter is the original kitchen of the house, with an old bread oven.

Nearby Brympton d'Evercy, 2.5 miles (4 km); Montacute House, 5 miles (8 km).

Barwick, near Yeovil, Somerset BA22 9TD
Tel (0935) 23902 **Fax** 20908
Location 2 miles (3 km) S of Yeovil off A37; car parking
Food & drink breakfast, dinner; residential and restaurant licence
Prices B&B £36-£46; DB&B £54-£64; bargain breaks
Rooms 6 double, 4 with bath, 2 with shower; all have TV, central heating, tea/coffee kit
Facilities sitting-room, bar, dining-room
Credit cards AE, MC, V
Children welcome if well behaved **Disabled** access difficult **Pets** dogs welcome
Closed Christmas
Proprietors Christopher & Veronica Colley

North Somerset

Number 3

This listed Georgian town house is well established as a good restaurant, and the Tynans have been running it as a small hotel for several years. Ann does the cooking – a short menu of sensitively executed dishes employing highly original combinations of flavours. Everything is freshly made, from the cheese straws served with pre-dinner drinks to the exquisite sorbets. Both the main house and the recently converted coach-house are richly decorated, with oil paintings in gilt frames, antiques and rich colours in the public areas, and carefully co-ordinated fabrics in the large and comfortable bedrooms. There is a welcoming residents' sitting-room on the first floor.

Nearby Abbey, Tor; Wells Cathedral, 5 miles (8 km).

3 Magdalene Street,
Glastonbury, Somerset
BA6 9EW
Tel (0458) 832129
Location in middle of town;
with garden and parking for
8 cars
Food & drink breakfast,
dinner; restaurant licence
Prices B&B £35-£55; dinner
£26
Rooms 6 double, all with bath;
family room by arrangement;
all rooms have phone, central
heating, tea/coffee kit, TV
Facilities bar, sitting-room,
garden
Credit cards MC, V
Children welcome
Disabled access difficult – two
steps to front entrance
Pets not accepted
Closed first three weeks Jan
Proprietors John and Ann
Tynan

Daneswood House

The exterior of this tall Edwardian house does not inspire confidence, with its pebble-dashing and fake beams. Don't be put off: inside is a welcoming, personal atmosphere and richly decorated bedrooms with traditional furniture. Less atmospheric, perhaps more comfortable, are those in a recently built wing, with mezzanine beds and spa baths. Food and wine are taken seriously. But the winding drive hints at the key attraction: a high setting affording splendid views over the Mendips.

Nearby Cheddar Gorge and caves, 2 miles (3 km).

Cuck Hill, Shipham, nr
Winscombe, Somerset BS25
1RD
Tel (0934) 843145 **Fax** 843824
Location 1.5 miles (2 km) off
A38, 13 (21 km) miles S of
Bristol; with 4-acre grounds
and ample car parking
Food & drink breakfast,
dinner; residential and
restaurant licence
Prices B&B £32.50-£56.25;
dinner £19
Rooms 12 double (4 twin), 10
with bath, 2 with shower; all
rooms have central heating,
TV, radio, tea/coffee kit
Facilities dining-room,
sitting-room, bar
Credit cards AE, DC, MC, V
Children accepted
Disabled no special facilities
Pets tolerated if small
Closed Christmas to New Year
Proprietor David and Elise
Hodges

North Somerset

Bowlish House

The somewhat austere look of this Palladian house seems to suggest that new arrivals should perhaps knock before barging in, but Bob and Linda Morley's regime behind the formal façade is anything but pompous. These days, the public rooms of the house have rather less of the slightly battered air of an ageing dowager – there are new sofas in the sitting-room – but the atmosphere is still relaxed and home-like rather than august.

The restaurant and its food are the main focus of interest. You can sink into pink armchairs for pre-dinner drinks in the panelled bar, before moving into a restfully painted dining-room, presided over by portraits of numerous 18thC worthies, to sample Linda Morley's polished culinary efforts. A stylish conservatory extension offers a congenial space for coffee and liqueurs overlooking the well-kept gardens at the rear of the house, where there is seating for the summer months.

Up the fine wood-panelled staircase (an imported but appropriate feature), there are just three bedrooms – all comfortably furnished, with large *en suite* bathrooms and a formidable array of giveaways.

Nearby Wells, 4 miles (6 km) – cathedral, Bishop's palace; Glastonbury, 7 miles (11 km) – Tor, abbey; Mendip Hills – walking, caving; Bath within reach.

Wells Road, Shepton Mallet, Somerset BA4 5JD
Tel (0749) 342022
Location just W of Shepton Mallet on A371; with walled garden and parking for 15 cars
Food & drink breakfast, dinner; full licence
Prices B&B £24; dinner £22.50
Rooms 3 double, all with bath; all rooms have central heating, TV, radio/alarm, tea/coffee kit
Facilities dining-room, bar, sitting-room, conservatory; croquet
Credit cards MC, V
Children welcome
Disabled access difficult
Pets welcome in bedrooms
Closed Christmas
Proprietors Bob and Linda Morley

Avon

Country house hotel, Hinton Charterhouse

Homewood Park

Homewood Park has been in these pages since 1988, and in the hands of Stephen and Penny Ross (now concentrating on the Queensberry – see page 48) won high praise from every other notable guide. So it comes as no surprise to find that the Gueunings have stuck to the same successful formula of mixing the informal with the solicitous in supremely elegant surroundings. A couple of years back a fire in the kitchens affected two of the bedrooms, which were redecorated in the same country-house style as the others – matching curtains, bedcovers and canopied bedheads in soft prints – while in the bathrooms Italian tiles and stencilling were introduced to give a slightly exotic air. Three others have now had the treatment.

Of course, there are changes – a landscape gardener has been advising on the garden, the greenhouses are being restored, and, although David Backhouse's bronzes still decorate the drawing room, a softer style of decoration has been introduced.

The Gueunings (he's Belgian) met at the hotel school in Lausanne and successfully ran The Manor House in Moreton-in-Marsh for 10 years, so no amateurs in charge here. Food is, as ever, first-rate under Tim Ford, although Sara's mother produces the home-made jams and tantalizing bottled fruits in liqueur for winter months.

Nearby American Museum, 4 miles (6 km); Bath, 5 miles (8 km).

Hinton Charterhouse, Bath, Avon BA3 6BB
Tel (0225) 723731 **Fax** 723820
Location 5 miles (8 km) S of Bath, close to A36; in 10-acre grounds with ample car parking
Food & drink breakfast, lunch, dinner; restaurant licence
Prices B&B £45-£80; dinner £29.50; bargain breaks
Rooms 15 double, all with bath and shower; all rooms have central heating, TV, phone, radio, hairdrier
Facilities sitting-room, bar, 3 dining-rooms; tennis, croquet
Credit cards AE, DC, MC, V
Children by arrangement
Disabled access easy; 2 ground-floor bedrooms
Pets not accepted
Closed never
Proprietors Frank and Sara Gueuning

Avon

Carpenters Arms

The English country inn at its best – or near enough. The flower-bedecked Carpenters Arms was formed many years ago in a row of 17thC miners' cottages, and has the essential pub requisites of stone walls, heavy oak beams, log fires and real ales. In other ways it is a world away from the norm. To find twelve spacious, prettily decorated rooms with *en suite* bathrooms above a pub is one distinction. Another is the food, for which the Arms is locally renowned. In the cosy restaurant the food is that bit more adventurous than in most pubs; in the informal Coopers Parlour the emphasis is squarely on simplicity and value.
Nearby Bristol; Bath 10 miles (16 km).

Stanton Wick, Pensford, Avon BS18 4BX
Tel (0761) 490202 **Fax** 490763
Location in rural setting, 7 miles (11 km) S of Bristol, just off A37 (follow signs from A368 which crosses A37 at Chelwood); with ample car parking
Food & drink full breakfast, lunch, dinner; full licence
Prices B&B £26.25-£45.50; dinner about £12-£20

Rooms 12 double, all with bath; all rooms have central heating, phone, TV, radio
Facilities restaurant, 3 bars
Credit cards MC, V
Children not suitable
Disabled access difficult
Pets not accepted in bedrooms
Closed Christmas Day; restaurant only, Sun evening and Mon lunch
Proprietor Nigel Pushman

Paradise House

The Cuttings' handsome Georgian house was sadly neglected before they took it over in the 1970s; they now take pride in showing it to hotel guide inspectors, so confident are they in what they have achieved. The house is a steep walk or a winding drive up the wooded hill to the south of the city. This accounts for one of the guest house's main attractions – the fine views shared by the secluded rear garden and several of the spacious, prettily decorated rooms.
Nearby Abbey, Roman Baths and Pump Room, Holburne Museum, Victoria Art Gallery (most within 10 min walk).

86-88 Holloway, Bath, Avon BA2 4PX
Tel (0225) 317723 **Fax** 482005
Location on S side of city off A367; in 0.5-acre gardens with three locking garages and ample street car parking
Food & drink full breakfast; no licence
Prices B&B £35-£65; 10% reduction for 5 nights or more
Rooms 9 double, 6 with bath, one with shower; one family

room, with bath and shower; all rooms have central heating, colour TV, phone, tea/coffee kit
Facilities breakfast room, sitting-room
Credit cards AE, MC, V
Children not suitable
Disabled access fair
Pets not accepted
Closed over Christmas
Proprietors Janet and David Cutting

Avon

Fountain House

Fountain House offers an unusual formula in a provincial British city, but one which seems to be gaining popularity: serviced apartments, combining the convenience of living and cooking space with the services of a bed-and-breakfast hotel. The building is a fine old Georgian townhouse, in the past split into two but recently re-united and renovated. The suites vary widely in size, shape and style – some are essentially open-plan (one has the bed on a mezzanine), others divided into several separate rooms. Furnishings are smartly luxurious, in a variety of modern and reproduction styles. Fountain House is well placed for restaurants, with some of the city's best within easy walking distance.
Nearby Assembly Rooms, Museum of Costume.

9-11 Fountain Buildings, Lansdown Road, Bath, Avon BA1 5DV
Tel (0225) 338622 **Fax** 445855
Location in middle of city, close to main shopping area
Food & drink breakfast
Prices B&B £60-£92
Rooms 14 suites, sleeping 2 to 5 people, all with one or 2 baths; all suites have kitchen, central heating, satellite TV, phone, hairdrier, entry-phone
Facilities suites are serviced daily as in a hotel
Credit cards AE, DC, MC, V
Children welcome
Disabled access possible; lift/elevator **Pets** accepted
Closed never
Proprietors Susan and Robin Bryan

Queensberry Hotel

This Bath hotel is slightly large for our purposes, but cannot be allowed to escape the net. Its owners, Stephen and Penny Ross, opened it in 1988 while still running the justly famous Homewood Park (see page 46). Predictably, they transformed its three Georgian terraced houses into one of the most relaxing, stylish and personal places to stay in the city. The sitting-room, beautifully furnished in muted colours, is small – but the bedrooms are spacious and equipped with easy chairs and breakfast tables. Not content with just rooms, the Rosses have added a smart basement restaurant, *The Olive Tree*, which is proving to be successful; emphasis is on simple flavours and satisfying portions.
Nearby Assembly Rooms, Museum of Costume, The Circus.

Russel Street, Bath, Avon BA1 2QF
Tel (0225) 447928 **Fax** 446065
Location in middle of city, close to main shopping area; paved gardens behind; daytime car parking restricted
Food & drink breakfast, dinner; restaurant and residential licence
Prices B&B £45-£89; winter break available Nov to Mar
Rooms 22 double, all with bath; all rooms have central heating, phone, colour TV
Facilities sitting-room, bar
Credit cards AE, DC, MC, V
Children welcome; cots available **Disabled** access possible; lift/elevator
Pets not accepted **Closed** one week Christmas/ New Year
Proprietors Stephen and Penny Ross

Avon

Bed and breakfast guest-house, Bath

Holly Lodge

Carrolle Sellick is well established on the Bath bed-and-breakfast scene, having run the highly regarded Haydon House for several years. She opened up in this larger Victorian house in 1986 having rescued it from dereliction, and has again produced a base for tired sightseers which is pretty and restful as well as thoroughly comfortable. There are grand views of Bath from the garden, breakfast room and some of the bedrooms, which are large and carefully furnished. The sitting-room too is spacious, with comfy sofas, antiques and fresh flowers. Breakfast is impressive, with home-made croissants and exotic-fruit platters as an alternative to the full English treatment. Strictly no smoking.
Nearby sights of central Bath.

8 Upper Oldfield Park, Bath, Avon BA2 3JZ
Tel (0225) 424042 **Fax** 481138
Location in residential area, half a mile (one km) SW of city centre off A367; in garden, with car parking
Food & drink full breakfast
Prices B&B £35-£65
Rooms 5 double, all with bath and shower, one single with shower; all have central heating, colour TV, phone, tea/coffee kit; most have trouser-press, hairdrier
Facilities sitting-room
Credit cards AE, DC, MC, V
Children accepted over age 10
Disabled access difficult
Pets not accepted
Closed never
Proprietor Carrolle Sellick

Town guest-house, Bath

Somerset House

The Seymours took the name of their established guest-house with them when they moved further up steep Bathwick Hill in 1985, and with it the formula for which they had become known: caring, personal service (not for those who seek anonymity), harmoniously furnished rooms and thoroughly good food – mainly traditional English in style, but with occasional excursions into foreign territory – at impressively modest prices. The Regency character of the building has been carefully preserved; it is a strictly no-smoking house.
Nearby Holburne Museum and Pulteney Bridge.

35 Bathwick Hill, Bath, Avon BA2 6LD
Tel (0225) 466451
Location on SE side of city; private car parking
Food & drink breakfast, dinner, lunch on Sun only; restaurant licence
Prices B&B £30; DB&B £48; reduction for 3 nights plus and for children sharing parents' room; bargain breaks Nov-May
Rooms 4 double, all with bath and shower; one single, with shower; 5 family rooms, all with bath and shower; all have central heating, phone, radio
Facilities 2 sitting-rooms (one with bar), dining-room
Credit cards AE, MC, V
Children welcome over 10
Disabled not suitable for severe disabilities
Pets small dogs only
Closed never
Proprietors J and M Seymour and family

Avon

Country guest-house, Bathford

Eagle House

No sign is displayed outside Eagle House, standing behind a stone wall and dignified wrought-iron gates, to suggest it is anything other than a fine, privately-owned, listed Georgian mansion. Inside, too, there is little to dispel that impression, particularly when sitting in the superb drawing-room which overlooks landscaped grounds and commands beautiful views across the Avon valley. John and Rosamund Napier are skilled hosts, combining professional service (John Napier trained at the Savoy and managed the Priory in Bath before moving here) with commendable informality – John firmly believes in trusting, not fussing over, his guests. The house is decorated without pomp – it is after all a guest-house rather than a full-blown hotel; the spacious bedrooms and adjoining bathrooms display simple wallpapers and an eclectic mix of furniture, ranging from the grand to the simple – some showing its age. Two additional bedrooms with a shared living-room and kitchen (for stays of 2 nights plus) have been created in a cottage in the old walled garden.

Nearby sights of Bath – abbey, Roman Baths; American Museum, 2.5 miles (4 km).

Church Street, Bathford, Bath, Avon BA1 7RS
Tel (0225) 859946
Location 2.5 miles (4 km) E of Bath, off A363, in village; in 2-acre gardens, with ample car parking
Food & drink breakfast; residential licence
Prices B&B £23-£39; £2.70 extra for full breakfast; children sharing parents' room charged only for breakfast
Rooms 3 double with bath, 2 with shower; one single with shower; 2 family rooms with bath, one also with shower; all rooms have central heating, colour TV, phone, tea/coffee kit, hairdrier
Facilities sitting-room, dining-room; croquet
Credit cards not accepted
Children welcome; cots, baby-sitting available
Disabled access difficult **Pets** dogs accepted
Closed 10 days over Christmas
Proprietors John and Rosamund Napier

Avon

Town guest-house, Bath

Sydney Gardens

Off the main tourist track in a quiet residential area of Bath overlooking a small park, Sydney Gardens is nevertheless conveniently close to Bath's popular sights. The large, Italianate Victorian house has been completely renovated by the Smithsons, and Stanley's own paintings adorn the walls. Bedrooms are individually and freshly decorated in well co-ordinated colours, and even those right at the top of the house have enough space for easy chairs. The breakfast room and sitting-room are light and gracious, and the smoking ban (in the whole house) ensures that non-smokers will enjoy their coffee and croissants.

Nearby Holburne Museum, canal towpath walk.

Sydney Road, Bath, Avon, BA2 6NT
Tel (0225) 464818
Location close to middle of town; in small garden with some private car parking and more on street
Food & drink full breakfast; no licence
Prices B&B £35-£59; reductions for 2 nights or more; winter breaks
Rooms 6 double, all with bath; all rooms have central heating, phone, colour TV, tea/coffee kit, hairdrier, radio alarm
Facilities sitting-room, breakfast room
Credit cards MC, V
Children welcome over 4
Disabled access difficult
Pets small dogs only by arrangement; must be kept in bedrooms
Closed Christmas and Jan
Proprietors Stanley and Diane Smithson

Country guest-house, Bathford

The Orchard

Few central Bath guest-houses can match the style and refinement of this detached Georgian house, in the attractive outlying village of Bathford, which the Londons have been running since the early 1980s. The bedrooms (no smoking) are large and uncluttered, with pleasant views over the secluded garden (which has an exceptional range of fine trees), and the spacious sitting-room is dotted with antiques. A log fire burns in cool weather, and there are plenty of books, magazines and games to hand. Breakfast is a wholesome affair served at one communal table.

Nearby Bath; American Museum, 2.5 miles (4 km).

80 High Street, Bathford, Bath, Avon BA1 7TG
Tel (0225) 858765
Location 3 miles (5 km) E of Bath, close to A363, in village; 1.5-acre grounds with ample car parking
Food & drink breakfast, no licence
Prices B&B £30
Rooms 4 double, all with bath and shower; all rooms have central heating, colour TV
Facilities sitting-room, dining-room
Credit cards not accepted
Children welcome over 11
Disabled access difficult
Pets not accepted
Closed Nov to Feb
Proprietors John and Olga London

Wiltshire

Chilvester Hill House

Running a guest-house is not the Dilleys' only job – Gill breeds beef cattle and John is a semi-retired consultant physician. They started taking guests into their solid Victorian home in the early 1980s, and since then have gone from strength to strength. The house has large rooms with high ceilings, elegantly furnished; family photos, books and ornaments mingle with antiques, velvet sofas and old prints. The three bedrooms are equally spacious, and carefully decorated in different floral styles. Meals are eaten at the family table: casseroles and roasts in winter, game in season, vegetables and salads from the garden.

Nearby Bowood; Avebury and Lacock, both 7 miles (11 km).

Calne, Wiltshire SN11 0LP **Tel** (0249) 813981 **Fax** 814217 **Location** in rural setting, 0.5 mile (1 km) W of Calne just off A4, signed to Bremhill; with gardens and car parking **Food & drink** breakfast, dinner by arrangement; residential licence **Prices** B&B £30-£50; dinner £18-£22; reductions for one week	**Rooms** 3 double, all with bath; all rooms have heating, TV, radio, tea/coffee kit **Facilities** dining-room, 2 sitting-rooms; swimming-pool **Credit cards** AE, DC, MC, V **Children** accepted over 12 years **Disabled** no special facilities **Pets** not accepted **Closed** one week low season **Proprietors** John and Gill Dilley

Fosse Farmhouse

A reader who had a cream tea at Caron Cooper's mellow stone farmhouse brought it to our attention. The scones were highly impressive; so is the rest of Caron's operation. Her background is in antiques and interior design, and it shows: the house is a delightful confection of antique furniture, stripped pine, ornaments and confidently chosen fabrics and colours. There are open log fires in the public rooms, antique lace bedspreads in the bedrooms. Caron is a cordon bleu cook; her three-course dinners offer no choice of main course, but vegetarians can be catered for.

Nearby Castle Combe, 2 miles (3 km); Cotswolds.

Nettleton Shrub, Nettleton, nr Chippenham, Wiltshire SN14 7NJ **Tel** (0249) 782286 **Fax** 783066 **Location** in countryside off B4039, 6 miles (10 km) NW of Chippenham; with 1.5 acre grounds, private car parking **Food & drink** full breakfast, lunch, dinner; residential and restaurant licence **Prices** B&B £37.50-£60; lunch from £7.50, dinner £22	**Rooms** 4 double, one with bath, 3 with shower; one single with shower, one suite, one family room with bath; all rooms have central heating, TV, tea/coffee kit, hairdrier **Facilities** dining-room, sitting-room, tea-room **Credit cards** AE, MC, V **Children** accepted **Disabled** access not easy **Pets** by arrangement **Closed** never **Proprietor** Caron Cooper

Wiltshire

Priory Steps

This is an amalgamation of a whole row of 17thC weavers' cottages, typical of Bradford, sympathetically decorated and furnished by Diana and Carey Chapman when they moved here from London in 1985. Each of the bedrooms has a decorative theme. Diana is a trained cook, and her three-course dinners (no choice, but any requirements happily met given notice) can be served either at a communal table in the dining-room or on the terrace overlooking the pretty two-level garden and the town.

Nearby Barton Tithe Barn; Bath, 8 miles (13 km).

Newtown, Bradford-on- Avon, Wiltshire BA15 1NQ
Tel (0225) 862230
Location close to middle of town, on N side; with car parking
Food & drink full breakfast, dinner; residential licence
Prices B&B £28-£42; dinner £15
Rooms 5 double, all with bath; all rooms have central heating, colour TV, tea/coffee kit
Facilities sitting-room, dining-room
Credit cards MC, V
Children accepted
Disabled access easy to one ground-floor bedroom, but dining-room on lower ground floor
Pets not encouraged
Closed never
Proprietors Carey and Diana Chapman

Bradford Old Windmill

Although it functioned only briefly, the Roberts' extraordinary home was built in 1807 as a windmill. The sitting-room and the principal bedroom each occupy a whole floor of the old tower; all the rooms are charmingly furnished, with stripped pine furniture and odds and ends from around the world. One round room has a round bed, and another room has a water bed. The vegetarian feasts the Robertses offer reflect their own interests and travels – dishes ranging from Mexican to Thai, and a choice of Continental, English, Healthy and American breakfasts. Smoking is not allowed. Take your own wine.

Nearby Barton Tithe Barn; Bath, 8 miles (13 km).

Masons Lane, Bradford-on-Avon, Wiltshire BA15 1QN
Tel (0225) 866842
Location just N of town centre; with cottage garden and parking for 4 cars
Food & drink full breakfast, dinner (Mon, Thur, Sat only)
Prices B&B £27.50-£50; dinner £18; reduction for children and 3 nights or more
Rooms 2 double, one with bath, one with shower; one single; one family room with shower; all rooms have central heating, colour TV, tea/coffee kit, alarm
Facilities sitting-room, dining-room
Credit cards not accepted
Children welcome over 6 years if well behaved
Disabled access difficult
Pets not accepted
Closed never **Proprietors** Peter and Priscilla Roberts

Wiltshire

Inn, Lacock

At the Sign of the Angel

Lacock and The Sign of the Angel go hand-in-hand: the 'perfect' English village (almost entirely in the preserving hands of the National Trust) and the epitome of the medieval English inn – half-timbered without, great log fires, oak panelling, beamed ceilings, splendid old beds and polished antique tables within.

There are many such inns sprinkled around middle England, but most are better enjoyed over a beer or two, or a meal, than overnight. Even here, the rooms vary in comfort and none could be called spacious. But they are all cosy and charming nonetheless, and full of character. The Angel is emphatically run as a small hotel rather than a pub – tellingly, there are no bars, and the residents' oak-panelled sitting-room on the first floor is quiet.

The Angel has belonged to the Levis family for 40 years, and is now run by son-in-law George Hardy with the help of village ladies. George also does the cooking – traditional English food such as roasts and casseroles. Breakfast offers old-timers such as junket and prunes as well as a huge cooked meal if you want it.

If the rooms in the inn itself are booked, don't turn down the cottage annexe, which is equally attractive and pleasantly secluded.

Nearby Lacock Abbey; Bowood House, 3 miles (5 km); Corsham Court, 3 miles (5 km); Sheldon Manor, 5 miles (8 km).

6 Church Street, Lacock, near Chippenham, Wiltshire SN15 2LA
Tel (0249) 730230 **Fax** 730527
Location 3 miles (5 km) S of Chippenham off A350, in middle of village; with gardens, and some car parking
Food & drink full breakfast, lunch, snacks, dinner Mon-Sat; cold supper on Sun; full licence
Prices B&B £37.50-£55; dinner £10-£27.50; buffet lunch from £2.50, Sun lunch £16-£22; bargain breaks
Rooms 10 double, all with bath; all have central heating, phone, tea/coffee kit
Facilities 2 dining-rooms, sitting-room **Credit cards** AE, MC, V **Children** over 12
Disabled access difficult
Pets dogs accepted, but not allowed in public rooms
Closed 22 Dec to 6 Jan
Manager George Hardy

Wiltshire

Manor house, Melksham

Shurnhold House

Yet another grand old house rescued from decay in the late 1980s and put to new use – in this case, a bed-and-breakfast guest-house, in business since late 1988. The house is a beautifully proportioned stone-built Jacobean affair dating from 1640. It sits quite close to a busy main road on the outskirts of an unremarkable town, but is well shielded by trees (look for the signs, because you will not spot the house) and well placed for touring in several directions.

Inside, all is as you would wish. A flagstone floor in the bar/sitting-room, oak beams, log fires and pretty floral fabrics here and in the breakfast room and sitting-room, which is full of books. Period furnishings are used wherever the opportunity arises and the budget allows. The beamed bedrooms are spacious, with restrained decoration – perhaps rich floral drapes against plain white walls – and several different styles of bed; several have fireplaces. Smoking is not allowed in the bedrooms.

Prices have been set at just the right level – higher than your typical B&B, but at half the rate of many 'country house hotels' occupying similarly splendid buildings. The licensed bar is an unusual feature for a B&B place.

Nearby Lacock, 2 miles (3.5 km); Bradford-on-Avon.

Shurnhold, Melksham, Wiltshire SN12 8DG
Tel (0225) 790555
Location in countryside, one mile (1.5 km) NW of Melksham on A365 to Box; in large garden with ample car parking
Food & drink breakfast; residential licence
Prices B&B £30-£45
Rooms 8 double, one family room, all with bath; all rooms have central heating, phone, TV, radio, hairdrier, tea/coffee kit
Facilities dining-room, sitting-room, bar/sitting-room
Credit cards MC, V
Children welcome
Disabled no special facilities
Pets dogs accepted by prior arrangement
Closed never
Proprietors Sue and Chris Mead

SOUTH-EAST ENGLAND

Hampshire

Country house hotel, Hurstbourne Tarrant

Esseborne Manor

The Yeos took over this polished and richly furnished turn-of-the-century house in 1988, putting day-to-day management in the hands of Frieda's son, Simon Richardson. Bedrooms are well equipped and prettily done up, the sitting-room spacious and relaxed, the sitting-room bar stylish, the dining-room elegant. Cooking is serious, extremely innovative and increasingly highly regarded; there is a daily set menu, with a short alternative *carte*.
Nearby Highclere Castle, 5 miles (8km); Stonehenge.

Hurstbourne Tarrant,
Andover, Hampshire
SP11 0ER
Tel (026476) 444 **Fax** 473
Location 7 miles (11 km) N of
Andover, on A343 1.5 miles
(2.5 km) N of village; in 4-acre
grounds with ample car
parking
Food & drink breakfast,
lunch, dinner; residential and
restaurant licence
Prices B&B £47.50-£84;
dinner £19.50; reductions for
2 nights or more
Rooms 12 double, all with
bath and shower; all rooms
have central heating, TV,
phone, clock, radio
Facilities bar, 2 sitting-rooms,
dining-room; tennis, croquet,
golf practice net
Credit cards AE, DC, MC, V
Children welcome over 12
Disabled access easy to
restaurant and one ground-
floor bedroom with wider
doors
Pets not accepted
Closed never
Proprietors Michael and
Frieda Yeo

Manor house hotel, Middle Wallop

Fifehead Manor

An inspection visit confirms that Mrs van Veelen continues to build on the fundamental strengths of her well established hotel – the character of the main red-brick building, the peace of its mature garden and the spaciousness of the bedrooms. Improvements to the decoration and furnishings (particularly in the once-dreary public areas) have paid great dividends, and chef Mark Robertson seems to go from strength to strength. The welcome is as warm as ever.
Nearby Museum of Army Flying; Stonehenge, 10 miles (16 km).

Middle Wallop, Stockbridge,
Hampshire SO20 8EG
Tel (0264) 781565 **Fax** 781400
Location 5 miles (8 km) SW of
Andover on A343; in gardens
with parking for 50 cars
Food & drink breakfast,
lunch, dinner; full licence
Prices B&B £40-£50; dinner
from £25; bargain breaks;
children sharing parents'
room £12 (under 5 free)
Rooms 10 double, all with
bath, 5 also with shower; 6
single, one with bath, 5 with
shower; all rooms have central
heating, TV, phone, radio
Facilities sitting-room, bar, 2
dining-rooms; croquet
Credit cards AE, DC, MC, V
Children welcome
Disabled access to 2 rooms
Pets welcome
Closed 2 weeks Christmas
Proprietor Mrs M van Veelen

Hampshire

Inn, Winchester

Wykeham Arms

This unusual back-street pub takes its name from the founder of
Winchester College, only yards away; the cathedral is also close
by, making this a natural port of call for senior members of the
choir. The Jamesons have created an appealing ambience, particularly in the cheerful bars, with their four log fires. The
bedrooms (with bathrooms and even a sauna squeezed into the
most unlikely spaces) have recently been totally refurbished.
There is a pleasant breakfast room, and the informal suppers are
in great demand; 22 interesting wines are served by the glass.
Nearby Cathedral, Venta Roman Museum, Winchester College.

75 Kingsgate Street,
Winchester, Hampshire
SO23 9PE
Tel (0962) 853834 **Fax** 854411
Location in middle of city,
between College and
cathedral, on corner of Canon
Street; small rear garden with
some car parking
Food & drink breakfast,
lunch, dinner; full licence
Prices B&B £36.25-£62.50;
dinner about £15

Rooms 7 double, all with bath;
all rooms have central
heating, phone, colour TV,
tea/coffee kit, radio/ alarm
Facilities 3 bars, sauna; patio
Credit cards AE, MC, V
Children welcome over 14
Disabled access difficult
Pets welcome
Closed restaurant only, Sun
Proprietors Graeme and Anne
Jameson

Country hotel, Petersfield

Langrish House

A secluded country house, rescued from ruin in 1980 by its
present owners. The rambling, pale stone building dates back to
the 16th century, though it is the Victorian Gothic extensions
which predominate from the sweeping gravel drive. The cellars
have been cleverly excavated to provide a cosy restaurant, breakfast room and sitting-areas. The sitting-room is small, but spotlessly kept and recently redecorated.
Nearby South coast, South Downs and Winchester within reach.

Langrish, Petersfield,
Hampshire GU32 1RN
Tel (0730) 66941 **Fax** 260543
Location 3 miles (5 km) W of
Petersfield, off A272; in 13-
acre grounds, with ample car
parking
Food & drink breakfast,
dinner (except Sun and bank
holidays); residential and
restaurant licence
Prices B&B £27.50-£48;
dinner from £12
Rooms 13 double, 5 single; all
with bath; all have central

heating, TV, radio, phone
Facilities 3 sitting-rooms,
dining-room, 2 bars
Credit cards AE, DC, MC, V
Children accepted
(baby-listening devices)
Disabled access easy for
ground-floor bedrooms;
difficult for dining-room
Pets accepted by prior
arrangement only
Closed one week after
Christmas
Proprietor Monique von
Kospoth

Hampshire

Town hotel, Wickham

Old House

The Old House has just about everything that we have been looking for in compiling this guide: a lovely setting – at a corner of the main square of one of the finest villages in Hampshire; a superb building – Grade II listed early Georgian; a delightful secluded garden full of roses; an immaculately kept and interesting interior, with antiques and 'objets' arranged to the best possible effect; and a restaurant serving far-above-average food – French regional in style, making excellent use of fresh ingredients. And, not least, there are the proprietors, Richard and Annie Skipwith, who keep a relaxed but attentive eye on the needs of the guests.

Nothing is over-stated – except perhaps the generous arrangements of fresh flowers which adorn all the public rooms. Bedrooms vary considerably – some are palatial, one or two rather cramped – but again a mood of civilized comfort prevails. Note however that the whole hotel (restaurant included) is closed on Sundays – which suggests that the business market is the dominant customer.

Nearby Portsmouth, 9 miles (14.5 km); South Downs; Winchester, Chichester within reach.

The Square, Wickham, Hampshire PO17 5JG
Tel (0329) 833049 **Fax** 833672
Location 2.5 miles (4 km) N of Fareham, on square in middle of village; car parking
Food & drink full breakfast, lunch, dinner; residential and restaurant licence
Prices B&B £42.50-£70; dinner from £20
Rooms 9 double, 3 single, one family room, all with bath; all rooms have central heating, TV, phone, trouser-press, hairdrier, radio/alarm
Facilities 2 sitting-rooms, dining-room, bar
Credit cards AE, DC, MC, V
Children very welcome; special meals provided
Disabled access easy to dining-room
Pets not accepted
Closed Sun; 2 weeks in Aug
Proprietor Richard Skipwith

Isle of Wight

Seaview Hotel

We wish there were more seaside hotels like this, catering for families but not compromising on standards of housekeeping, hospitality and, particularly, food and wine, for which Nicola Hayward (a former professional wine-taster) has built a high (indeed, award-winning) reputation. The Seaview is also the central pub of the village, making it all the more attractive for most visitors. It is a mainly Victorian/Edwardian building.

Nearby Flamingo Park, one mile (1.5 km); Bembridge Maritime Museum, 4 miles (6 km).

High Street, Seaview, Isle of Wight PO34 5EX
Tel (0983) 612711 **Fax** 613729
Location near the beach in seaside village 3 miles (5 km) E of Ryde; with car parking
Food & drink breakfast, lunch, dinner; pub meals; full licence
Prices B&B £40-£60; dinner from £16
Rooms 14 double, 12 with bath and 2 with shower; 2 suites both with bath; all have central heating, phone, TV, radio, baby-listening
Facilities 2 sitting-rooms (one non-smoking), dining-room, bar, public bar
Credit cards AE, DC, MC, V
Children very welcome – special meals and rooms provided
Disabled 2 ground-floor bedrooms, but doors narrow
Pets welcome if well behaved, except in public rooms
Closed restaurant only, Sun dinner
Proprietors N and N Hayward

Winterbourne

This spacious house is of 18thC origin, and much is made of the time Dickens spent here writing; but 'Dickensian' is the last adjective that springs to mind. Elegant, polished and formal are among the first, along with peaceful: the house and immaculate grounds (with streams and pools) are deliciously secluded. Many of the rooms are in a separate coach-house, giving sea views. The set four-course meals are not notably ambitious, but freshly prepared with local ingredients, and include a vegetarian option.

Nearby beach; Botanic Gardens, Ventnor, one mile (2 km).

Bonchurch, Isle of Wight
Tel (0983) 852535 **Fax** 853056
Location in Bonchurch, 0.5 miles (one km) off A3055; with 4-acre grounds and ample car parking
Food & drink breakfast, dinner, lunch by request; full licence
Prices B&B £39-£43; DB&B £52-£57; reductions for children sharing
Rooms 14 double (5 twin), 3 single, one family room, all with bath or shower; all have phone, TV, radio; most have central heating **Facilities** sitting-room, dining-room, bar
Credit cards AE, DC, MC, V
Children welcome; baby-listening, babysitting by arrangement; no under 5s in dining-room **Disabled** not suitable **Pets** dogs accepted but must be kept on leads
Closed Nov to Mar
Proprietors TA and PM O'Connor

Surrey

Langshott Manor

Coming upon this exquisite brick-and-timber Elizabethan manor-house, in its own grounds amid the suburban sprawl of Horley, is akin to discovering a rare orchid in a swamp. As likely as not, you'll be greeted by the three friendly house labradors; Geoffrey Noble may be raking the extensive lawns. Once inside, surrounded by oak panelling, the only sound is of a clock ticking.

Through the cold winter of 1986-87, the Noble family lived up to their name, draining ponds and restoring the house to its current immaculate state. Each of the rooms is named after one of the children; each has a distinct character, but all are luxuriously furnished and well equipped. Dinner – traditional and wholesome English food with Elizabeth David overtones – is now served at separate tables, with the grand oak dining-table now reserved for larger parties.

The Nobles seem to have thought of everything, down to the courtesy car to take you to and from the airport if necessary. For a family-run house, Langshott is not cheap. But you get what you pay for.

Nearby Gatwick airport; Ashdown Forest; Hever castle, Chartwell.

Langshott, Horley, Surrey
RH6 9LN
Tel (0293) 786680
Location 0.75 miles (one km)
E of A23, 2.5 miles (4 km) N
of Gatwick Airport; in 3-acre
gardens with ample car
parking
Food & drink breakfast,
lunch, dinner; residential and
restaurant licence
Prices B&B £57-£101; dinner
£25
Rooms 7 double, all with bath;

all rooms have central
heating, TV, radio
Facilities dining-room,
sitting-room, library, gallery;
croquet, clock golf
Credit cards AE, DC, MC, V
Children accepted; but ponds
dangerous for toddlers
Disabled no special facilities
Pets not accepted
Closed Christmas Day
Proprietors Geoffrey, Patricia
and Christopher Noble

West Sussex

Town guest-house, Chichester

Suffolk House

Since they took over in 1990, the Pages have made this Georgian-style townhouse a welcoming and comfortable haven. House-keeping is excellent, with close attention to detail. After revitalising the airy bedrooms and bathrooms, they last year created an inviting sitting-room; this is non-smoking, like the dining-room where traditional English and French dishes are served. There is also a neat walled garden.
Nearby Cathedral, festival theatre.

3 East Row, Chichester, West Sussex PO19 1PD
Tel (0243) 778899 **Fax** 787282
Location off East Street, in middle of city, with walled garden; parking on street, or in private space 5 mins away
Food & drink breakfast, lunch, dinner; residential and restaurant licence
Prices B&B £32.50-£46.50; lunch from £6, dinner from £12.50; children half-price

Rooms 6 double, 4 single, 2 family rooms, all with bath; all rooms have central heating, phone, TV, radio, hairdrier
Facilities sitting-room, dining-room, bar
Credit cards AE, DC, MC, V
Children very welcome
Disabled 4 ground-floor rooms
Pets not allowed in dining-room **Closed** never
Proprietors Michael and Rosemary Page

Country hotel, Midhurst

Park House

Although Park House has been run as a hotel for nearly forty years, it still retains the atmosphere of a private country house – thanks to the careful attention of Ioné O'Brien. Set in nine-acre gardens, it is a 16thC mansion with Victorian additions. The large, elegant public rooms include a drawing-room lined with books and ornaments, and a long dining-room with polished tables that can be fitted together. Bedrooms are individually furnished and overlook the gardens and grass tennis-courts. Ioné and her helpers produce satisfying dinner-party food.
Nearby Petworth, 6 miles (10.5 km); Chichester, 12 miles (19 km)

Bepton, Nr Midhurst, West Sussex GU29 0JB
Tel (0730) 812880 **Fax** 815643
Location in countryside, close to B2226 and just N of village of Bepton, 3 miles (5 km) SSW of Midhurst; with 9 acres of gardens and ample car parking
Food & drink full breakfast, lunch, dinner; residential and restaurant licence
Prices B&B £52-£54; DB&B £69-£72; lunch £13.50; dinner from £17.50; reductions for 4 nights or more

Rooms 9 double, one single, all with bath; all rooms have central heating, phone, TV, radio, hairdrier
Facilities dining-room, sitting-room, bar, TV room; swimming-pool, 2 grass tennis courts, croquet, 9 hole pitch and putt course
Credit cards AE, MC, V
Children welcome
Disabled one ground-floor bedroom **Pets** accepted except in dining-room
Closed never
Proprietor Mrs Ioné O'Brien

West Sussex

Ockenden Manor

There have been many changes for the better here since Anne Goodman took over this attractive 16th/17thC manor house – notably in the richly harmonious decorations. Bedrooms are spacious and individual (and crammed with giveaways), and staff friendly and obliging. Despite its size, the hotel is run in a personal way, is comfortable, and convenient for Gatwick and Brighton. Dinner, served in the oak-panelled restaurant with painted ceiling and stained glass windows, is another highlight.
Nearby Nyman's Garden, 3 miles (5 km).

Ockenden Lane, Cuckfield, West Sussex RH17 5LD
Tel (0444) 416111 **Fax** 415549
Location 2 miles (3 km) W of Hayward's Heath close to middle of village, off A272; in 9-acre grounds, with ample car parking
Food & drink breakfast, lunch, tea, dinner; residential licence
Prices B&B £45-£90; dinner from £26.50; half-price meals for children under 10
Rooms 21 double, all with bath; one single with shower; all have central heating, TV, phone, radio, trouser-press, hairdrier
Facilities sitting-room, bar, dining-room, function room
Credit cards AE, DC, MC, V
Children welcome
Disabled access easy to restaurant
Pets not accepted
Closed never
Proprietor Mrs Anne Goodman

The King's Head

One of our favourite recipes for a satisfying stay in the country at reasonable prices: a pub full of character and with an ambitious kitchen, and adequately comfortable and bright bedrooms. Chef Jeremy Ashpool, who owned the restaurant, has left – but his successor, Jackie Young, appears to be keeping up the good work, producing inventive, modern dishes. We look forward to reports on the new regime. The pub is a welcoming place, but it is a pub, with no hotel-like facilities such as sitting-rooms.
Nearby Nyman's Gardens, 3 miles (5 km).

South Street, Cuckfield, Sussex RH17 5VY
Tel (0444) 454006
Location in middle of village on A272, near church; with garden; no private car parking
Food & drink breakfast, bar snacks; lunch, dinner in separate restaurant; full licence
Prices B&B £22.50-£42; dinner from £6
Rooms 9 double (4 twin), one with bath, 7 with shower, one with handbasin; all rooms have central heating, phone, TV, tea/coffee kit
Facilities 2 bars, restaurant, family room
Credit cards AE, MC, V
Children welcome
Pets tolerated
Disabled access difficult
Closed Christmas dinner
Proprietor Peter Tolhurst

West Sussex

Gravetye Manor

The country house hotel, now so much a part of the tourist scene in Britain, scarcely existed when Peter Herbert opened the doors of this serene Elizabethan house just over 35 years ago. It is scarcely surprising that in that time he and his team have got their act thoroughly polished; but it is remarkable that Gravetye is not in the least eclipsed by younger competitors. Standards in every department are unflaggingly high. Service consistently achieves the elusive aim of attentiveness without intrusion, while the ambitious food – eclectic, but predominantly French and English – is about the best in the county.

The pioneering gardener William Robinson lived in the house for half a century until his death in 1935. Great care is taken to maintain the various gardens he created; Robinson was also responsible for many features of the house as it is seen today – the mellow oak panelling and grand fireplaces in the calm sitting-rooms, for example. Bedrooms – all immaculately done out – vary in size from the adequate to the enormous, and prices range accordingly.

Nearby Wakehurst, 3 miles (5 km); Nyman's Gardens, 6 miles (10 km).

Vowels Lane, near East Grinstead, West Sussex RH19 4LJ
Tel (0342) 810567 **Fax** 810080
Location 4.5 miles (7 km) SW of East Grinstead by B2110 at Gravetye; in 30 acre grounds with ample car parking
Food & drink breakfast, lunch, dinner; restaurant and residential licence
Prices B&B £73.50-£112; dinner £31-£60
Rooms 16 double, 2 single, all with bath; all rooms have central heating, TV, phone, radio, hairdrier
Facilities 2 sitting rooms, bar, dining-room; croquet, trout fishing
Credit cards MC, V
Children welcome over 7, and babes in arms
Disabled access difficult
Pets not accepted
Closed never
Proprietors Herbert family

West Sussex

Country house hotel, Storrington

Little Thakeham

We stray well outside our normal price limits here to embrace a house of irresistible character – an Edwin Lutyens Tudor-style manor built in 1902-3 and considered one of his finest. The Ractliffs have been running it since 1980 as a refined and luxurious hotel of rare quality. The centrepiece is a double-height sitting-room with a vast fireplace and minstrel's gallery, and the furnishings – some by Lutyens himself – are of a high standard throughout. The Elizabethan theme continues into the part-paved, part-grassy gardens – 'beautifully laid out and kept up', says a satisfied visitor.

Nearby Parham House; Arundel Castle; Petworth; Sussex Downs.

Merrywood Lane, Storrington, West Sussex RH20 3HE **Tel** (0903) 744416 **Fax** 745022 **Location** 1.5 miles (2.5km) N of Storrington, close to B2139; in garden with ample car parking **Food & drink** full breakfast; lunch and dinner by arrangement; full licence **Prices** B&B £75-£95; dinner £32.50 **Rooms** 9 double, all with bath; all rooms have central heating, Teletext TV, phone **Facilities** sitting-room, bar, restaurant; tennis, heated swimming-pool, croquet; helipad **Credit cards** AE, DC, MC, V **Children** welcome **Disabled** access fair **Pets** not accepted **Closed** Christmas, New Year **Proprietors** Tim and Pauline Ractliff

---

Country guest-house, Chichester

Crouchers Bottom

The Fodens cannot explain the name of their converted farm-house – a stalker's affliction, perhaps? – but they have created in it a relaxed and welcoming atmosphere for guests. Bedrooms, which are in a separate converted coach house, and in which there is no smoking, are prettily decorated, with thoughtful use of space. The sitting-room in the main house has been extended to make room for a 'garden restaurant'. Over breakfast, the Fodens' goose provides a lively cabaret in the orchard outside.

Nearby Fishbourne Palace, Chichester, 2 miles (3 km).

Birdham Road, Apuldram, Chichester, West Sussex PO20 7EH **Tel** (0243) 784995 **Fax** 539797 **Location** in countryside 2 miles (3km) S of Chichester on the A286 **Food & drink** breakfast, dinner, snack lunches by arrangement; residential and restaurant licence **Prices** B&B £33-£51; dinner £19; reductions for 3 nights or more **Rooms** 6 double, 5 with bath, one with shower; all rooms have colour TV, tea/coffee kit, radio alarm, hairdrier, phone **Facilities** sitting-room, dining-room **Credit cards** MC, V **Children** accepted **Disabled** access easy – 4 ground-floor bedrooms, one specially adapted **Pets** by arrangement **Closed** Christmas week **Proprietors** Ronald and Pamela Foden

East Sussex

Coutry house hotel, Rushlake Green

Stone House

Having moved (after running the extremely successful Priory Hotel) to their ancestral family home, a glorious 16thC manor house, Peter and Jane Dunn have not been able to resist opening their doors to guests again. The fact that their current enterprise is on a much smaller scale means that Jane has time to do what she enjoys most – cooking, and looking after her house guests individually. Her relaxed and friendly demeanour belies a very sure touch, and Stone House is run with great competence – which means it is much in demand for house parties, Glynebourne visitors (luxury wicker picnic hampers can be prepared), shooting weekends (Peter can organize Land Rovers, dogs and guns) and even small executive conferences.

Bedrooms are beautifully decorated; two have exceptionally fine antique four-posters and are particularly spacious (the bathrooms can double as sitting rooms). Televisions are hidden so as not to spoil the period charm. This is an excellent place in which to sample authentic English country living at its most gracious – log fires and billiards, woodland walks and croquet – together with the atmosphere of a home rather than a hotel.

Nearby Battle; Glyndebourne 15 miles (24 km).

Rushlake Green, Heathfield, East Sussex TN21 9QJ
Tel and Fax (0435) 830726
Location just off village green 8 miles (13 km) NW of Battle, in large grounds with ample car parking
Food & drink full breakfast, afternoon tea, dinner; residential licence
Prices B&B £50-£81.25; dinner £24.95
Rooms 8 double (5 twin), all with bath; all rooms have central heating, telephone, radio, TV
Facilities sitting-room, library, dining-room; billiards/snooker; croquet, fishing, shooting
Credit cards not accepted
Children welcome over 9
Disabled not suitable
Pets welcome, in bedrooms only
Closed Christmas to mid-Jan
Proprietors Peter and Jane Dunn

East Sussex

Town hotel, Brighton

The Twenty One

This tall Victorian town house in quiet Kemptown proves that a small hotel can be beautifully furnished and caringly run without charging guests the earth. The bedrooms are light and harmonious, and well equipped – one with a special emphasis on Victorian furnishings, including a splendid four-poster bed (but note that this is a room without en suite bathroom). Public rooms are smartly done out in a rich, modern style, and the dining-room is particularly prettily decorated. Dinner – ordered 24 hours in advance – is a rich three-course set meal with a French flavour.

Nearby Royal Pavilion; Sea World.

21 Charlotte Street, Brighton, East Sussex BN2 1AG
Tel (0273) 686450 **Fax** 607711
Location just off seafront road in Brighton; with free on-street parking
Food & drink breakfast, dinner; residential licence
Prices B&B £23-£50; dinner £15.50
Rooms 6 double, 5 with shower; all rooms have central heating, colour TV, phone, tea/coffee kit, radio, hairdrier
Facilities sitting-room, dining-room
Credit cards AE, MC, V
Children welcome over 12
Disabled not suitable
Pets not accepted
Closed restaurant only, Sun and Mon
Proprietors David and Jan Power

Country house house, Battle

Powdermills

The extensive grounds, complete with lakes and woodland, are only one attraction of this elegant Georgian house. The Cowplands are big in the antiques trade, and have assembled an interesting variety of period pieces – though without spoiling the comfortable, lived-in feel of the sitting-rooms. Some bedrooms have antiques, too, while others are more modern. Guests dine in the Orangery (also open to non-residents). Food is *nouvelle* in style and includes locally caught fish and game.

Nearby Bodiam, 6 miles (10 km); Bateman's, 8 miles (13 km).

Powdermill Lane, Battle, East Sussex TN33 0SP
Tel (0424) 775511 **Fax** 774540
Location on S side of town; in 50-acre grounds with ample car parking
Food & drink full breakfast, tea, dinner; lunch by arrangement; full licence
Prices B&B £35-£50; dinner from £16.50; low-season reductions; bargain breaks
Rooms 15 double, 2 suites; all with bath and shower; all rooms have central heating
Facilities sitting-rooms, library, separate restaurant, function room; outdoor swimming-pool, fishing; riding and golf nearby
Credit cards AE, MC, V
Children welcome if well behaved
Disabled access easy
Pets dogs welcome if well behaved **Closed** restaurant only, Sun dinner
Proprietors Douglas and Julie Cowpland

East Sussex

Country guest-house, Ticehurst

East Lymden

This fine Lutyens-style Edwardian house, surrounded by acres of glorious mature gardens with many rare trees and plants, also serves as the hub of a 220-acre working sheep farm. When her four children flew the nest, Gini FitzGerald decided in 1990 to open her home to guests, who can benefit from the covered Edwardian swimming-pool, croquet lawn and tennis court.

Inside, all is serene, and quite un-farm-like. The drawing room, library (with TV), candle-lit dining-room and bedrooms are elegant and beautifully decorated; there are fresh flowers throughout. Gini looks after her guests well, and nothing seems too much trouble. Meals are cooked in the Aga, and vegetables are home-grown; tea and cakes are provided in the afternoon (lunches are available by arrangement). The three bedrooms are exceptionally light and spacious, and have been kept without telephone or television to reinforce the get-away-from-it-all atmosphere; they do, however, have ample hot water for baths, whatever the time. It's altogether a delightfully relaxing place for a short or not-so-short stay, and well situated for sightseeing.

Nearby Batemans, Scotney Castle, 4 miles (6 km); Bodiam Castle, 6 miles (10 km); Sissinghurst 10 miles (16 km).

Ticehurst, Wadhurst, East Sussex TN5 7JB
Tel (0580) 200397 **Fax** 201093
Location SW of village off B2099, 9 miles (14 km) SE of Tunbridge Wells; in large gardens, with ample car parking
Food & drink full breakfast, lunch by arrangement, afternoon tea, dinner; no licence
Prices B&B £35-£40; dinner £18; reductions for three nights or more

Rooms 3 double, all with bath; all have central heating, radio, tea/coffee kit, hairdrier
Facilities sitting-room, library with TV, dining-room; croquet, tennis, heated and covered swimming-pool
Credit cards MC, V
Children welcome over 12
Disabled not suitable
Pets by arrangement – but not allowed in bedrooms
Closed Nov to Mar
Proprietor Gini FitzGerald

East Sussex

Town hotel, Brighton

Topps

The untiring Collinses continue to improve these two terraced Regency houses. Recently they have enlarged the rear bedrooms and have replaced some of the more routine furniture with splendid antiques. The result is a hotel of exceptional comfort and mounting style – the size of the bedrooms and the equipment of the bathrooms come in for special commendation: 'you could arrive without a suitcase and find everything you need'. There is a modest restaurant in the basement.

Nearby Royal Pavilion; seafront.

17 Regency Square, Brighton, East Sussex BN1 2FG
Tel (0273) 729334 **Fax** 203679
Location in heart of town opposite West Pier; large public car park opposite
Food & drink full breakfast, dinner (except Wed and Sun); residential and restaurant licence
Prices B&B £38-£64; dinner from £18.95; reductions for 2 nights
Rooms 13 double, one single; all with bath; all rooms have central heating, colour TV, phone, tea/coffee kit, minibar, trouser-press, hairdrier
Facilities sitting-room, dining-room
Credit cards AE, DC, MC, V
Children welcome
Disabled access difficult
Pets not accepted
Closed never
Proprietors Pauline and Paul Collins

Country guest-house, Frant

The Old Parsonage

At the heart of the charming village of Frant, and set in three acres of gardens, The Old Parsonage is a fine Georgian country house beautifully renovated by Tony and Mary Dakin. The tall and spacious reception rooms are filled with plants and decorated with lithographs and watercolours as well as Mary's unusual tapestries and Tony's photos of village scenes. The style is gracious – Persian rugs, crystal chandeliers and antiques – and the enormous conservatory is exceptionally bright and airy. The freshly decorated bedrooms (two with four-posters) have large bathrooms (one, with sunken bath, is almost a sitting-room).

Nearby Tunbridge Wells; Penshurst Place 7 miles (11 km).

Frant, Tunbridge Wells, TN3 9DX
Tel (0892) 750773
Location near church in village 3 miles (5 km) S of Tunbridge Wells, in large gardens with ample car parking
Food & drink full breakfast
Prices B&B £24.50-£39
Rooms 3 double (one twin), all with bath; all rooms have central heating, TV, radio, hairdrier
Facilities sitting-room, breakfast room, conservatory
Credit cards not accepted
Children welcome
Disabled not suitable
Pets accepted in bedrooms
Closed never
Proprietors Tony and Mary Dakin

East Sussex

Country hotel, Battle

Little Hemingfold Farmhouse

Don't be misled by the word 'farmhouse': apart from the setting there is not much that is agricultural about this substantial, rambling building, part 17thC, part early Victorian.

The house has a peaceful setting in 40 acres of farm and woodland; it is surrounded by gardens, and overlooks a pretty 2-acre trout lake (the Slaters are happy to lend fishing rods). Inside, intriguing nooks and crannies give the house a special charm. The two sitting-rooms and the cosy dining-room all have log fires. So do 4 of the 9 bedrooms that are accommodated in the converted coach house and stables grouped around a flowery courtyard; all the rooms are individually furnished in pleasantly rustic style, and some have exposed beams.

Allison and Paul emphasize fresh ingredients in their traditional cooking. A highly satisfied visitor calls them 'hard-working, friendly, and inconspicuous unless called upon'.

Nearby Bodiam Castle, 6 miles (10 km); Great Dixter, 6 miles (10 km); Rye, Sissinghurst within reach.

Telham, near Battle, East Sussex, TN33 0TT
Tel (0424) 774338
Location 1.5 miles (3 km) SE of Battle, off A2100; in 40-acre garden, with trout lake, fields and woods; ample car parking
Food & drink breakfast, light lunch, dinner; restaurant licence
Prices B&B £30-£35; DB&B £46-£52; reductions for 2 nights or more
Rooms 12 double, one family room; 10 with bath; all rooms have central heating, colour TV, phone, tea/coffee kit, radio clocks, electric blankets; 4 rooms have log-burning stoves
Facilities 2 sitting-rooms, dining-room, bar; boating, trout-fishing, tennis
Credit cards AE, MC, V
Children welcome
Disabled access very difficult
Pets small dogs accepted in garden rooms
Closed never
Proprietors Paul and Allison Slater

East Sussex

The Old Vicarage

Paul and Julia Masters have built up a faithful following for this
Tudor-Georgian house which they took over in 1988. The house
has an excellent position – central but peaceful, next to St
Mary's church – and the Masters have added other attractions.
The bedrooms are prettily decorated in Laura Ashley papers and
fabrics, and all now have private bathrooms. Breakfast is a highlight and includes local Ashbee sausages, freshly baked scones,
home-made marmalades and tea from a Rwanda plantation.
Maps and guidebooks abound for those interested in exploring
but note that the cobbled streets hereabouts are awkward for
anyone unsteady on their feet. 'Delightful' is a recent verdict.
Nearby Great Dixter, 6 miles (10 km); Ellen Terry Museum.

66 Church Square, Rye, East
Sussex, TN31 7HF
Tel (0797) 222119 **Fax** 227466
Location on A259 near
middle of town; with small
walled garden, parking
arrangements
Food & drink full breakfast,
no licence
Prices B&B £18-£28
Rooms 6 double, one with
bath, 4 with shower; one suite;
all rooms have central
heating, TV, tea/coffee kit,
hairdrier
Facilities sitting-room,
dining-room
Credit cards not accepted
Children welcome over 10
Disabled not suitable
Pets not accepted
Closed never
Proprietors Paul and Julia
Masters

Netherfield Place

Netherfield Place gives the appearance of a Georgian mansion,
but was in fact built in 1924. It has been open as a hotel for 11
years, the last eight in the competent hands of the Colliers. The
bedrooms are tastefully decorated with luxurious fabrics; most
have fine views of the gardens. Public rooms are stylish but lack
the intimacy of less grand establishments.
Nearby Great Dixter, 6 miles (10 km); Bodiam Castle, 6 miles (10
km); Bateman's, 6 miles (10 km); Rye within reach.

Netherfield, Battle, East
Sussex TN33 9PP
Tel (0424) 774455 **Fax** 774024
Location 3 miles (5 km) NW
of Battle, 2 miles (3 km) off
A2100; in 30-acre grounds
with parking for 30 cars
Food & drink full breakfast,
lunch, dinner; full licence
Prices B&B £45-£65; dinner
£22.50
Rooms 10 double, 4 single, all
with bath; all rooms have
central heating, colour TV,
phone, radio
Facilities 2 sitting-rooms, bar,
dining-room; tennis court,
croquet lawn
Credit cards AE, DC, MC, V
Children welcome if well
behaved
Disabled access easy to
dining-room
Pets not generally accepted;
small breeds by arrangement
Closed Christmas and New
Year
Proprietors H and M Collier

East Sussex

Town house hotel, Rye

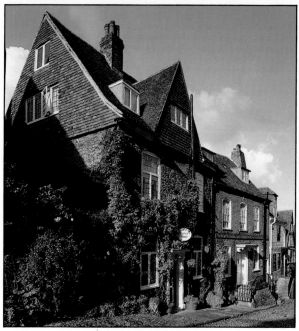

Jeake's House

This splendid 17thC house has been lovingly restored to make a delightful small hotel – a verdict confirmed by a recent visitor. The beamed bedrooms overlook either the old roof-tops of Rye or Romney Marsh stretching to the sea. Bedsteads are brass or mahogany, bedspreads lace, furniture antique. Downstairs, a galleried ex-chapel makes the grandest of breakfast rooms. A roaring fire greets guests on cold mornings, and Jenny Hadfield serves either a traditional breakfast or a vegetarian alternative. There are a comfortable sitting-room and a bar in the main body of the chapel, with books and pictures lining the walls.

Nearby Great Dixter, 6 miles (10 km); Ellen Terry Museum.

Mermaid Street, Rye, East Sussex TN31 7ET
Tel (0797) 222828 **Fax** 222623
Location in middle of Rye; with public car parking nearby
Food & drink full breakfast; residential licence
Prices B&B £19.50-£27.50; reductions for 4 nights plus, and for children sharing
Rooms 8 double, 7 with bath; one single; 2 family rooms with bath; one suite with bath; all rooms have central heating, phone, TV, radio
Facilities dining-room, 2 sitting-rooms, bar
Credit cards AE, MC, V
Children welcome; baby listening/sitting service
Disabled not suitable
Pets dogs accepted in bedrooms by arrangement
Closed never
Proprietors Francis and Jenny Hadfield

71

SOUTH-EAST ENGLAND

West Kent

Country guest-house, Cranbrook

Hancocks Farmhouse

Bridget and Robin Oaten's home – a delightful, listed, 16thC timber-framed building, with an impeccable flowery garden – is a very welcoming place, with a relaxed atmosphere. The sitting-room, complete with large inglenook, is refined and cosy; it serves as a breakfast room, too (and can accommodate guests at individual tables). The bedrooms are simply but comfortably furnished: one has a fine old four-poster, and another has a spacious sitting area. But concern for visitors' well-being is the key: 'It is difficult to speak too highly of the Oatens,' say a quartet of cycling reporters who arrived wet through.
Nearby Sissinghurst, 3 miles (5 km); Scotney, 5 miles (8 km).

Tilsden Lane, Cranbrook, Kent TN17 3PH
Tel (0580) 714645
Location about 2 miles (3 km) SE of village, in large garden, with ample car parking
Food & drink full breakfast, sandwiches by arrangement, tea, dinner; no licence
Prices B&B £20-£27; dinner £15

Rooms 3 double, 2 with bath, one with shower; all have central heating
Facilities sitting-room
Credit cards not accepted
Children accepted over 9
Disabled one ground-floor room **Pets** well-behaved dogs by arrangement **Closed** never
Proprietors Bridget and Robin Oaten

Country guest-house, Biddenden

Birchley

It's a familiar story. The children leave home, and the parents are left with time and empty bedrooms on their hands. Taking in guests fills both voids. The Randalls opened their doors in 1990, having carefully refurbished their three available rooms in pretty, frilly styles. Their home, set in secluded grounds, is the splendid timber-framed Tudor part of a house massively extended in Edwardian times. The gardens are Jennifer's great passion, and in a way Drummond's – he's building a miniature railway out there. Breakfast is served at an ancient table before a carved inglenook in the heavily beamed dining-room, and there is also a panelled sitting-room. Smoking is not allowed.
Nearby Sissinghurst, 4 miles (6.5 km); Leeds and Bodiam castles.

Fosten Green Lane, Biddenden, Ashford, Kent TN27 8DZ
Tel & fax (0580) 291413
Location in countryside, one mile (1.5 km) S of Biddenden; in large grounds with car parking
Food & drink breakfast, dinner (on request)
Prices B&B £25-£35; dinner £15; reductions for 3 or more nights

Rooms 3 double, one with bath, 2 with shower; all have TV, central heating, hairdrier, tea/coffee kit
Facilities dining-room, sitting-room; covered heated swimming-pool
Credit cards MC, V **Children** accepted over 12 **Disabled** access difficult **Pets** not accepted **Closed** Christmas
Proprietors Jennifer and Drummond Randall

West Kent

Country guest-house, Bethersden

Little Hodgeham

Most small hotels reflect the personality of their owner but some are virtually extensions of that personality; Little Hodgeham falls squarely into the latter category. Erica Wallace dominates this picture-postcard Tudor house, and although evidence of her care, attention and hard work abounds, it is the vitality of her character that makes a lasting impression on guests. (Ms Wallace is not past putting a greetings card on the bed of a couple arriving for a wedding anniversary celebration, and preparing heart-shaped mousses for that evening's first course.)

The lovingly restored house has just three bedrooms, all beautifully and carefully co-ordinated, right down to the choice of flowers. The split-level four-poster room is particularly striking. The sitting-room has a massive open fireplace, exposed beams and furnishings in complementary colours. The dining-room is small and intimate, the cooking displaying Erica's untutored 'natural feel for food'. The gardens, duck pond included, are immaculately kept (and now lit at night).

Nearby Sissinghurst Castle gardens, 8 miles (13 km); many other grand houses and gardens within reach.

Smarden Road Bethersden, Kent TN26 3HE
Tel (0233) 850323
Location 2 miles (3 km) NW of Bethersden, 8 miles (13 km) W of Ashford by A28; in garden, with car parking
Food & drink full breakfast, dinner; residential licence
Prices DB&B £49.50; £45 for 4 nights or more; reduction for children sharing parents' room
Rooms 3 double, 2 with bath, one with shower; all rooms have central heating, tea/coffee kit, hairdrier, radio
Facilities sitting-room, dining-room, TV room; carp fishing, small outdoor swimming-pool
Credit cards not accepted
Children accepted; usually fed earlier than adults
Disabled not suitable
Pets accepted by arrangement
Closed mid-Sep to late-Mar
Proprietor Erica Wallace

West Kent

Manor house, Cranbrook

The Old Cloth Hall

Mrs Morgan's warmth of welcome has made her many friends among the guests who have made their way up the sweeping gravelled drive to this splendid 15thC half-timbered manor, which can count Queen Elizabeth I as one of its visitors.

Diamond-paned windows look out on to 13 acres of glorious Kentish gardens – magnificent rhododendrons and azaleas, a sunken rose garden, swimming-pool, tennis court, and a superb croquet lawn to complete the picture.

The interior, as you would expect, is also rather special. There are log fires in the inglenooks; the oak floors and panelling gleam; and the antiques, fine chintz fabrics, porcelain and flower arrangements are all evidence of Mrs Morgan's appreciation of how to make her home look its best. She is also a cook – house specialities include boeuf en croute, stuffed leg of lamb, home-made soups. The bedrooms, furnished with antiques, are exceptionally pretty, and offer a very high standard of comfort; one has a beautifully draped 6ft-wide four-poster.

A couple who spent their autumnal wedding night at the Old Cloth Hall report in glowing terms on everything from the tranquil setting to the fruit fresh from the garden.

Nearby Sissinghurst gardens 2 miles (3 km); Scotney Castle gardens 7 miles (11 km).

Cranbrook, Kent TN17 3NR
Tel (0580) 712220
Location in countryside one mile (1.5 km) E of Cranbrook on road to Tenterden; in grounds of 13 acres with ample car parking
Food & drink full breakfast, dinner; lunch by arrangement; no licence
Prices B&B £33-£65; dinner £20
Rooms 3 double, 2 with bath, one with shower; all rooms have central heating, hairdrier, TV
Facilities sitting-room, dining-room; swimming-pool, tennis-court, croquet
Credit cards not accepted
Children tolerated
Pets not accepted
Disabled not suitable
Closed Christmas
Proprietor Mrs Katherine Morgan

West Kent

Country guest-house, Boughton Monchelsea

Tanyard

'Exactly the sort of place you are looking for – a most interesting building in a beautiful setting, not far from a busy town, run by a committed and sensitive proprietor and with top-class food.'

This report from a regular visitor pays proper tribute to Tanyard's setting and the contribution Jan Davies makes to the well-being of her guests, but underplays the attractions of the house itself. It is a dream of a building – timber-framed, built around 1350 and entirely without symmetry; red tiles and muted yellow paint outside, sparkling white between the mellow exposed beams within – set in a lovely country garden with glorious views across the Weald of Kent.

It is furnished with a cheerful mix of modern and antique pieces – all very natural and home-like – and both the sitting-room and dining-room have large inglenook fireplaces. All the bedrooms are spacious, and there is one large open-plan suite.

With the completion of a new kitchen, Jan is opening a restaurant in the old kitchen, serving limited-choice menus (about four dishes per course).

Nearby Boughton Monchelsea Place; Leeds Castle, 4 miles (6 km).

Wierton Hill, Boughton Monchelsea, near Maidstone, Kent ME17 4JT
Tel (0622) 744705 **Fax** 741998
Location 4.5 miles (7 km) S of Maidstone, just off B2163; in 4-acre grounds with ample car parking
Food & drink full breakfast, dinner; restaurant licence
Prices B&B £37.50-£95; dinner £23
Rooms 4 double, 3 with bath, one with shower; one single; one suite with spa bath; all rooms have central heating, TV, phone, tea/coffee kit, radio
Facilities dining-room, sitting-room, bar
Credit cards MC, V
Children welcome over 6
Disabled not suitable
Pets not accepted
Closed dates not known
Proprietor Jan Davies

West Kent

Frith Farm House

No longer a true farmhouse, Frith is an extremely civilized late-Georgian building reached by a sweeping gravel drive amidst carefully tended lawns and gardens. The Chesterfields have furnished and decorated their home with flair: elegantly draped fabrics in bold, deep colours complement the antiques and the fine collections of china, and the sitting-room (with log fire) and dining-room are subtly lit and atmospheric. Bedrooms, also in deep colours, are handsome (one has a four-poster), and are provided with hot water bottles, mineral water, biscuits and sweets – touches which illustrate Susan Chesterfield's care for her guests (who are requested not to smoke).

Nearby Canterbury, 15 miles (24 km); Chilham, 9 miles (14 km).

Otterden, Eastling, nr Faversham, Kent ME13 0DD
Tel (0795) 890701
Location 2 miles SW of village, 6 miles SW of Faversham; in six acres of grounds, with ample car parking
Food & drink full breakfast, packed lunch, dinner; no licence **Prices** B&B £19.50 to £24.50; dinner from £15; reductions for 2 nights or more **Rooms** 3 double (2 twin), all with shower and WC; all have central heating, radio, TV, tea/coffee kit, hairdrier
Facilities sitting-room, dining-room; riding by arrangement
Credit cards not accepted
Children welcome over 12
Disabled not suitable **Pets** not accepted **Closed** never
Proprietors Susan and Markham Chesterfield

Brattle House

In their mainly Georgian, tile-hung and weatherboarded house, the Rawlinsons have created extremely comfortable accommodation with a home-from-home atmosphere. All is bright, spruce and pretty, with pine furniture, soft flowery patterns and white walls. The light, low-beamed sitting-room looks out over the garden, and the attractive dining-room (candle-lit at night) has a beautifully polished antique table. Maureen Rawlinson loves pampering her guests, and pays great attention to detail. Breakfast is hearty, and includes local sausages and farm eggs; at dinner, vegetarians can be well catered for. No smoking.

Nearby narrow-gauge railway; Sissinghurst 6 miles (10 km).

Cranbrook Road, Tenterden, Kent TN30 6UL
Tel (05806) 3565
Location half a mile (1 km) W of town; in 9-acre garden, with car parking
Food & drink full breakfast, packed lunch, dinner; no licence
Prices B&B £27; reduced rates for 4 nights; dinner £15.50
Rooms 3 double (one twin), all with shower; all rooms have central heating, radio, tea/coffee kit, hairdrier
Facilities sitting-room, dining-room, conservatory
Credit cards not accepted
Children welcome over 12
Disabled not suitable
Pets not accepted **Closed** Christmas and New Year
Proprietors Maureen and Alan Rawlinson

East Kent

Manor house hotel, St Margaret's-at-Cliffe

Wallett's Court

The Oakleys started doing bed and breakfast in their handsome old manor house in 1979, moved on to doing country suppers, and now have a full-blown restaurant, open to non-residents. There are four compact, pine-furnished rooms in a converted barn, and three grander ones in the main house, with abundant beams and brickwork in the best Kent tradition, and robust antique furniture. Both rooms and meals are excellent value.

Nearby Walmer Castle, 3 miles (5 km); Kent Downs.

West Cliffe, St Margaret's-at-Cliffe, Dover, Kent CT15 6EW
Tel (0304) 852424 **Fax** 853430
Location 3 miles (5 km) NE of Dover on B2058, off A258; with garden and ample car parking
Food & drink full breakfast, dinner; residential and restaurant licence
Prices B&B £25-£55; dinner from £19.50
Rooms 5 double, all with bath, 3 with shower; 2 family rooms, both with shower; all rooms have central heating, tea/coffee kit
Facilities sitting-room, 2 dining-rooms, playroom, table-tennis; tennis court
Credit cards MC, V
Children welcome
Disabled access difficult to dining-room; one annexe bedroom suitable
Pets accepted in one bedroom, but not public rooms
Closed one week autumn and spring; Christmas
Proprietors Chris and Lea Oakley

Converted oast house, Chartham

Thruxted Oast

There is nothing more Kentish than a red-brick oast-house; here you can stay in one, last used for hop-drying 20 years ago and rescued from decay in the late 1980s by the Derouets. It is effectively a terrace of five oasts, and each of the three bedrooms occupies one; the rooms are spacious (2 armchairs in each) and welcoming, with patchwork quilts and stripped pine furniture, and are equipped with countless little extras (perhaps betraying Hilary's background as an air stewardess). The sitting-room is similarly appealing, with an open fire. You are welcomed as part of the family here, taking breakfast in the kitchen. Smoking is not allowed in the rooms.

Nearby Canterbury; Chilham castle and gardens, 4 miles (6 km).

Mystole, Chartham, Canterbury CT4 7BX
Tel (0227) 730080
Location in peaceful valley, 4 miles (6.5 km) SW of Canterbury just off A28; with garden and parking for 6 cars
Food & drink full breakfast
Prices B&B £36.50; reductions for 7-night stay
Rooms 3 double, all with bath; all rooms have central heating, phone, TV, radio, hairdrier
Facilities sitting-room; croquet
Credit cards AE, DC, MC, V
Children accepted over 8 years by arrangement
Disabled access difficult **Pets** not accepted **Closed** Christmas
Proprietors Tim and Hilary Derouet

Berkshire

Inn, Yattendon

Royal Oak

'Hotel and restaurant', says the sign on the front of this cottagey, mellow red-brick inn, lest you mistake it for a mere pub. Certainly, the Royal Oak is no longer a common-or-garden local: its two restaurants have a style and elegance not usually associated with ale and darts. But the Oak still has a small bar where residents and non-residents alike can enjoy a choice of real ales without having a meal.

Next to the bar dining area is the light, relaxed and comfortable sitting-room (with newspapers and books within easy reach of its sofas) and beyond that the dining-room, with its elegant reproduction furniture and elaborate designer decoration. Bedrooms are prettily decorated and equipped with every conceivable extra. Another attraction is the garden, recently replanted and a delight during the summer months.

As the guide went to press, we learned that the Oak has changed hands for the second time in recent years. Alan Campbell has installed a new Michelin-starred chef, Graham Newbould, and is embarking on a complete redecoration of the hotel. We look forward to seeing the results.

Nearby Basildon Park, 3 miles (5 km); Donnington Castle, 6 miles (10 km); Snelsmore Common, 6 miles (10 km).

The Square, Yattendon, near Newbury, Berkshire RG16 0UF **Tel** (0635) 201325 **Fax** 201926 **Location** 7 miles (11 km) NE of Newbury, in middle of village; walled garden and separate parking for 30 cars **Food & drink** full breakfast, lunch, dinner; full licence **Prices** B&B £30-£70; dinner £15-£20 (bar), £25-£30 (restaurant – must be booked in advance); weekend breaks **Rooms** 5 double, all with bath; all rooms have colour TV, radio, phone, hairdrier **Facilities** dining-room, sitting-room, 3-roomed bar/dining-room **Credit cards** AE, DC, MC, V **Children** welcome **Disabled** access easy to restaurant and bar but otherwise difficult **Pets** accepted by prior arrangement **Closed** never **Manager** Alan Campbell

London

The Gore

We make no apology for including a hotel as big as this when it is run by the team who opened Hazlitt's (page 84). In 1990 they bought this Victorian town house (long established as a hotel) set in a wide tree-lined street near Kensington Gardens, and since then have given it the Hazlitt treatment: the bedrooms are furnished with period antiques, the walls are covered with old prints and oils, and they have recruited a young and friendly staff, trained to give efficient but informal service. Catering is in the hands of rising star Antony Worrall-Thompson – you have a choice of the Mediterranean-style Bistrot or the 'gourmet' restaurant next door, 190 Queen's Gate.

Nearby Kensington Gardens, Hyde Park; Albert Hall; Harrods.

189 Queen's Gate, London SW7 5EX
Tel (071) 584 6601
Fax 589 8127
Location just S of Kensington Gardens; metered parking and public car park nearby
Food & drink breakfast, lunch, dinner; full licence
Prices B&B £76-£120
Rooms 31 double, 23 single (32 baths and 22 showers); all rooms have central heating, phone, TV, minibar, radio, hairdrier, safe
Facilities sitting-room, bar, restaurant, bistro
Credit cards AE, DC, MC, V
Children welcome; babysitting
Disabled lift/elevator; steps to front entrance **Pets** by arrangement **Closed** never
Proprietors Peter McKay and Jeannie Duncan

Five Sumner Place

Amid the growing number of swanky 'townhouse hotels' in central London, where B&B in the cheapest double costs £65 or more per person, it is reassuring to find something slightly more modest. This place has no pretensions to hotel status – there are no signs outside, and you get a key to the permanently locked front door – and the rooms are not as individual as some. But standards of comfort and maintenance are high, and the location is a good one. Breakfast (a buffet) is in a pleasant conservatory, and there is a small patio.

Nearby South Kensington museums; Knightsbridge; Albert Hall; Kensington Gardens.

5 Sumner Place, London SW7 3EE
Tel (071) 584 7586
Fax 823 9962
Location in residential street off Old Brompton Road; with small rear garden, public car park nearby; nearest tube South Kensington
Food & drink buffet breakfast; room service
Prices B&B £42-£62
Rooms 10 double (5 twin), 3 single, all with bath or shower; all rooms have phone, TV, radio, minibar
Facilities conservatory breakfast room
Credit cards AE, MC, V
Children welcome
Disabled no special facilities
Pets not accepted
Closed never
Proprietor John Palgan

London

Town guest-house, Knightsbridge

L'Hotel

Opened in 1983 by David Levin, who is owner of the much-praised Capital Hotel next door, L'Hotel adds a touch of glamour to the tarnished image of the big-city bed-and-breakfast. Some may baulk at paying high prices for a place with so few facilities, despite the pretty decor and professional staff. But others treasure the fact that L'Hotel is unaffected and simple, yet clearly in the luxury class. 'We always stayed in top London hotels,' said one glamorous guest, 'but we find we miss none of their vast array of facilities here; nor do we miss the way they are monopolized by businessmen.'

Far from being a businessman's enclave, this is a hotel which welcomes children – unusual for a small, up-market establishment – and sees husbands driven mad by their wives' habit of 'just popping into Harrods' next door. Bedrooms at L'Hotel have been decorated by Margaret Levin in a rustic yet feminine style. They vary hardly at all – none is large – but the three most pleasant are those which sport gas log fires. The reception area has a colonial American feel, with stencilled walls. Guests take breakfast in their rooms or in the smart cream-and-brown Metro wine bar in the basement, which is also open to non-residents and serves light French country dishes.

Nearby Hyde Park; Knightsbridge; Buckingham Palace.

28 Basil Street, London SW3 1AT	all with bath and shower; all rooms have central heating, radio, TV, phone, minibar, tea/coffee kit
Tel (071) 589 6286	
Fax 225 0011	
Location between Sloane Street and Harrods; paying car park opposite	**Facilities** wine bar
	Credit cards AE, DC, MC, V
	Children welcome
Food & drink breakfast; snacks, lunch, dinner available in wine bar	**Disabled** not suitable
	Pets accepted by arrangement
Prices B&B £62.50-£145	**Closed** restaurant only, Sun lunch and dinner
Rooms 11 double, one suite;	**Proprietor** David Levin

London

Dorset Square

This striking hotel stands on the south side of the fine Regency garden square which was the original site of Lord's cricket ground. Outside is a discreet brass plaque bearing the hotel's name; inside, a delightful evocation of a traditional English country house – the work of co-owner Kit Kemp. The sensation that absolutely nothing has been left to chance may be slightly unnerving – even the receptionist is dressed in cricket flannels – but there is no denying that the whole effect is captivating. Colefax chintzes, striped wallpapers and clever paint effects are mixed with flair in the small public rooms, along with an abundance of flowers and pictures. Bedrooms – whose solid marble bathrooms include de luxe American showers that practically knock you over – are all fresh and supremely elegant, with not a jarring note to be found. The restaurant, situated in the basement, is beautifully decorated with murals of cricketing and ballooning scenes, and serves modern English dishes.

Don't expect a sleepy, easy-going country-house atmosphere to go with the surroundings at Dorset Square. This is a slick city hotel with a carefully contrived image and a dynamic young management team.

Nearby Regent's Park; Madame Tussaud's; Oxford Street.

39 Dorset Square, London NW1 6QN
Tel (071) 723 7874
Fax 724 3328
Location close to Marylebone station, in square with access to 2-acre private gardens, garaged parking close by
Food & drink breakfast, lunch, dinner, full room service; full licence
Prices B&B £57-£98
Rooms 31 double, 6 single; all with bath and/or shower; all rooms have central heating, colour TV with satellite, clock/ radio, minibar, phone; some rooms have air-conditioning
Facilities sitting-room, dining-room, bar
Credit cards AE, MC, V
Children welcome
Disabled access easy to ground-floor bedrooms
Pets not accepted
Closed never
Manager Sally Holt

81

London

Town hotel, Notting Hill

Pembridge Court

Over the past few years this gracious early Victorian town house has been lovingly refurbished to offer well-equipped, spacious bedrooms as well as friendly, personal service. The sitting-room is prettily furnished and features a large collection of framed Victorian fans, lace gloves and miscellaneous clothes on the walls. The basement restaurant and bar, Caps, is decorated with school and club caps and offers good food and cheerful service.
Nearby Kensington Gardens; Kensington shops.

34 Pembridge Gardens, London W2 4DX
Tel (071) 229 9977
Fax 727 4982
Location a short walk N of Notting Hill Gate, in residential street with garage for 2 cars; nearest tube Notting Hill Gate
Food & drink breakfast, snacks, dinner; restaurant and residential licence
Prices B&B £55-£115; dinner about £16

Rooms 18 double, all with bath; 3 single with bath and shower; all rooms have central heating, colour TV, radio, phone, hairdrier
Facilities restaurant, bar, sitting-room
Credit cards AE, DC, MC, V
Children very welcome
Disabled access difficult
Pets accepted if well behaved
Closed never
Manager Valerie Gilliat

Town hotel, Notting Hill

Portobello Hotel

An established favourite with the film, fashion and popular music industries, and other night owls, with a 24-hour bar and restaurant for the exclusive use of guests. Pastel decoration with cane armchairs in the bar and garden chairs in the marble-tiled dining-room give a fresh, light air. The sitting-room is a mixture of styles, with modern sofas, a large leather-top desk, parlour palms in Victorian *jardinières*, and stripped French doors draped with brillant red livery. Bedrooms range from compact 'cabins' to spacious suites dominated by heavy, carved four-posters. Bathrooms are often small but have recently been refurbished.
Nearby Kensington Gardens; Kensington High Street.

22 Stanley Gardens, London W11 2NG
Tel (071) 727 2777
Fax 792 9641
Location in residential area N of Holland Park; nearest tube: Holland Park or Notting Hill Gate
Food & drink breakfast (in room); other meals available 24 hours a day
Prices B&B £50-£85; meals widely variable
Rooms 9 double, 9 single; all

with shower; 7 suites with bath; all rooms have central air heating, cable TV, phone, minibar, hairdrier, tea/coffee kit
Facilities dining-room, sitting-room, bar
Credit cards AE, DC, MC, V
Children welcome if well behaved
Disabled lift/elevator
Pets welcome if well behaved
Closed one week at Christmas
Manager John Ekperigin

London

Bed and breakfast guest-house, South Kensington

Number Sixteen

Number Sixteen is one of London's most characterful luxury bed-and-breakfast establishments. The original building has spread along its early Victorian South Kensington terrace, to encompass four adjoining houses – all extensively refurbished in the last couple of years.

Public rooms and bedrooms alike are brimful of pictures, including a huge eye-catching abstract in the reception room. Downstairs there are always big bowls of fresh flowers – sweet peas or roses perhaps – and the large rear patio garden is well kept and full of colour. Inside, the decoration is richly traditional and harmonious. A series of small sitting-rooms with Victorian moulded ceilings, polished antiques and luxurious drapes, lead to an award-winning conservatory, from where, on summer days, you can sit and admire the profusion of flowers outside.

Bedrooms are generously proportioned, comfortable and stylish, largely furnished with period pieces or reproductions; some have French windows opening on to the garden. Bathrooms are tiled and functional. Breakfast is served in your room. The hotel has no dining-room but there are plenty of restaurants on the Old Brompton Road nearby.

Nearby South Kensington museums; Knightsbridge; Sloane Square; Kensington Gardens.

16 Sumner Place, London SW7 3EG
Tel (071) 589 5232
Fax 584 8615
Location just off Old Brompton Road; small garden, but no private car parking; nearest tube South Kensington
Food & drink breakfast; residential licence
Prices B&B £42.50-£95
Rooms 36 double, 26 with bath;10 single with shower; all rooms have central heating, minibar, hairdrier, phone; TV, radio available
Facilities sitting-room, bar, conservatory
Credit cards AE, DC, MC, V
Children accepted over 12
Disabled not suitable
Pets not accepted
Closed never
Manager Jane Roberts

London

The Fielding Hotel

Most of the Fielding's guests come back time after time; they agree that finding another hotel of comparable price in such an enviable position (the heart of Covent Garden) would not be easy. It is an 18thC listed building with diamond-paned windows and flower-filled window boxes in a quiet pedestrian street. Martin Braham knows everything there is to know about the latest plays and operas; he shares the cosy reception with Smokey, a sociable African Grey parrot. The bedrooms have pretty floral curtains and pine furnishings, and the public areas light wallpaper and beechwood chairs.

Nearby Royal Opera House, Covent Garden; West End.

4 Broad Court, Bow Street, London, WC2B 5QZ
Tel (071) 836 8305
Fax 497 0064
Location in pedestrian zone opposite Royal Opera House; no private car parking
Food & drink breakfast; residential licence
Prices B&B £42-£75
Rooms 9 double, 8 with shower; 10 single, 9 with shower; 2 family rooms, one with bath, one with shower; 4 suites one with bath, 3 with shower; all rooms have central heating, phone, TV, radio
Facilities breakfast room, lobby/bar
Credit cards AE, DC, MC, V
Children accepted
Disabled 5 ground-floor rooms
Pets not accepted
Closed Christmas
Manager Martin Braham

Hazlitt's

There is no quarter of central London with more character than Soho, now lively and fashionable; and there are few places to stay with more character than Hazlitt's, formed from three 18thC terraced houses off Soho Square. Character is the name of the game here. Old prints line the walls; Victorian taps grace the bathrooms; furniture is chosen more for its antiquity and decorative value than its function. Continental breakfast is served in the rooms. There is no shortage of good restaurants nearby.

Nearby Oxford Street; Royal Opera House, theatres, cinemas.

6 Frith Street, Soho Square, London W1V 5TZ
Tel (071) 434 1771
Location between Oxford Street and Shaftesbury Avenue; 2 public car parks within 2 minutes' walk
Food & drink breakfast, snacks
Prices B&B £74.50-£118.50
Rooms 15 double, all with bath; 7 single, 6 with bath, one with shower; one suite with bath; all rooms have central heating, phone, TV, hairdrier
Facilities sitting-room
Credit cards AE, DC, MC, V
Children welcome; cots and baby-sitting available
Disabled access difficult
Pets dogs accepted by prior arrangement
Closed Christmas
Manager Sture Rydman

South-west Wales

Country hotel, Brechfa

Ty Mawr

This long, low 16thC house, standing at right angles to the main street of a tiny village in deepest Dyfed, has fine views of the surrounding wooded hillsides, dotted with sheep. Inside, much thought has clearly gone into decorating the cosy public rooms, which include an immaculate bar with rough stone walls and smart pine fittings, and a welcoming sitting-room with an open log fire. Bedrooms are comfortable and pleasantly rustic. The Tudhopes' restaurant (beamed, stone-walled, dotted with antiques) has earned itself a good reputation. The emphasis is on regional specialities.

Nearby Brecon Beacons; Cardigan Bay within reach.

Brechfa, Dyfed SA32 7RA
Tel (0267) 202332 **Fax** 202437
Location 10 miles (16 km) NE of Carmarthen, on B4310, in village; with garden, and ample car parking
Food & drink full breakfast, dinner, light lunch; full licence
Prices B&B £34-£44; dinner from £16; bargain breaks
Rooms 5 double, all with bath; all rooms have central heating
Facilities sitting-room, bar, dining-room
Credit cards AE, MC, V
Children welcome – cot available; play area
Disabled not suitable
Pets dogs welcome if well behaved **Closed** 2 weeks Nov/Dec; 2 weeks Jan/Feb
Proprietors Dick and Beryl Tudhope

Country hotel, Haverfordwest

Sutton Lodge

The decorative scheme of stripped pine and delicate country-style papers and fabrics suits this early 19thC house very well. The bedrooms are large and handsome, with splendid cast-iron baths and brass fittings, the public rooms calm and mellow. Breakfast is a wholesome feast, and dinner an impressive affair of four set courses. A reader's report confirms that 'Stan and Paul provide an extraordinary level of personal attention, and the facilities and food are superior to many more expensive places.'

Nearby Pembrokeshire Coast Path; offshore islands.

Portfield Gate, Haverfordwest, Pembrokeshire SA62 3LN
Tel (0437) 768548 **Fax** 760826
Location one mile (1.5 km) W of Haverfordwest; ample car parking
Food & drink full breakfast, dinner; residential and restaurant licence
Prices B&B £42; dinner £21
Rooms 3 double, all with bath; all rooms have central
heating, colour TV, radio, tea/coffee kit
Facilities sitting-rooms, dining-room, conservatory
Credit cards not accepted
Children welcome over 14
Disabled no special facilities
Pet at proprietors' discretion
Closed mid-Dec to Apr
Proprietors Paul Rodwell and Stanford Moseley

South-west Wales

Country house hotel, Reynoldston

Fairyhill

From the time the Fraynes – the owners until 1993 – opened Fairyhill as a hotel in April 1985, it has been well worth seeking out as a quiet and utterly civilized retreat, only about 25 minutes from the end of the M4.

Set in 24 acres of grounds – much of which is still semi-wild (the brochure unabashedly advertises a wildlife sanctuary) – the three-storey Georgian building has a series of spacious, simply furnished public rooms on the ground floor, leading to the conservatory-cum-dining-room, where assiduous and friendly local waitresses serve food from an interesting menu with distinctly *nouvelle* touches – though there are interesting local dishes too, including cockles and laver bread. Bedrooms vary greatly in size and style, some being fairly modern, others more traditional – though they are all comfortable and well-equipped.

New owners took over in October 1993; reports on the new regime would be welcome.

Nearby Loughor Castle, 7 miles (11 km); scenic coast of Gower Peninsula; Swansea within reach.

Reynoldston, Gower, near Swansea, West Glamorgan SA3 1BS
Tel (0792) 390139 **Fax** 391358
Location 12 miles (19 km) W of Swansea, one mile (1.5 km) NW of village; in 24-acre park and woodland, with ample car parking
Food & drink breakfast, lunch, dinner; restaurant and residential licence
Prices B&B £37.50-£75; lunch from £9, dinner from £20
Rooms 9 double, all with shower, 2 also with bath; all rooms have central heating, colour TV, phone
Facilities sitting-room, bar, 2 dining-rooms, conference room, sauna; trout fishing
Credit cards AE, MC, V
Children accepted
Disabled access easy to restaurant, but no ground-floor bedrooms
Pets accepted, but not in public rooms
Closed Boxing Day
Proprietors P and J Camm, P Davies and A Hetherington

South-west Wales

Country guest-house, Fishguard

Tregynon Country Farmhouse

The Heards' blissfully isolated retreat has matured nicely since its doors were opened in 1982. Three bedrooms are in the main 16thC stone farmhouse, the others in adjacent cottages; furnishing throughout is suitably cosy-rustic. Fires blaze in winter. Jane learnt to cook at the knee of her French grandmother, and her food is a highlight: satisfying, traditionally based and wholesome, with proper care taken of vegetarians. There is a well rounded wine list. Children eat at tea-time, preserving adult peace at the dinner table. No smoking in the dining-room or bedrooms.
Nearby walks, wildlife, beaches.

Gwaun Valley, Fishguard, Pembrokeshire SA65 9TU
Tel (0239) 820531 **Fax** 820808
Location isolated in country -side 7 miles (11 km) SE of Fishguard, 3 miles (5 km) S of Newport (get directions)
Food & drink breakfast, packed lunch, dinner; residential and restaurant licence
Prices B&B £23-£32; dinner £14.75-£19.75
Rooms 4 double, 4 family rooms, all with bath or shower; all have central heating, phone, colour TV, baby-listening, hairdrier, tea/coffee kit
Facilities sitting-room, 2 dining-rooms, bar
Credit cards MC, V (3% surcharge) **Children** welcome
Disabled access possible
Pets not accepted
Closed 2 weeks in winter
Proprietors Peter and Jane Heard

Country hotel, Wolf's Castle

Wolfscastle Country Hotel

Andrew Stirling is a qualified squash coach who has the luxury of a court he can call his own; but this welcoming country hotel has plenty of other, less specialized attractions, too. The relaxed, unpretentious style of the well-run, much-extended Victorian house has won many friends – staff are picked for personality as much as skills – and its furnishings are gradually being improved. The wide-ranging menus use sound fresh ingredients.
Nearby Pembrokeshire coast.

Wolf's Castle, Haverfordwest, Dyfed SA62 5LZ
Tel (043787) 225 **Fax** 383
Location 8 miles (12 km) N of Haverfordwest on A40; with ample car parking
Food & drink full breakfast, bar lunch, dinner; restaurant and residential licence
Prices B&B £32.50-£42; 10% reduction for 4 nights or more
Rooms 16 double, 4 single; all with bath; all rooms have central heating, phone, colour TV, radio/alarm, tea/coffee kit
Facilities sitting-room bar, dining-room, banqueting-suite; squash, tennis
Credit cards AE, MC, V
Children welcome
Disabled not suitable
Pets small dogs accepted by arrangement
Closed never
Proprietor Andrew Stirling

South-west Wales

Penally Abbey

The setting is the key attraction of this Gothic country house, converted to a hotel in 1985. It gives easy access to the lively little resort of Tenby, but stands secluded in its own extensive wooded gardens, giving views of the splendid Pembrokeshire coastline; when the weather permits, you can even enjoy the views while taking breakfast on the terrace. Food is freshly prepared, satisfying and eaten by candlelight. Most of the bedrooms have four-poster beds, and antique furniture dotted around.
Nearby Tenby; Pembrokeshire coast.

Penally, near Tenby, Pembrokeshire, Dyfed SA70 7PY
Tel (0834) 843033 **Fax** 844714
Location in village 1.5 miles (2.5 km) SW of Tenby; with ample car parking
Food & drink breakfast, dinner; residential and restaurant licence
Prices B&B £42-£56; DB&B £64-£78
Rooms 10 double, one single; all with bath and shower; all rooms have central heating, TV, phone
Facilities sitting-room, dining-room, bar, billiards room; indoor pool
Credit cards MC, V
Children accepted, if well behaved
Disabled access possible: 2 ground-floor bedrooms in coach house
Pets not accepted **Closed** never **Proprietors** Mr and Mrs S T and E Warren

Stone Hall

The Watsons bought this white-painted stone manor house in 1982 and opened their doors as a hotel and restaurant at the end of 1984. For Francophile gastronomes, it is becoming something of a Mecca, thanks to the guiding hand of Martine Watson, who not only is French but also employs French chefs and waiters. The house retains its ancient character, with much stone and old oak in evidence. Bedrooms are notable mainly for spaciousness.
Nearby St David's Cathedral; Pembrokeshire coast within reach.

Welsh Hook, Wolf's Castle, Haverfordwest, Dyfed SA62 5NS
Tel (0348) 840212 **Fax** 840815
Location in countryside 1.5 miles (2.5 km) W of A40, between Haverfordwest and Fishguard; in large secluded grounds, with ample car parking
Food & drink full breakfast, dinner; residential and restaurant licence
Prices B&B £31.50-£48; dinner £15-£16
Rooms 3 double, 2 with bath, one with shower; 2 single, one with bath, one with shower; all rooms have central heating, colour TV, tea/coffee kit
Facilities sitting-room, bar, 2 dining-rooms
Credit cards AE, MC, V
Children welcome; meals available at special times
Disabled access difficult
Pets not accepted
Closed 2 weeks early Dec
Proprietors Alan and Martine Watson

Brecon Beacons & Wye

Manor house hotel, Three Cocks

Old Gwernyfed

Roger and Dawn Beetham ran this splendid Elizabethan manor house 'very quietly' after taking over the lease from Roger's parents in 1979; but in 1986 the opportunity arose to buy Old Gwernyfed outright, and the two of them have since set about making it 'the best personal small hotel around'.

Happily, the improvements so far have not interfered with the historic character of the place. Decoration is kept to a minimum and the slightly haphazard collection of grand old furniture goes on growing. The four newest bedrooms, created where the kitchens used to be, have the same high ceilings and sense of space of the larger of the old rooms (which range in size from very small to positively enormous). The public rooms are especially impressive – the oak-panelled sitting-room is overlooked by a minstrel's gallery, the dining-room has a vast fireplace with a wood-burning stove. Period music is played as a background to Dawn's original and satisfying dinners ('designed for people who have just walked half of Offa's Dyke' says our inspector), with some choice at beginning and end.

Nearby Brecon Beacons; Hay-on-Wye, 5 miles (8 km).

Felindre, Three Cocks
Brecon, Powys LD3 0SG
Tel (0497) 847376
Location 11 miles (18 km) NE of Brecon, off A438, in open countryside; in 13-acre grounds and gardens with ample car parking
Food & drink breakfast, dinner; packed lunch by arrangement; restaurant and residential licence
Prices B&B £26-£43; dinner £18.25; reductions for stays of 3 nights, and for children sharing room

Rooms 9 double, 7 with bath, one with shower; 2 single, one with bath; 3 family rooms, all with bath
Facilities dining-room, sitting-room, games room, bar; croquet
Credit cards not accepted
Children accepted if well behaved
Disabled access difficult
Pets accepted if well behaved, but not in public rooms
Closed Jan and Feb
Proprietors Dawn and Roger Beetham

Brecon Beacons & Wye

Country guest-house, Abergavenny

Llanwenarth House

While the Weatherills have put tremendous efforts into rescuing this dignified house, they have taken great care to keep the personal touches. Amanda, Cordon Bleu-trained, supervises the kitchen, where the emphasis is on home-grown and local ingredients. The well-furnished bedrooms and public rooms are notably spacious and comfortable, and many enjoy lovely views of the peaceful Usk valley.

Nearby Brecon Beacons National Park; Offa's Dyke path.

Govilon, Abergavenny, Gwent NP7 9SF
Tel (0873) 830289 **Fax** 832199
Location 4 miles (6 km) SW of Abergavenny, off A465; in 9-acre grounds, with ample car parking
Food & drink breakfast, dinner; restaurant and residential licence
Prices B&B £31-£36; dinner £21; reductions for 2 nights or more
Rooms 5 double, 3 with bath, 2 with shower; all rooms have central heating, TV, radio, tea/coffee kit
Facilities sitting-room, dining-room; croquet
Credit cards not accepted
Children welcome over 10
Disabled access easy – one ground-floor bedroom
Pets dogs accepted if well behaved, but not in public rooms
Closed Feb
Proprietors Bruce and Amanda Weatherill

Country inn, Three Cocks

Three Cocks Hotel

There is no disputing the charm of this ivy-covered 15thC coaching inn, built around a tree (still in evidence in the kitchen) in the Welsh hills. The sitting-rooms have an 'olde worlde' feel; one is oak-panelled and towny, the other beamed and rustic. Bedrooms are small but quaint, with dark oak furniture and pale fabrics. But what makes the Three Cocks stand out is Marie-Jeanne's Belgian influences over both the food and atmosphere. Continental specialities and rich creamy sauces regularly crop up on the menu and a large selection of Belgian beers is offered.

Nearby Brecon Beacons; Hay-on-Wye (second-hand book shops), 5 miles (8 km); Hereford (Mappa Mundi).

Three Cocks, nr Brecon, Powys, LD3 OSL
Tel (0497) 847215
Location in village, 11 miles (18 km) NE of Brecon on A438; with ample car parking
Food & drink breakfast, lunch, dinner; full licence
Prices B&B £30; bar snacks from £5, dinner £24; reductions for 2 nights and for children sharing
Rooms 7 double, 6 with bath, one with shower; all rooms have central heating
Facilities dining-room, breakfast room, 2 sitting-rooms, TV room **Credit cards** MC, V **Children** welcome; cot and high-chair available
Disabled access difficult
Pets not accepted
Closed Dec to mid-Feb; restaurant only, Tue
Proprietors Michael and Marie-Jeanne Winstone

Mid Wales

Ynyshir Hall

Regular visitors to Ynyshir Hall will know that in the 1980s it repeatedly changed hands. But the present incumbents have been here since 1989 and, happily, seem to know what they are about. Both are ex-teachers, Joan of geography, Rob of design and art – and his paintings now decorate the walls of the whole house. Given Rob's background, you might expect the decoration of the hotel to be rather special, too – and you would not be disappointed. The colour schemes are adventurous, the patterns bold, the use of fabrics opulent, the attention to detail striking. The bedrooms are named after famous artists, and furnished accordingly.

The white-painted house dates from the 16th century, but is predominantly Georgian and Victorian. It stands in glorious landscaped gardens with grand views across the Dovey estuary.

Food is fruitily imaginative but not over-complex – based on local ingredients, with English and French as well as Welsh influences at work.

Nearby Llyfnant valley; Aberystwyth, 11 miles (18 km).

Eglwysfach, Machynlleth, Powys SY20 8TA
Tel (0654) 781209 **Fax** 781366
Location 11 miles (18 km) NE of Aberystwyth, just off A487; in 12-acre grounds with ample car parking
Food & drink breakfast, lunch, dinner; residential and restaurant licence
Prices B&B £40-£60; meals from £20; reductions for 4 nights or more
Rooms 6 double, 5 with bath, one with shower; 3 suites; all rooms have central heating, phone, TV
Facilities dining-room, sitting-room, bar, conservatory
Credit cards AE, MC
Children accepted over 9
Disabled access easy; one ground-floor room
Pets dogs accepted in one bedroom **Closed** Jan; restaurant only, Sun evening and Mon **Proprietors** Rob and Joan Reen

Mid Wales

Country guest-house, Llanbrynmair

Barlings Barn

Only two sounds disturb the peace of this secluded Welsh farm-house – the baas of the sheep on the surrounding hillsides, and the thwacks, squeaks and anguished cries which accompany the game of squash. Terry Margolis is a qualified squash coach, and has his own court, built to no-compromise standards.

It is the perfect peace of the place that keeps it in these pages despite the Margolis's steady move towards a self-catering set-up – meals are no longer served, but you can order home-cooked frozen meals to consume in your own accommodation. You can stay in a wing of the main cottage, which is charmingly rustic, with oak beams and stone walls, and a wood-burning stove; in the 'Loft'; or in one of two 'Barnlets' – 2-storey self-contained suites. The modest, spring-fed swimming-pool is a flowery sun-trap.

Nearby Riding, walking, fishing; Snowdonia; Aberdovey beach.

Llanbrynmair, Powys SY19 7DY
Tel (0650) 521479 **Fax** 521520
Location 2 miles (3 km) NE of Llanbrynmair in private lane off road to Pandy; with garden and ample car parking
Food & drink home-cooked frozen meals
Prices from £120 for 3 nights off-season in a 'Barnlet' to £450 for a week in the cottage in high season
Rooms 4 suites – 2 'Barnlets' sleeping 2/4, main cottage wing sleeping 4/6, and the 'Loft' sleeping 4/6; all rooms have central heating
Facilities squash, heated swimming-pool, sauna, solarium
Credit cards not accepted
Children very welcome
Disabled not suitable
Pets accepted by arrangement
Closed never
Proprietors Terry and Felicity Margolis

Mid Wales

Lasswade House

A three-storey Edwardian house overlooking fields on the outskirts of Llanwrtyd Wells. The Udalls took over here in 1993, and are delighted to arrange pony trekking, fishing or any other local activities. There is a spacious sitting-room, with comfortable sofas; the individually styled bedrooms are light and airy, with well-kept bathrooms. Diners can expect large helpings of mildly adventurous, mainly French/English dishes and a choice of 30 or so wines which are well described and fairly priced.

Nearby RSPB bird reserves, mountain walks; Brecon Beacons.

Station Road, Llanwrtyd Wells, Powys LD5 4RW
Tel (05913) 515 **Fax** 611
Location SE of middle of village, close to railway station; in garden amid fields with ample car parking
Food & drink breakfast, dinner; residential and restaurant licence
Prices B&B £27.50; DB&B £40; bargain breaks
Rooms 6 double, 3 with bath, 3 with shower; all rooms have central heating, colour TV, phone, radio, alarm, tea/coffee kit, hairdrier
Facilities sitting-room, dining-room
Credit cards MC, V
Children by arrangement
Disabled access easy to dining-room and sitting-room only
Pets dogs welcome if well behaved
Closed never
Proprietors Jack and Beryl Udall

The Ffaldau

We first came upon this listed 16thC house, sheltered by the Radnorshire hills, shortly after the Knotts opened for business in the summer of 1985. We were welcomed into the kitchen, where preparations for dinner were aromatically under way, with encouraging warmth and openness, and it is no surprise that the Ffaldau is now firmly on its feet. Oak beams, log fires and pretty country-style decorations give an inviting air to the house. The bedrooms have been thoroughly revamped in recent years, as has the upstairs sitting-room. Readers have written to commend the Knotts' welcome and their 'superb', 'generous' food.

Nearby Llandrindod Wells, 4 miles (6 km).

Llandegley, Llandrindod Wells, Powys LD1 5UD
Tel (0597) 851421
Location 4 miles (6 km) E of Llandrindod Wells on A44; ample car parking
Food & drink full breakfast, dinner; residential and restaurant licence
Prices B&B £18-£25; dinner from £10.50-£18
Rooms 4 double, 2 with bath, 2 with shower; all have tea/coffee kit, central heating, hairdrier
Facilities sitting-room, bar, dining-room
Credit cards MC, V
Children welcome over 10
Disabled access easy but no ground-floor bedrooms
Pets not accepted
Closed never **Proprietors** Leslie and Sylvia Knott

North Wales

Seaside hotel, Abersoch

Porth Tocyn

This whitewashed, slate-roofed establishment, looking out over the sea from the Lleyn peninsula towards Snowdonia, is a rare animal. The Fletcher-Brewers, who have owned it for 45 years, call it a country house hotel; but it is not what most people would understand by the term. Porth Tocyn certainly contains as many antiques as the typical country house hotel and is run with as much skill and enthusiasm as the best of them. But the building – an amalgam of several old lead-miners' cottages, much extended over the years – makes for a cosy, home-like atmosphere. And the seaside position has naturally encouraged the Fletcher-Brewers to cater well for children as well as parents keen to enjoy the hotel's civilised attractions. Chief among these is the excellent dinner-party-style food; don't go expecting to lose weight. Bedrooms don't have quite the polish of the public areas, but are excellent value.

Nearby Plas Yn Rhiw 6 miles (10 km); Criccieth Castle 14 miles (23 km); Snowdonia within reach.

Bwlchtocyn, Abersoch, Pwllheli, Gwynedd LL53 7BU
Tel (0758) 713303 **Fax** 713538
Location 2.5 miles (4 km) S of Abersoch; in 25 acres of farm land and gardens with ample car parking
Food & drink breakfast, lunch, dinner, picnics; residential and restaurant licence
Prices B&B £32-£57; DB&B £55-£80
Rooms 13 double, 3 single, one family room; all with bath and shower; all rooms have central heating, TV, phone

Facilities cocktail bar, TV room, dining-room, 6 sitting-rooms; tennis, outdoor heated swimming- pool
Credit cards MC
Children welcome, but those under 7 usually take high tea instead of dinner
Disabled access easy – one step into hotel and 3 ground-floor bedrooms
Pets accepted by arrangement
Closed early Nov to week before Easter
Proprietors Fletcher-Brewer family

94

North Wales

Inn, Dolgellau

George III

This 300-year-old inn, separated for a century from the nearby Mawddach estuary by a railway, now has access to the shore once again – and the bonus of space in the disused station a few yards away for some spacious, well-furnished bedrooms to add to those in the main building. The sitting-room has beams and an ingle-nook, while the main Welsh Dresser bar has wooden settles and oak tables; in summer the 'cellar' bar comes into play. After more than 30 years in the hands of the Hall family, the George was taken over by the Cartwrights in 1993. Reports, please.

Nearby Fairbourne Railway, 6 miles (10 km); Snowdonia.

Penmaenpool, Dolgellau, Gwynedd LL40 1YD
Tel (0341) 422525 **Fax** 423565
Location 2 miles (3 km) W of Dolgellau on A493; on edge of Mawddach estuary, with ample car parking
Food & drink breakfast, lunch, dinner, snacks; full licence
Prices B&B £35-£44; dinner about £16; children sharing room £5; winter breaks
Rooms 12 double, 10 with bath, one with shower; all rooms have central heating, colour TV, phone, tea/coffee kit, trouser-press, hairdrier
Facilities sitting-room, 2 bars, dining-room; fishing
Credit cards AE, MC, V
Children welcome if well behaved
Disabled access good
Pets welcome if well behaved
Closed never
Proprietors Julia and John Cartwright

Country house hotel, Dolgellau

Borthwnog Hall

Facing south over the beautiful Mawddach estuary and sur-rounded by mature gardens, this elegant little Regency house enjoys a glorious position. It is an unusual hotel; there are only three rooms and the house is superbly furnished as only a home can be, but it is run on hotel lines – there is a civilized sitting-room for guests, with an open fire, and a proper dining-room with a wide choice of food and an award-winning wine list. The library has been turned into an art gallery, full of paintings, sculpture and pottery.

Nearby fishing, walking, trekking, narrow-gauge railways.

Bontddu, Dolgellau, Gwynedd LL40 2TT
Tel (034149) 271 **Fax** 682
Location beside estuary, on A496 4 miles (6 km) W of village; in gardens with private car parking
Food & drink breakfast, dinner; restaurant and residential licence
Prices B&B £42-£48, DB&B £54-£60; reductions for children, bargain breaks
Rooms 3 double (2 twin), all with bath or shower; all rooms have central heating, TV, radio, alarm
Facilities sitting-room, dining-room, bar
Credit cards MC, V
Children welcome
Disabled access difficult
Pets accepted by arrangement
Closed Christmas
Proprietors Derek and Vicki Hawes

North Wales

Country hotel, Llanberis

The Pen-y-Gwryd Hotel

High up in the desolate heart of Snowdonia, this small coaching inn is a place of pilgrimage for mountaineers – the team which made the first ascent of Everest in 1953 came here to train for the expedition (and still come back for reunions). Mr and Mrs Pullee, whose family have owned the hotel for the last 40 years, take pride in describing the hotel, its bedrooms, its food – even the Victorian bathrooms – as old-fashioned.

Nearby Snowdon Mountain Railway, 5 miles (8 km); Snowdonia.

Nant Gwynant, Gwynedd LL55 4NT
Tel (0286) 870211
Location 5 miles (8 km) SW of Llanberis, at junction of A498 and A4086, in isolated setting; garden, car parking
Food & drink full breakfast, bar lunch, tea, dinner; full licence
Prices B&B from £19; dinner from £12; reductions for 3 nights or more

Rooms 16 double, 3 single; one family room with bath; all have central heating
Facilities sitting-room, bar, dining-room, games room
Credit cards not accepted
Children welcome
Disabled access easy **Pets** well behaved dogs welcome
Closed early Nov to New Year; weekdays Jan and Feb
Proprietors Mrs C B Briggs and Mr & Mrs B C Pullee

Country hotel, Talyllyn

Minffordd

'Minffordd has the happiest atmosphere of all the places where I have stayed,' says a reporter, 'probably because the exceptional Pickles family itself is so happy.' The rambling, relaxed building is not remarkable architecturally or decoratively. But the Pickles take a tremendous pride in making it as comfortable and welcoming to visitors as possible. Son Jonathan is the chef; he has established a reputation for his rich modern and traditional British dishes. No smoking is allowed except in the bar.

Nearby Ascent of Cader Idris; Talyllyn Railway, 5 miles (8 km).

Talyllyn, Tywyn, Gwynedd LL36 9AJ
Tel (0654) 761665 **Fax** 761517
Location 8 miles (13 km) S of Dolgellau at junction of A487 and B4405; parking for 12 cars
Food & drink full breakfast, dinner; residential and restaurant licence
Prices DB&B £49-£59; reductions for 2 nights or more in low season and for children sharing parents' room

Rooms 6 double, 5 with bath and shower, one with shower; all rooms have central heating, phone, radio, tea/coffee kit, hairdrier
Facilities bar, sitting-room, dining-room, sun room
Credit cards DC, MC, V
Children welcome over 3
Disabled access difficult
Pets not accepted
Closed Jan and Feb; also Nov, Dec except for weekends
Proprietors Pickles family

North Wales

Country house hotel, Talsarnau

Maes-y-Neuadd

The name, pronounced 'Mice-er-Nayath', means Hall in the Field, which is no longer a fair description of an amiable granite-built house set in grounds rich with rhododendrons and ringed by woods. But fields are not far away: all around is spellbinding hill scenery.

Maes-y-Neuadd is a civilized and welcoming country hotel, run with great care and flair by the four partners, all of them new to the business when they took over the hotel in 1981 and each of them now in charge of one aspect of it. Over the decade since they arrived, they have refurbished the whole house, mixing antique and modern furniture with panache. Both public rooms and bedrooms vary in vintage and style, from cottagey to elegant Georgian; leather Chesterfields in the beamed 14thC bar will not please purists.

The hotel has a long-standing reputation for offering satisfying and wide-ranging meals – daily-changing set menus of five courses, making extensive use of local lamb, game and fish but always including a vegetarian dish as well.

Nearby Ffestiniog Railway, 2.5 miles (4 km); Snowdonia.

Talsarnau, near Harlech, Gwynedd LL47 6YA
Tel (0766) 780200 **Fax** 780211
Location 3 miles (5 km) N of Harlech, close to B4573; in 8-acre grounds with parking for 50 cars
Food & drink full breakfast, lunch, dinner; residential and restaurant licence
Prices DB&B £75-£114; reduction for children sharing parents' room; winter breaks
Rooms 14 double, 12 with bath and shower, one with bath; one single with shower; 2 suites with bath and shower; all rooms have central heating, TV, phone
Facilities sitting-room, bar, dining-room, conservatory
Credit cards AE, DC, MC, V
Children welcome, but no under 8's at dinner
Disabled access good – wheelchair hoist; 3 ground-floor bedrooms
Pets accepted by arrangement
Closed 10 days mid-Dec
Proprietors June and Michael Slatter, Olive and Malcolm Horsfall

North Wales

Seaside hotel, Llandudno

St Tudno

The Blands are meticulous in attending to every detail of this seafront hotel, which they have been improving for 22 years now, with 21st celebrations continuing into 1994. The pretty rooms, each decorated differently in designer wallpapers and matching fabrics, have found the balance between Victorian charm and modern facilities. A long list of thoughtful extras add to the comfort, including complimentary wine. The air-conditioned dining-room is light and inviting, with a profusion of plants and cane-backed chairs. The daily changing *carte*, based on the best local ingredients, deserves serious study in the comfortable bar, and the cooking is right on target. All of this would be difficult to resist even without the bonus of the hotel's young and helpful staff. Guests are requested not to smoke in the period-style sitting-room or the dining-room.

Nearby Dry ski slope, 0.5 miles (1 km); Conwy Castle, 3 miles (5 km); Bodnant Gardens, 7 miles (11 km); Snowdonia.

Promenade, Llandudno, Gwynedd LL30 2LP
Tel (0492) 874411 **Fax** 860407
Location on seafront opposite pier and promenade gardens; small garden and private parking for 10 cars; unrestricted street parking
Food & drink breakfast, lunch, dinner; residential and restaurant licence
Prices B&B £35-£89, dinner £25; reductions for children sharing parents' room; reduced DB&B rates for 2 nights or more
Rooms 15 double, 13 with bath, 2 with shower; 2 single with bath; 4 family rooms, all with bath; all rooms have central heating, satellite TV, phone, radio/alarm, fridge, tea/coffee kit, hairdrier
Facilities bar, 3 sitting-rooms, dining-room; covered heated swimming-pool
Credit cards AE, DC, MC, V
Children very welcome; baby-listening, cots, highchairs and high tea available (dinner not suitable for very young)
Disabled access fairly easy except for wheelchairs; lift/elevator to most bedrooms
Pets small well behaved dogs accepted at proprietors' discretion
Closed never
Proprietors Martin and Janette Bland

North Wales

Dolmelynllyn Hall

The father-and-daughter team of Jon Barkwith and Jo Reddicliffe completely refurbished this mainly 19thC (originally 16thC) house with considerable style when they arrived here in 1988. Confident colour schemes are successfully teamed with Victorian antiques in some areas, more modern furnishings in others, to create a warmly comfortable atmosphere. Bedrooms are individually decorated (and individually described on the tariff); many have splendid views across the terraced gardens. Jo's daily changing menus are highly successful, adding invention to traditional local recipes, and there is a sensibly balanced wine list.

Nearby fishing, walking, narrow-gauge railways; Snowdon.

Ganllwyd, Dolgellau, Gwynedd LL40 2HP
Tel & **fax** (034140) 273
Location in countryside, on A470 5 miles (8 km) N of Dolgellau; in large grounds with private car parking
Food & drink breakfast, dinner; lunch by arrangement; restaurant and residential licence
Prices B&B £37.50-£47.50, DB&B £52.50-£62.50 (2 days min)

Rooms 8 double, 3 single, all with bath or shower; all rooms have central heating, phone, radio, TV, hairdrier, tea/coffee kit
Facilities sitting-room, dining-room, conservatory bar, library; fishing **Credit cards** AE, MC, V **Children** welcome over 8 **Disabled** not suitable
Pets accepted in certain bedrooms **Closed** Dec to Feb
Proprietors Jon Barkwith and Jo Reddicliffe

Tyddyn Llan

The Kindreds restored this solid 18thC house in the Berwyn mountains in the early 1980s, converting it into an inviting hotel – with books and magazines on hand, and antiques and paintings dotted around. It is very much a home, despite the number of guests it can accommodate. The kitchen has a high reputation: inventive menus change regularly and make good use of local ingredients. The hotel has four miles of fishing on the Dee.

Nearby Bala Lake and Railway, 8 miles (13 km); Snowdonia.

Llandrillo, near Corwen, Clwyd LL21 0ST
Tel & **fax** (049084) 264
Location 5 miles (8 km) SW of Corwen off B4401; with ample car parking
Food & drink breakfast, lunch, tea, dinner; restaurant and residential licence
Prices B&B £44-£60; DB&B £70-£95; reductions for 2 nights or more and for children sharing room
Rooms 10 double, 8 with bath,

2 with shower; all rooms have central heating, phone, radio; TV on request
Facilities sitting-room, bar, restaurant; croquet, fishing
Credit cards MC, V
Children welcome
Disabled not suitable
Pets dogs accepted by arrangement, and not in public rooms
Closed one week in Feb
Proprietors Bridget and Peter Kindred

Hereford & Worcester

The Green Man

This substantial old timber-framed inn successfully plays the dual roles of popular country pub and small hotel. Bedrooms vary widely: the four-poster room, with its exposed beams, is snugly traditional; others, which have been modernized, are light and airy. There is not much sitting space apart from the oak-beamed bars, but the large lawned garden has tables and benches. Modest but tasty food is served both in the bars and in the smartly converted barn which forms the dining-room.

Nearby Ross-on-Wye, 3 miles (5 km); Hereford

Fownhope, near Hereford, Hereford and Worcester HR1 4PE
Tel (0432) 860243
Location 8 miles SE of Hereford on B4224, in village; with garden and parking for 75 cars
Food & drink full breakfast, bar or packed lunch, tea, dinner, snacks; full licence
Prices B&B £24-£31; reductions for children sharing parents' room; bargain breaks
Rooms 12 double, 4 with bath, all with shower; 3 family rooms, 2 with bath, all with shower; all rooms have central heating, tea/coffee kit, TV, trouser-press
Facilities 2 bars, dining- room, sitting-room
Credit cards AE, MC, V
Children welcome; cots, high-chairs available
Disabled access easy to public rooms and to ground- floor bedroom across courtyard
Pets welcome
Closed never
Proprietors Arthur and Margaret Williams

The Cottage in the Wood

Three buildings make up this glossy little hotel. There are bedrooms in all three, taking the hotel over our usual size limit; but the smartly furnished Georgian dower house at its heart is intimate, calm and comfortable. The setting is the key – superb views across the Severn Valley to the Cotswolds.

Nearby Malvern Hills; Eastnor Castle, 5 miles (8 km).

Holywell Road, Malvern Wells, Hereford and Worcester WR14 4LG
Tel (0684) 573487 **Fax** 560662
Location 2 miles (3 km) S of Great Malvern off A449; ample car parking
Food & drink full breakfast, lunch, tea (Sat, Sun), dinner; residential and restaurant licence
Prices B&B £47.50-£74; dinner about £24; reductions for 2 nights or more
Rooms 19 double, all with bath, 12 also with shower; one single with bath; all have central heating, phone, TV, tea/coffee kit, hairdriers
Facilities sitting-room, bar, dining-room; conference suite
Credit cards AE, MC, V
Children welcome; cots
Disabled not ideal; ground-floor rooms in annexe **Pets** accepted (not main building)
Closed never **Proprietors** John and Sue Pattin

Hereford & Worcester

Country guest house, Ledbury

Grove House

Although Grove House dates back to the 15th century it has the appearance of a Georgian farm manor-house, complete with courtyard, red-brick outhouses and stables. By keeping the number of rooms down to three, the Rosses have preserved entirely the atmosphere of a private home. (That the plumbing preserves one of the weaknesses of a private home – an occasional shortage of hot water – is less laudable but easily forgiven.)

The origins of the house are more evident inside, with timber framing in the walls and red oak panelling in the dining-room, where logs are burned in winter. The bedrooms are large, comfortable and carefully furnished with antiques – two with four-posters – and our anonymous inspector records with delight that hot water bottles are slipped between the crisp cotton sheets in the late evening. There are fresh cut flowers, and towels are not stinted. Guests have the use of a large, separate sitting-room.

Ellen Ross is an excellent cook who aims higher than is usual in such small establishments, aided by the produce of her own large vegetable garden. After help-yourself drinks in the sitting-room, dinner is served at a single long table.

Nearby Eastnor Castle, 1.5 miles (2.5 km); Malvern Hills.

Bromsberrow Heath, Ledbury, Herefordshire HR8 1PE
Tel (0531) 650584
Location 3 miles (5 km) S of Ledbury off A417, close to M50; ample car parking
Food & drink full breakfast, dinner; no licence
Prices B&B £34-£43; dinner £21
Rooms 3 double, all with bath, one also with shower; all rooms have central heating, TV, tea kit, clock/ radio, hairdrier
Facilities sitting-room, dining-room; tennis, riding (by arrangement), outdoor swimming-pool, boating-pond
Credit cards not accepted
Children accepted
Disabled not suitable
Pets can stay in car
Closed 17 Dec to 4 Jan
Proprietors Michael and Ellen Ross

Hereford & Worcester

Country house hotel, Ledbury

Hope End

It was 1975 when Patricia Hegarty inherited the shell of Hope End – a handsome red-brick 18thC house with exotic embellishments which had been the childhood home of Elizabeth Barrett – and 1979 before she and husband John were ready to open their doors. They quickly established Hope End as one of the most distinctive hotels in the country.

Whereas many country house hotels are made in a single mould, Hope End is the Hegartys' own creation. It may disappoint seekers after luxury and style; but it certainly satisfies those in search of comfort and relaxation. The Hegartys' watch-words are simplicity and quality – whether in Patricia's excellent cooking (employing a striking range of home-grown vegetables and herbs) or in the decoration and furniture – some of it antique, some stripped pine, some locally crafted.

All the bedrooms are inviting, but the biggest are splendidly spacious. They are dotted around three wings of the house, with two separate from the main building – the Garden Cottage offers its own little sitting-room, for complete seclusion. The rambling house affords three sitting-rooms, all with sofas and log fires, the largest a splendid, spacious room on the first floor.

Nearby Eastnor Castle, 5 miles (8 km); Malvern Hills; Worcester, Hereford and Gloucester all within easy reach.

Hope End, Ledbury, Hereford and Worcester
HR8 1JQ
Tel (0531) 633613 **Fax** 636366
Location 2.5 miles (4 km) N of Ledbury; in 40 acres of wooded parkland with ample car parking
Food & drink full breakfast, dinner; residential and restaurant licence
Prices B&B £49.50-£131; dinner £30; reduction for 2 nights or more
Rooms 9 double, all with bath; all rooms have central heating, tea/coffee kit, phone
Facilities 3 sitting-rooms, dining-room
Credit cards MC, V
Children welcome over 12
Disabled access difficult
Pets not accepted
Closed mid-Dec to mid-Feb
Proprietors John and Patricia Hegarty

Hereford & Worcester

Country house hotel, Chaddesley Corbett

Brockencote Hall

The present Brockencote Hall is of Victorian origin and more or less Georgian in style, but it lies at the heart of a 300-year-old estate that provides a grand setting of mature and varied trees. The Anglo-French Petitjeans, trained hoteliers both, opened it as a hotel in 1986, having renovated and furnished it with great taste and style. The pine- and maple-panelled library is particularly welcoming. Bedrooms are splendidly spacious, with carefully coordinated colour schemes. Cooking is appropriately ambitious.
Nearby walks in grounds; Worcester, 15 miles (24 km).

Chaddesley Corbett, nr Kidderminster, Hereford & Worcester DY10 4PY
Tel (0562) 777876 **Fax** 777872
Location in countryside, on A448 4 miles (6 km) SE of Kidderminster; in large grounds, ample car parking
Food & drink breakfast, lunch dinner; full licence
Prices B&B £45-£75; DB&B £60-£87

Rooms 13 double, all with bath; all rooms have central heating, phone, radio, TV
Facilities sitting-room, dining-room, library
Credit cards AE, DC, MC, V
Children welcome if well behaved **Disabled** no special facilities **Pets** not welcome
Closed never
Proprietors Joseph and Alison Petitjean

Country house hotel, Bromsgrove

Grafton Manor

This ancient red-brick manor house is very much a family affair – father John and twins Nicola and Simon in the kitchen, mother June and elder son Stephen running the front of house. They opened their doors as a restaurant in 1980, and the imaginative four-course dinners are still the best for miles around; a recently created formal herb garden behind the house makes its contribution. Bedrooms are richly furnished and thoroughly equipped, and the heart of the house is the lofty old Great Parlour, now the bar/sitting-room, complete with Steinway grand piano.
Nearby Hagley Hall, 6 miles (10 km).

Grafton Lane, Bromsgrove, Hereford and Worcester B61 7HA
Tel (0527) 579007 **Fax** 575221
Location 2 miles (3 km) SW of Bromsgrove off B4090; in 11-acre gardens, with ample car parking
Food & drink breakfast, lunch, dinner; residential licence
Prices B&B £75-£150; dinner £28.50
Rooms 6 double (2 twins), one single, two suites; all with

bath; all rooms have central heating, coal gas fires, colour TV with teletext, radio/alarm, hairdrier, phone
Facilities sitting-room/bar, dining-room; croquet
Credit cards AE, DC, MC, V
Children welcome if well behaved
Disabled access
Pets not accepted; kennels can be provided
Closed never
Proprietors Morris family

Hereford & Worcester

Holdfast Cottage

'Cottage' seems to be stretching things a bit – and yet, despite its size, this Victorian farmhouse does have the cosy intimacy of a cottage, encouraging the friendly informality which the previous owners, the Beetlestones, sought and which the new owners, Stephen and Jane Knowles, also hope to achieve.

Inside, low oak beams and a polished flagstone floor in the hall conform to the cottage requirement; beyond there, headroom improves – though flowery decoration emphasizes the cottage status. Bedrooms are light and airy, with carefully co-ordinated fabrics and papers; some bathrooms are small. Outside, the veranda with its wisteria keeps the scale of the house down. The garden beyond – again scarcely cottage-style – adds enormously to the overall appeal of the place, with its lawns, shrubberies, fruit trees and delightful 'wilderness'.

The daily-changing *carte* is based on continental as well as traditional English dishes, employing the best local produce.

Nearby Eastnor Castle, 4 miles (6 km); Worcester, Hereford and Gloucester all within easy reach.

Welland, near Malvern,
Hereford and Worcester
WR13 6NA
Tel (0684) 310288
Location 4 miles (6.5 km) S of
Great Malvern on A4104; with
ample car parking
Food & drink full breakfast,
dinner; residential and
restaurant licence
Prices B&B £34-£54; dinner
£17; bargain breaks
Rooms 7 double, all with bath;
1 single with shower; all rooms
have central heating, colour
TV, radio/alarm, phone,
hairdrier
Facilities sitting-room, bar,
dining-room, conservatory;
croquet
Credit cards MC, V
Children welcome
Disabled access difficult
Pets allowed indoors
Closed never
Proprietors Stephen and Jane
Knowles

Hereford & Worcester

Country hotel, Kington

Penrhos Court

It is almost 20 years now since Daphne Lambert opened a restaurant in a small converted barn rescued from decay here at Penrhos Court. More recently, the restoration of the whole group of medieval buildings has been completed, culminating in the thirteenth-century cruck hall. The food is still an attraction – honest, traditionally based, French-influenced – though it is perhaps the buildings that are special. Bedrooms are comfortable, though furnishings have less character than the surroundings; ground-floor ones have individual patio gardens.

Nearby Hergest Croft Garden and Park Wood, 3 miles (5 km); Offa's Dyke Path.

Kington, Herefordshire HR5 3LH
Tel (0544) 230720 **Fax** 230754
Location one mile (2 km) E of Kington on A44; with 6-acre grounds and ample car parking
Food & drink breakfast, lunch, dinner; full licence
Prices B&B £40-£120; lunch/dinner £15-£25
Rooms 12 double (9 twin), 4 family rooms, all with bath; all rooms have central heating, phone, satellite TV, radio, hairdrier
Facilities 3 dining-rooms, 2 sitting-rooms, bar
Credit cards AE
Children welcome
Disabled access easy
Pets not accepted
Closed never
Proprietors Martin Griffiths and Daphne Lambert

Country hotel, Eyton

The Marsh

The Marsh hovers in status between the home that takes guests and the proper hotel. It is tipped into the latter category by the polished approach of the enthusiastic Gillelands, and the fact that the place operates as a restaurant. Jacqueline's eclectic five-course menus have acquired a good reputation; if staying two nights you have the option of a more modest fixed meal. But the real appeal is the house: a 14thC timbered and stone-floored marvel, lovingly restored, with richly decorated bedrooms and a splendid fragrant garden.

Nearby Eye Manor, 2.5 miles (4 km).

Eyton, Leominster, Herefordshire HR6 0AG
Tel (0568) 613952
Location 2 miles (3km) NW of Leominster, 1.5 miles (2 km) W of B4361; in 1.5-acre gardens with car parking
Food & drink breakfast, lunch by arrangement, dinner; residential and restaurant licence
Prices B&B £50-£74; lunch £17.50-£18.50, dinner £27.50
Rooms 4 double (one twin), all with bath; one single with shower; all have radio, central heating, phone, TV, hairdrier
Facilities dining-room, bar, sitting-room, conference room
Credit cards AE, DC, MC, V
Children tolerated; baby-listening available
Disabled access difficult
Pets not accepted **Closed** never **Proprietors** Martin and Jacqueline Gilleland

West Gloucestershire

The Old Vicarage

Some visitors to this handsome Georgian vicarage marvel at the Bulls' juggling act – keeping the guests, hens, herbs and vines happy all at once. Others have prescribed concentration on fewer goals. But there is agreement that the Old Vicarage is a warm, welcoming house, full of character as well as flowers and antiques. There is a pretty sitting-room, and bedrooms are simply furnished but charmingly decorated with plenty of flowers. The Bulls are enthusiastic cooks, and offer quite a wide choice of traditional and innovative dishes at dinner – served in dinner-party style at a single table. Although they do not possess a licence they will happily uncork wine at no charge.

Nearby walks to river Severn; Forest of Dean, Wye valley.

Awre, Newnham, Gloucestershire GL14 1EL **Tel** (0594) 510282 **Location** 3 miles (5 km) SE of Newnham, off A48, on edge of village; in 4-acre grounds with adequate car parking **Food & drink** full breakfast, dinner; no licence **Prices** B&B £19-£21; dinner £14.50	**Rooms** 3 double, one with shower; 2 single; all rooms have tea/coffee kit **Facilities** sitting-room, dining-room **Credit cards** not accepted **Children** accepted over 11 **Disabled** access difficult **Pets** not accepted **Closed** Christmas **Proprietors** May and Nick Bull

Tudor Farmhouse

The chatty Fletchers' lovely 14thC stone farmhouse is prettily decorated and neatly furnished – with a new injection of fresh fabrics and decoration last year. A fine oak staircase spirals up to the rooms in the main house, which include two four-posters. Three rooms are across the courtyard behind. The sitting- and dining-rooms have exposed stone and beams, the former an open fireplace, the latter elegant rose-pink table linen. There is a set-price dinner menu that changes weekly, and a vegetarian menu. Breakfast is a minor feast.

Nearby Monmouth Castle, 5 miles (8 km); Wye valley.

Clearwell, near Coleford Gloucestershire GL16 8JS **Tel** (0594) 833046 **Fax** 837093 **Location** 5 miles (8 km) SE of Monmouth on B4231; parking for 15 cars **Food & drink** full breakfast, dinner; residential and restaurant licence **Prices** B&B £24.50- £42.50; dinner from £12.50; short breaks **Rooms** 9 double, one suite, all	with bath; all rooms have central heating, colour TV, tea/coffee kit, radio/alarm, phone, hairdrier **Facilities** sitting- room/bar, dining-room, conservatory **Credit cards** AE, MC, V **Children** welcome **Disabled** access easy **Pets** accepted in cottage annexe **Closed** never **Proprietors** Deborah and Richard Fletcher

West Gloucestershire

Country hotel, Corse Lawn

Corse Lawn House

This tall, red-brick Queen Anne house, set back across common land from what is now a minor road, must have been one of the most refined coaching inns of its day. Should you arrive in traditional style, you could still drive your coach-and-four down the slipway into the large pond in front of the house, to cool the horses and wash the carriage.

The Hines have been here since the late 1970s, first running the house purely as a restaurant, later opening up four rooms and in recent years adding various extensions (carefully designed to blend with the original building) to provide more and more bedrooms as well as more space for drinking, eating and sitting. The Falstaffian Denis Hine – a member of the famous French Cognac family – and son Giles extend a warm welcome to guests, while Baba Hine cooks. Her repertoire is an eclectic mix of English and French, modern and provincial dishes, all carefully prepared and served in substantial portions; there are fixed-price menus (with a vegetarian alternative) at both lunch and dinner as well as a *carte*, all notably good value.

Bedrooms are large, with a mixture of antique and modern furnishings and the atmosphere of the house is calm and relaxing. Breakfasts are a home-made feast.

Nearby Tewkesbury Abbey, 5 miles (8 km); Malvern Hills.

Corse Lawn, Gloucestershire
GL19 4LZ
Tel (0452) 780479 **Fax** 780840
Location 5 miles (8 km) W of
Tewkesbury on B421; in
12-acre grounds with ample
car parking
Food & drink full breakfast,
lunch, tea, dinner; full licence
Prices B&B £45-£80; lunch
from £16, dinner £23.50
Rooms 19 double (2 suites),
all with bath and shower; all
rooms have central heating,
colour TV, phone, tea/coffee
kit, hairdrier, trouser-press
Facilities 3 sitting-rooms, bar,
restaurant, 2 meeting rooms;
croquet, tennis, putting,
swimming pool **Credit cards**
AE, DC, MC, V **Children**
welcome if well behaved
Disabled access easy to public
rooms and 5 ground-floor
bedrooms **Pets** dogs allowed
in bedrooms **Closed** never
Proprietors Denis, Baba Hine
and Giles Hine

Country guest-house, Stinchcombe

Drakestone House

Drakestone House takes you back to turn-of-the-century rural England – an Edwardian country house complete with dovecote; landscaped gardens bordered by neatly trimmed yew hedges; and views of green fields and the Welsh mountains. There's a warm welcome from Hugh and Crystal St John-Mildmay, whose family home this is. They serve breakfast before a log fire on chilly days, and trays of tea in the friendly sitting-room. They will also produce dinner if arranged in advance.

Nearby Slimbridge Wildfowl Trust, 4 miles (6 km); Owlpen Manor, 4 miles (6 km); Cotswold villages.

Stinchcombe, near Dursley, Gloucestershire GL11 6AS
Tel (0453) 542140
Location 3 miles (5 km) NW of Dursley, off B4060; ample car parking in courtyard
Food & drink full breakfast; dinner by prior arrangement; no licence, take your own wine
Prices B&B £22; dinner £15; reduction for children
Rooms 3 double, one with shower; all rooms have central heating
Facilities sitting-room, dining-room
Credit cards not accepted
Children welcome
Disabled access difficult
Pets not allowed in house
Closed Nov to Mar
Proprietors Hugh and Crystal St John-Mildmay

Country house, Painswick

Painswick Hotel

Somerset and Hélène Moore (who used to run Flitwick Manor on page 123) moved in 1991 to this distinctly upmarket Georgian rectory tucked away in the back lanes of a prosperous village. The graceful proportions of the rooms – beautifully and expensively furnished with an elegant mix of classy reproductions, antiques and well chosen objects, the serenity of the gardens, and the fine views of the westerly Cotswold scarp all contribute to an upmarket hotel of great attractions.

Nearby Cotswold villages; Gloucester 5 miles (8 km).

Kemps Lane, Painswick, Gloucestershire GL6 6YB
Tel (0452) 812160 **Fax** 814059
Location near middle of village, 3 miles (5 km) N of Stroud on A46; with car parking in front of hotel
Food & drink breakfast, dinner, Sun lunch; full licence
Prices B&B £42.50-£60; Sun lunch £14.75, dinner £22.50; reductions for children sharing parents' room
Rooms 13 double, all with bath; 2 single, one with bath, one with shower; 4 family rooms, all with bath; all rooms have central heating, phone, TV, radio, tea/coffee kit
Facilities sitting-room, 2 dining-rooms, bar; croquet
Credit Cards AE, MC, V
Children welcome; cots, high chairs, baby-listening devices available
Pets only by prior arrangement
Disabled access difficult
Closed never
Proprietor Somerset Moore

Cotswolds

Malt House

It is easy to miss this 17thC Cotswold house (in fact a conversion of three cottages) in a tiny hamlet comprising little more than a church and a pub. Once found, the Malt House is delightful – with low beamed ceilings, antique furniture and leaded windows overlooking a dream garden, where the family cats potter contentedly about.

The bedrooms, most of which overlook the gardens, are comfortable and prettily decorated, with pleasant old furniture and, in some cases, antique or 4-poster beds. The Browns, who took over the hotel in 1992, may be new to the business but they have obviously taken it in their stride. You are welcomed as part of the family and there is always someone on hand to chat or give advice on where to go.

Guests breakfast and dine around a communal antique table in front of an inglenook in the beamed dining-room. The Browns' son Julian, who is an experienced chef, comes in to cook 4-course meals, based on fresh ingredients from the kitchen gardens.

Nearby Batsford Park Arboretum, 3 miles (5 km); Sezincote Garden, 4.5 miles (7 km); Snowshill Manor, 5 miles (8 km); Stratford-upon-Avon, 12 miles (19.5 km); Cotswold villages; Cheltenham.

Broad Campden, Chipping Campden, Gloucestershire GL55 6UU
Tel (0386) 840295 **Fax** 841334
Location one mile (1.5 km) SE of Chipping Campden just outside village; in 4.5 acre paddocks, orchard and garden, with ample car parking
Food & drink full breakfast, dinner; restaurant licence
Prices B&B £37.50-£55.50; dinner from £20

Rooms 5 double, 4 with bath; one single; all rooms have central heating, TV, radio, tea/coffee kit
Facilities sitting-room, dining-room; croquet
Credit cards MC, V
Children welcome if well behaved; high tea provided
Disabled access difficult
Pets not accepted
Closed Christmas/New Year
Proprietors Nick and Jean Brown

Cotswolds

Country hotel, Broadway

Collin House

In the decade that John Mills (formerly an engineer-business-man) has owned and run this 16thC stone house, it has steadily blossomed into one of the most appealing and genuine charming small hotels in this guide. Collin House feels lived-in and evolving – far removed from the instant designer-kit style of country hotel so prevalent in the monied Cotswolds.

Tucked well away from commercialized Broadway in several acres of secluded grounds, it is a haven of peace. The sitting-room and bar are warm, agreeable places to sit, read, talk or consider the appetizing dishes chalked up daily on the bar blackboard, or on the handwritten menu presented for more formal eating in the candlelit dining-room. All the bedrooms are prettily furnished and decorated, and like the rest of the house full of interesting items – rugs, vases, books, pictures – many collected on forays to local auctions. The extensive gardens come into their own in fine weather.

One report this year is critical of service. From our own experience of John Mills' hospitality, we are confident that the problem was an isolated one.

Nearby Snowshill Manor, 2.5 miles (4 km); Batsford Park Arboretum, 6 miles (10 km); Sudeley Castle, 6 miles (10 km).

Collin Lane, Broadway,
Worcestershire WR1 7PB
Tel (0386) 858354
Location one mile (1.5 km)
NW of Broadway, off A44; in
spacious grounds with ample
private car parking
Food & drink full breakfast,
lunch, dinner; restaurant and
residential licence
Prices B&B £44-£49.50;
dinner £15-£23; reductions for
5 nights or more (Apr to Oct)
and 2 nights or more (Nov to
Mar)

Rooms 6 double, 5 with bath,
one with shower; one single,
with shower; all rooms have
central heating, tea/coffee kit
Facilities sitting-room, bar,
dining-room; swimming-pool,
croquet
Credit cards MC, V
Children welcome; by prior
arrangement under 6
Disabled no special facilities
Pets not accepted
Closed Christmas
Proprietor John Mills

Cotswolds

Charingworth Manor

A splendid Cotswold manor house, dating from the fourteenth century but open as a hotel only since 1988, set in lovely gardens with distant country views. We cannot resist it, despite its large number of rooms and high prices. The decoration and furnishings of the beamed rooms, upstairs and downstairs, are deliciously restrained and beautifully detailed, carefully avoiding designer excesses; even the bathrooms have character. Food is now less fashionable, more traditional than it was. The 'leisure spa' is a stylish recent addition.

Nearby Chipping Campden, Hidcote Manor gardens.

Charingworth, nr Chipping Campden, Gloucestershire GL55 6NS
Tel (038678) 555
Location 3 miles (5 km) E of Chipping Campden on B4035; with 50-acre grounds and ample car parking
Food & drink full breakfast, lunch, dinner; full licence
Prices B&B £55-£105; DB&B from £70; lunch £12-£15, dinner £27.50
Rooms 21 double, 3 suites, all with bath; all have central heating, phone, TV, radio, hairdrier, trouser-press, safe
Facilities dining-room, sitting-rooms; heated indoor swimming-pool, sauna, steam room, solarium, tennis
Credit cards AE, DC, MC, V
Children welcome; baby-sitting by arrangement
Disabled access difficult
Pets by arrangement
Closed never
Manager Simon Henty

Bay Tree

This creeper-covered 16thC building, away from Burford's busy high street, is no longer in the hands of a hotel group but is personally run by its owner, Michael Porter. There are 20 spacious individual bedrooms, complete with beams and every conceivable luxury; numerous cosy sitting corners, well furnished with antiques and ancient tapestries; and an immaculate garden with its neat yew hedges, fish ponds and barbecue area. The dining-room offers first-class food and an extensive wine list.

Nearby Minster Lovell Hall, 5 miles (8 km); Cotswold villages.

Sheep Street, Burford, Oxfordshire OX18 4LW
Tel (0993) 822791 **Fax** 823008
Location just off Burford high street, near junction of A40 and A424; parking for 20 cars
Food & drink full breakfast, lunch, dinner; full licence
Prices B&B £55-£75; dinner £19.50; reductions for children sharing parents' room
Rooms 13 double (3 four-poster), 2 single, 5 suites/family rooms, all with bath and shower; all rooms have central heating, colour TV, phone, hairdrier
Facilities 3 sitting-rooms, 2 bars; conservatory
Credit cards AE, DC, MC, V
Children welcome
Disabled access easy to dining-room only
Pets by prior arrangement
Closed never
Proprietor Michael Porter

Cotswolds

Country guest-house, Withington

Halewell

Elizabeth Carey-Wilson opened her lovely Cotswold-stone house to guests in the early 1980s, and has managed to keep the atmosphere of a gracious family home entirely intact. The house, part of it an early 15thC monastery, forms a picture-postcard group around a courtyard. Mrs Carey-Wilson treats her guests as friends. Breakfast is whenever you will after 9 o'clock, but she serves her set dinner – usually a roast or a grill – at a single table at a set time (couples are split).

Nearby Chedworth Roman Villa, 1.5 miles (2.5 km).

Withington, near Cheltenham, Gloucestershire GL54 4BN
Tel (024289) 238
Location 8 miles (13 km) SE of Cheltenham S of A40, on edge of village; ample car parking
Food & drink full breakfast, dinner; residential licence
Prices B&B £38.50-£49.50; dinner £17.50; reductions for 2 nights, and for children
Rooms 6 double, all with bath, some also with shower; all have central heating, colour TV, radio, tea/coffee kit
Facilities 2 sitting-rooms, bar, dining-room; heated outdoor swimmmg-pool (summer), trout lake
Credit cards MC, V
Children welcome
Disabled access good – special ground-floor suite
Pets accepted by arrangement
Closed never **Proprietor** Elizabeth Carey-Wilson

Country hotel, Cleeve Hill

Cleeve Hill

'Ideal for a few relaxing days in the Cotswolds. The views from the bedroom and breakfast room were breathtaking, and the bedroom was very comfortable, tastefully decorated. Most important was the friendly, helpful attitude of John and Marion Enstone – always available, but melting unobtrusively into the background when not required.' This report from a very experienced 'scout' leaves little to add. The house, near the summit of Cleeve Hill, is Edwardian in style, and the Enstones (ex-BA cabin crew) have refurbished it entirely since they bought it in 1991. Omelettes are a breakfast speciality. No smoking is permitted.

Nearby Cheltenham; Sudeley Castle, 5 miles (8 km).

Cleeve Hill, Cheltenham, Gloucestershire GL52 3PR
Tel (0242) 672052
Location in countryside, on B4632, 4 miles (6 km) NE of Cheltenham; with terraced garden and parking for 12 cars
Food & drink breakfast; residential licence
Prices B&B £27.50-£45; reductions for children sharing and for 2 nights
Rooms 7 double (2 twin), one single, one family room, all with bath; all rooms have central heating, TV, phone, radio, hairdrier
Facilities sitting-room with bar, dining-room
Credit cards AE, MC, V
Children accepted
Disabled access difficult
Pets not accepted
Closed never
Proprietors John and Marion Enstone

Cotswolds

Bibury Court

Until recently this beautiful Jacobean mansion was run along house party lines by the tireless Collier family; now a manager has been installed, but not much else has changed. You won't get luxury accommodation or 5-star service, but you will get atmospheric bedrooms (some with four-poster beds), panelled public rooms with open fires and antique furniture, a friendly welcome, seven acres of garden to explore and 'honest cooking with eastern and antipodean variations'.

Nearby Arlington Row, Arlington Mill museum, trout hatchery; Bath, Oxford, Stratford all within reach.

Bibury, Cirencester, Gloucestershire GL7 5NT **Tel** (0285) 740337 **Fax** 740660 **Location** in village on B4425, 6 miles (10 km) NE of Cirencester; with garden and ample car parking **Food & drink** breakfast, lunch, dinner; full licence **Prices** B&B £34-£53; lunch from £5, dinner from £17 **Rooms** 20 double (14 twin), 18 with bath, 2 with shower; all have central heating, phone, hairdrier, TV, tea/coffee kit **Facilities** sitting-room, dining-room, bar; fishing, croquet **Credit Cards** AE, DC, MC, V **Children** welcome **Pets** accepted in bedrooms **Disabled** access difficult **Closed** Christmas **Proprietors** Miss P J Collier, Mr and Mrs A Johnston

Lamb Inn

Richard and Kate Cleverly's inn is not a luxurious place, but it epitomizes what this guide is all about – they run it (as they have for over a decade) with energy, verve and good humour; the features of the 300-year-old inn are retained and extensions have been made using original stone and beams; respectable beers such as Wadworths 6X, Tanglefoot and Flowers IPA are on tap; the furniture is comfortable; the bedrooms are well equipped and prettily decorated (two with four-posters); there is a delightful garden; food is home-cooked, and it is very reasonably priced.

Nearby Stow-on-the-Wold, 5 miles (8 km); Burford, 6 miles (10 km); Shipton-under-Wychwood, 9 miles (14 km).

Great Rissington, Bourton-on-the-Water, Gloucestershire GL54 2LJ **Tel** (0451) 820388 **Location** 4 miles (6 km) SE of Bourton-on-the-Water, 3 miles (5 km) N of A40; in gardens with ample car parking **Food & drink** full breakfast, light (or packed) lunch, dinner; full licence **Prices** B&B £18-£28; dinner from £10.50; bargain breaks **Rooms** 13 double, 5 with bath, 6 with shower; 2 suites; all rooms have central heating **Facilities** sitting-room with TV, bar; indoor heated swimming-pool **Credit cards** MC, V **Children** welcome, but not in bar **Disabled** not suitable **Pets** dogs welcome in bedrooms if well behaved **Closed** Christmas Day and Boxing Day **Proprietors** Richard and Kate Cleverly

Cotswolds

Manor house hotel, Chadlington

The Manor

The Grants are no novices to the hotel business – they used to run Kirkby Fleetham Hall in North Yorkshire, before moving south to this imposing, mainly 18thC manor house in the heart of the Cotswolds.

In the five years since they came here, they have thoroughly redecorated the place, taking great care to preserve the atmosphere of a private country house. 'There's not one piece of wallpaper I haven't personally put up,' says David proudly and, to his credit, the decoration is strikingly smart throughout. Bedrooms are palatial, with large beds, luxurious bathrooms and plenty of sitting space as well. They are named after birds, and 'Skylark' is perhaps the most impressive with its circular ceiling, possibly once part of the original entrance hall. All look out on to the gardens and rolling hills beyond.

The sitting-room and drawing-room have equally good views across the Cotswolds, and are very grand – certainly not the kind of place to bring dogs or riotous children. The dining-room is also formal, with polished tables against a dark pink background. Chris's dinners are imaginative (broad bean and hazelnut soup, perhaps, followed by calves' livers in gin and lime), and allow some choice.

Nearby Bleinheim/Woodstock, 5 miles (8 km); Cotswolds; Oxford, 15 miles (24 km).

Chadlington, Oxfordshire OX7 3LH
Tel (0608) 76711
Location beside church in village, 3 miles (5 km) SE of Chipping Norton; with 18 acres of grounds and ample car parking
Food & drink breakfast, dinner
Prices B&B £50-£65; dinner £25.50
Rooms 7 double, all with bath; all rooms have central heating, phone, TV
Facilities sitting-room, 2 dining-rooms, library
Credit cards MC, V
Children accepted if well behaved
Pets not accepted
Disabled not suitable
Closed never
Proprietors David and Chris Grant

Cotswolds

Inn, Burford

The Lamb

If you want some respite from Burford's summer throng, you won't do better than the Lamb, only a few yards behind the High Street, but a veritable haven of tranquillity – particularly in the pretty walled garden.

Inside the creeper-clad stone cottages, you won't be surprised to find traditional pub trappings (after all, the Lamb has been an inn since the 15thC), but you may be surprised to discover 12 spacious beamed bedrooms, decorated with floral fabrics and antiques. All are different – 'Shepherds', for example, has a vast antique four-poster bed and a little attic-like bathroom, 'Malt' (in what was once the neighbouring brewery) has a smart brass bed and large stone mullion windows.

The hotel is run by Caroline and Richard De Wolf, with the help of Caroline's mother Bunty. It's very much a family enterprise, although they employ two chefs (one French) to produce impressive-sounding, daily-changing meals. These are served in the dining-room, looking on to the geranium-filled patio. Coffee can be taken in here, or in the sitting-room or TV room, both of which have comfortable chairs and sofas grouped around open fires. The Lamb manages to combine the convivial atmosphere of a pub with that of a comfortable hotel.

Nearby Minster Lovell Hall, 5 miles (8 km); Cotswold villages.

Sheep Street, Burford OX8 4LR
Tel (099382) 3155
Location in village, with car parking for 6 in courtyard
Food & drink breakfast, lunch, dinner; full licence
Prices B&B £30-£70; bar meals about £5.95, restaurant meals (3-course) £18.50; midweek and weekend breaks
Rooms 13 double, 12 with bath, one with shower; all rooms have central heating; some rooms have hairdrier, television
Facilities bar, 3 sitting-rooms, dining-room
Credit cards MC, V
Children welcome; baby listening service
Disabled 3 ground-floor bedrooms **Pets** dogs in room by prior arrangement
Closed 25 and 26 December
Proprietors Mr and Mrs R M De Wolf

Cotswolds

The Shaven Crown

The Shaven Crown, as its name suggests, has monastic origins; it was built in 1384 as a hospice to nearby Bruern Abbey, and many of the original features remain intact – most impressively the medieval hall, with its beautiful double-collar braced roof and stone walls decorated with tapestries and wrought ironwork.

The hall forms one side of the courtyard garden, which is decked with flowers and parasols, and on a sunny day is a lovely place to enjoy the Brookes' wholesome pub lunches. Some of the bedrooms overlook the courtyard, others are at the front of the house and suffer from road noise – though this is unlikely to be a problem at night. The Brookes family (parents, son and daughter-in-law) have decorated the rooms sympathetically, leaving the low ceilings, uneven floorboards, exposed beams and open fireplaces intact. Some of the furniture is rather mundane and the bathrooms ordinary.

Dinner is taken in the oak-beamed dining-room which leads off the hall. The menu offers plenty of choice and changes with the seasons – it is not elaborate, but the food is interesting and competently cooked. And if you still have the energy after 4 or 5 courses, you can join the locals in the narrow chapel-like bar, or adjourn to the hall, which doubles as a (rather drafty) sitting-room.

Nearby North Leigh Roman Villa, 6 miles (10 km).

Shipton-under-Wychwood, Oxfordshire OX7 6BA
Tel (0993) 830330
Location in middle of village; ample car parking
Food & drink full breakfast, lunch, dinner; full licence
Prices B&B £33-£53; dinner from about £18.50; reduced weekly rates, bargain breaks
Rooms 7 double, with bath; one single, with bath; one family room, with bath; all rooms have central heating, TV, tea/coffee kit
Facilities restaurant, bar, medieval hall; bowling green
Credit cards MC, V
Children welcome
Disabled good access – one ground-floor bedroom
Pets allowed in bar but not in bedrooms
Closed never
Proprietors Brookes family

Cotswolds

Country guest-house, Lower Brailes

Feldon House

The Withericks both escaped the world of commercial catering to renovate their charming house on the fringes of the Cotswolds. For most travellers, Feldon House is a bed-and-breakfast establishment – and a thoroughly welcoming and comfortable one it is, too. But it is even more attractive to those who opt to take lunch or dinner. Allan Witherick does not run a restaurant in the conventional sense, but caters for single parties of up to 12 in the small dining-room, and up to three couples in the conservatory. His fixed menus (which can of course take account of individual preferences) tend towards English food, based on fresh ingredients, all delightfully presented.

The house is a modest one, with a red-brick Victorian façade. Inside, it has been carefully decorated, with stripped woodwork, muted colours and antique furniture. Bedrooms are pretty and comfortably furnished, and provide all the necessary creature comforts; two are in the main house, the others are in the old coach house. The gardens, front and rear, are leafy and colourful, and beautifully kept without being formal. A delightful place, and a good alternative to the pricier hotels in and around Stratford-upon-Avon. Golf enthusiasts will be pleased to hear that an 18-hole course is open in the village.

Nearby Upton House and gardens, 5.5 miles (9 km); Broughton Castle, 8 miles (13 km); Cotswold villages; Stratford-upon-Avon.

Lower Brailes, near Banbury,
Oxfordshire OX15 5HW
Tel (0608) 685580
Location 10 miles (16 km) W
of Banbury on B4035, in
middle of village; in garden
with parking for 9 cars
Food & drink full breakfast,
lunch, dinner (not Sun);
restaurant and residential
licence
Prices B&B £21-£46; lunch
£17.95, dinner £22.95;
reductions for 2 nights or
more

Rooms 4 double, all with bath;
all rooms have central
heating, phone, TV, radio,
tea/cofee kit; hairdrier and
trouser-press available
Facilities 2 sitting-rooms,
dining-room, conservatory
Credit cards AE, MC, V
Children welcome over 11
Disabled access difficult
Pets accepted by prior
arrangement
Closed 2 weeks autumn
Proprietors Allan and Maggie
Witherick

Cotswolds

Swalcliffe Manor

Judith and Francis Hitching opened the doors of their beautiful
and historic house to guests in 1985 – and have not looked back.
No wonder. Swalcliffe Manor boasts a host of unrivalled features
– a Tudor great hall with huge log fireplace, a fine medieval
undercroft, an enormous Georgian sitting-room, a dining-room
with a long Elizabethan refectory table, and bedrooms which are
widely different but all captivating, with views over the secluded
gardens. Judith runs the house almost single-handedly – though
'Francis is a good butler' – and has won awards for her gourmet
cooking. Dinner might include scallops with ginger and onions,
boned and stuffed chicken *en croute*, elderflower sorbet and
raspberry *coulis*. Breakfast is large, and comes complete with
home-made jams.

Nearby Blenheim Palace, Hidcote Gardens; Stratford-upon-Avon
and Cotswold villages within reach.

Swalcliffe, Banbury,
Oxfordshire OX15 5EH
Tel (029578) 348
Location 5 miles (8 km) W of
Banbury, next to church; in
4.5-acre grounds, with ample
car parking
Food & drink full breakfast,
tea, dinner; no licence
Prices B&B £20-£30; dinner
from £16
Rooms 4 double, 3 with bath
(one with four-poster bed);
one single; all rooms have
central heating, tea/coffee kit
Facilities sitting-rooms,
dining-room, great hall with
piano and TV; croquet,
swimming-pool
Credit cards not accepted
Children welcome over 7 if
well behaved
Disabled not suitable; steep
stairs, polished floors
Pets not accepted
Closed mid-Dec to Mar
Proprietors Judith and Francis
Hitching

Andrews Hotel

Lots of people stop at Andrews for a lavish cream tea; few
venture upstairs in this timbered 15thC inn to discover 8 smartly
decorated rooms. Some have low beams, some 4-posters; all are
done out in expensive fabrics and have gleaming bathrooms.
Breakfast is all home-made and elegantly presented.

Nearby Cotswold villages.

High Street, Burford,
Oxfordshire 0X18 4QA
Tel (0993) 823151 **Fax** 823240
Location in middle of
Burford; no private car
parking
Food & drink full breakfast,
cream tea; restaurant licence
Prices B&B £30-£40;
reductions for 2 nights plus
Rooms 6 double, 3 with bath,
3 with shower; one single, one
family room, both with bath;
all have central heating, TV
Facilities breakfast room,
sitting-room; terrace
Credit cards MC,V
Children welcome
Disabled one ground-floor
room **Pets** not accepted
Closed Christmas
Proprietor Trevor Gibbons

Cotswolds

Country house hotel, Tetbury

Calcot Manor

This 15thC Cotswold farmhouse has been functioning as a hotel since 1984. Brian and Barbara Ball have now retired but their son, Richard, and a team of dedicated staff continue to provide the highest standards of comfort and service while preserving a calm and relaxed atmosphere. The lovely old house itself was a sound choice – its rooms are spacious and elegant without being grand – and the setting amid lawns and old barns, surrounded by rolling countryside, is all you could ask for. The original bedrooms have been redecorated and three new ones have been added – furnishings and decorations are carefully harmonious, with rich fabrics and pastel colours throughout. In 1993 a cottage was converted into four new family suites, designed specifically for parents travelling with young children.

Food is a highlight. The young chef, Ben Davies, has retained for the hotel a prized Michelin star, with his original and elaborate cooking.

Nearby Chavenage, 1.5 miles (2.5 km); Owlpen Manor, 3 miles (5 km); Westonbirt Arboretum, 4 miles (6 km); Slimbridge, 6 miles (10 km)

Near Tetbury, Gloucestershire GL8 8YJ
Tel (0666) 890391 **Fax** 890394
Location 3 miles (5 km) W of Tetbury on A4135; in 4-acre grounds with ample car parking (2 under cover)
Food & drink full breakfast, lunch, dinner; residential and restaurant licence
Prices B&B £44-£68; dinner £18-£26
Rooms 15 double, all with bath and shower (6 with spa bath); 4 family suites; all rooms have central heating, colour TV, phone, radio, hairdrier
Facilities 2 sitting-rooms, dining-room; heated outdoor swimming-pool, croquet
Credit cards AE, DC, MC, V
Children welcome; baby-listening
Disabled access good to all ground-floor public rooms; 4 ground-floor bedrooms
Pets not accepted
Closed never
Proprietor Richard Ball

Cotswolds

Cotswold House

Robert and Gill Greenstock set themselves a monumental task of redecorating Cotswold House from top to bottom when they took it over in 1988. The patient application of their motto – 'attention to detail' – is everywhere in evidence.

Using local craftsmen, they have restored the magnificent spiral staircase to its former glory and have filled the public rooms with antiques, collector's items and hand-painted murals. There are two dining-rooms; the All Day Eaterie (café-bar and adjoining courtyard) serving brasserie-style meals and cream teas, and the 'grand' dining-room (marble pillars, classy fabrics, French windows overlooking the garden) where interesting *à la carte* dinners are served – often with piano accompaniment. The sitting-rooms are large and airy, and decorated in Regency style.

Each of the 15 bedrooms has a different theme, carried through to the last detail; the Military room is full of regimental souvenirs, the Indian room has dome-shaped mirrors and bed-heads, Aunt Lizzie's is romantically lacy, and the latest addition, the Colonial Room has all the trappings of an American residence at the turn of the century, including hand-stencilled walls and a canopied four-poster bed. All rooms have impeccable bathrooms and beautiful flower arrangements.

Nearby Broadway, 4 miles (6.5 km).

The Square, Chipping Campden, Gloucestershire **Tel** (0386) 840330 **Fax** 840310 **Location** in main street of town; with garden and parking for 12 cars **Food & drink** full breakfast, lunch, dinner; full licence **Prices** B&B £45-£70; lunch around £9, Sun lunch £15, dinner £15 or £25; weekend and midweek breaks **Rooms** 12 double, all with bath (one four-poster bed); 3 single, 2 with bath, one with shower; all rooms have central heating, phone, satellite TV, hairdrier, radio **Facilities** 2 sitting-rooms, bar; croquet **Credit cards** AE, MC, V **Children** accepted over 8 **Disabled** access difficult **Pets** not accepted **Closed** Christmas **Proprietors** Mr and Mrs Robert Greenstock

Oxfordshire

Country inn, Clanfield

The Plough

There is no disguising the slightly corporate-contract look of the furnishings of this glossy little inn, which is part of the small Hatton Hotels group. But equally there is no denying the comfortable and relaxing ambience that the interior designer has created, and the welcoming atmosphere that the staff add to it. The building is a mellow Cotswold-stone manor-house, and not surprisingly some of the rooms are on the small side – though some bathrooms include whirlpool baths. There is no sitting-room apart from the bar/lounge. The food is as sophisticated as the decoration.

Nearby Cotswolds; Oxford, 25 miles (40 km).

Bourton Road, Clanfield, Oxfordshire OX8 2RB
Tel (036781) 222 **Fax** 596
Location in village 4 miles (6 km) N of Faringdon; with garden and private car parking
Food & drink breakfast, dinner; restaurant and residential licence
Prices B&B £40
Rooms 6 double, all with bath

or shower; all rooms have central heating, phone, TV, hairdrier, trouser-press
Facilities dining-room, bar/lounge
Credit cards AE, DC, MC, V
Children welcome over 7
Disabled access difficult
Pets not accepted
Closed never
Manager Jean Dunstone

Town hotel, Woodstock

Feathers

An amalgam of four tall 17thC town houses of mellow red brick, now an exceptionally civilized town hotel. The public rooms are full of character, the individually decorated bedrooms elegant and comfortable – though some are on the small side. Antiques, pictures, books, flowers and plants abound. One visitor was full of praise for the way the staff managed to make a weekend 'entirely relaxing, without intruding in the way that hotel staff so often do'. Excellent food.

Nearby Blenheim Palace; Oxford, 7 miles (11 km).

Market Street, Woodstock, Oxfordshire OX20 1SX
Tel (0993) 812291 **Fax** 813158
Location in middle of town; with courtyard garden and limited private car parking
Food & drink breakfast, lunch, dinner; full licence
Prices B&B £49-£85; dinner from £23.50
Rooms 13 double with bath; 3 suites with bath; one single

with shower; all rooms have central heating, colour TV, phone, radio
Facilities bar, 2 sitting-rooms, dining-room, restaurant; conservatory
Credit cards AE, DC, V
Children welcome
Disabled access difficult
Pets accepted by arrangement
Closed never
Manager Tom Lewis

Oxfordshire

Bath Place

It came as a relief, a couple of years ago, to find at last an entry for downtown Oxford. Bath Place is a tight group of carefully restored 17thC cottages, opened as a hotel in 1989 and about as centrally placed as you could wish. It does not have much in the way of sitting-space, but for sightseers that is not likely to matter greatly, and there are compensations: well equipped and tasteful bedrooms, a smart bar and restaurant, and – most important – adventurous modern cooking by chef Peter Cherrill, who has made quite a name for himself in the area.

Nearby Sheldonian Theatre; Oxford colleges.

4-5 Bath Place, Holywell St, Oxford OX1 3SU
Tel (0865) 791812 **Fax** 791834
Location in small mews off Holywell St in heart of city; with parking for 5 cars
Food & drink breakfast, lunch, dinner; residential and restaurant licence
Prices B&B £42-£62; lunch £14, dinner £14-£40
Rooms 8 double, 5 with bath, 3 with shower; 2 suites, one with bath, one with shower; all rooms have central heating, phone, TV, minibar, radio
Facilities dining-room, bar, sitting-area **Credit cards** AE, DC, MC, V **Children** accepted
Disabled no special facilities
Pets by arrangement **Closed** never; restaurant only, Sun dinner, Mon, Tue lunch; 2 weeks in Aug; 2 days after Christmas **Proprietors** Yolanda and Kathleen Fawsitt

Beetle and Wedge

Kate and Richard Smith established their reputation at the Royal Oak in Yattendon (see page 78). This larger Victorian inn, in a superb position on the Thames, offers more scope in every way, and they are steadily realising its potential. The public rooms have been tastefully refurbished, and the restaurant has made a name for itself. The riverside Boathouse offers less formal meals in a wine-bar-style setting, and there is an outdoor restaurant when weather allows. By now the gradual refurbishment of the bedrooms – with 'lovely' bathrooms – should be complete.

Nearby Thames valley; Oxford.

Moulsford-on-Thames, Oxford OX10 9JF
Tel (0491) 651381 **Fax** 651376
Location overlooking Thames, 2 miles (3 km) N of Goring on A329; with car parking
Food & drink full breakfast, lunch, dinner; full licence
Prices B&B £42.50-£100; meals £19.50; weekend breaks; reductions for children
Rooms 10 double, all with bath (one suite); all rooms have central heating, phone, TV, radio, hairdrier, tea/coffee kit
Facilities restaurant, sitting-room, boathouse bar
Credit cards AE, DC, MC, V
Children accepted **Disabled** access easy; some ground-floor rooms and adapted toilets
Pets by arrangement only
Closed Christmas Day; restaurant only, Sun evening, Mon Lunch and evening
Proprietors Richard and Kate Smith

Bedfordshire

Flitwick Manor

Although Flitwick Manor – now in the hands of Greentime Ltd since the departure of Somerset and Hélène Moore – has crept way above our normal price limits, we can't resist leaving it in these pages, as it stands out as something of an oasis in the relative desert of Bedfordshire.

Built between the 17th and 19th centuries, thoroughly modernized in 1936, and converted to a hotel 1984, this red-brick manor stands at the end of an authentically crunchy, tree-lined drive. The house overlooks parkland that extends far beyond its own substantial gardens. The public rooms are all highly individual: the mellow panelled bar/sitting-room; the library with ornamental plaster; the dining-room in elegant Regency style; the music room recently done out in Gothic style. Bedrooms are spacious and beautifully furnished in varying traditional styles, with many antique pieces.

The food, prepared by Duncan Poyser, is described as 'Modern English' and enjoys a good reputation. There are fixed-price menus and vegetarian options.

Nearby Woburn Abbey, 4.5 miles (7 km); Chilterns.

Church Road, Flitwick, Bedfordshire MK45 1AE
Tel (0525) 712242 **Fax** 718753
Location 2 miles (3 km) S of Ampthill, on S side of village, close to A5120; in 6.5-acre grounds with ample car parking
Food & drink breakfast, lunch, dinner; full licence
Prices B&B £65-£150; dinner from £28.50
Rooms 12 double, all with bath; 3 single, all with bath; all rooms have central heating, colour TV, phone, radio, hairdrier, minibar
Facilities dining-room, bar, library, sitting-room, music room; croquet, putting, tennis, fishing
Credit cards AE, MC, V
Children welcome if well behaved
Disabled access good – separate entrance for wheelchairs; 3 ground-floor rooms
Pets welcome (cost extra)
Closed never
Manager Sonia Banks

Warwickshire

Chapel House

This predominantly Georgian building, once the dower house to the now-demolished Atherstone Hall, is a successful blend of period elegance and modern comforts. The light and airy Garden Room is used mainly for breakfast; the main dining-room has elegantly laid separate tables, and is open to non-residents throughout the week. Chef Gary Thompson is in charge of the kitchen, and does a sound job with fresh ingredients – 'first-class,' says a recent visitor, 'prepared and presented with thought and care'. The cottagey second-floor bedrooms are welcoming; the sitting-room and conservatory are comfortable and peaceful.
Nearby Coventry and Lichfield within reach.

Friars Gate, Atherstone, Warwickshire CV9 1EY
Tel (0827) 718949 **Fax** 717702
Location 5 miles (8 km) NE of Nuneaton; off A5 in town square; car parking in street
Food & drink full breakfast, dinner; restaurant licence
Prices B&B £24.50-£50; dinner from £14.95
Rooms 7 double, 3 with bath, 4 with shower; 5 single, one with bath, 4 with shower; all have central heating, TV, phone, radio
Facilities sitting-room, 2 dining-rooms
Credit cards DC, MC, V
Children welcome over 8
Disabled easy access to dining-room **Pets** not accepted **Closed** Christmas
Proprietors David and Pat Roberts

Mallory Court

Allan Holland and Jeremy Mort have put the emphasis in this converted country manor – built at the turn of the century in Lutyens style – unashamedly on luxury, from the oak-panelled dining-room, where the tables are laid with silver and crystal, to the spacious, individually decorated bedrooms. Dinner is imaginative with a very reasonably-priced table d'hôte.
Nearby Warwick Castle, 2 miles (3 km); Kenilworth Castle, 5 miles (8 km); Stratford-upon-Avon, 9 miles (14.5 km).

Harbury Lane, Bishops Tachbrook, Royal Leamington Spa, Warwickshire CV33 9QB
Tel (0926) 330214 **Fax** 451714
Location 2 miles (3 km) S of Leamington, just off B4087 in 10-acre grounds, with ample parking and garages for 3 cars
Food & drink breakfast, lunch, tea, dinner; full licence
Prices B&B £72.50-£140; dinner from £30
Rooms 10 double, all with bath, 6 also with shower; one suite, with bath; all rooms have central heating, colour TV, hairdrier, radio
Facilities sitting-rooms, dining-room, garden room; outdoor swimming-pool, tennis, squash, croquet
Credit cards AE, MC, V
Children welcome over 9
Disabled access difficult
Pets not accepted
Closed never
Proprietors Allan Holland and Jeremy Mort

Warwickshire

Town hotel, Stratford-upon-Avon

Stratford House

For a central position in Stratford, this lovely old Georgian house is hard to beat – a mere stone's throw from the Royal Shakespeare Theatre, with the rest of historical Stratford right on the doorstep. Its previous owners ran Stratford House as a B&B place for many years before adding a restaurant in 1986. Sylvia Adcock 'retired' from a larger hotel in 1987 to take it over. The sitting-room at the front of the house is intimate and home-like while the Shepherd's Garden Restaurant at the back has a delightful conservatory, which opens on to a flowery walled garden where diners can eat alfresco, if the weather permits. Jonathan George's cooking is geared to a short, mildly adventurous and regularly changing menu. Some of the bedrooms are on the small side, but all have recently been refurbished.

Nearby Shakespeare's birthplace and tomb, Royal Shakespeare Theatre (all in Stratford); Warwick and Cotswolds within reach.

Sheep Street, Stratford-upon-Avon, Warwickshire CV37 6EF
Tel (0789) 268288 **Fax** 295580
Location in middle of town with walled courtyard; car parking can be arranged nearby
Food & drink full breakfast, lunch, dinner; residential and restaurant licence
Prices B&B £34.50-£61; dinner from £15.50; bargain breaks
Rooms 9 double, 6 with bath, 2 with shower; one single with bath; one suite with bath; all rooms have central heating, colour TV, tea/coffee kit, phone, radio/alarm
Facilities dining-room, sitting-room, bar
Credit cards AE, DC, MC, V
Children welcome, preferably over 5
Disabled access easy – 3 ground-floor bedrooms (though no wide doorways)
Pets not accepted
Closed Christmas
Proprietor Sylvia Adcock

Warwickshire

Country house hotel, Ettington

Ettington Manor

A classic Wolsey Lodge – a wisteria-clad Tudor manor house with beams, oak panelling, stone flagged floors and open fires – where you are treated as house guests and 'expected to behave as such'. Meals are eaten around one table in the beamed dining-room (although a 'table for two' in a separate room can be arranged). Julie (a trained cordon bleu cook) produces a four-course dinner as well as 'theatre suppers' for those going to Stratford. Bedrooms are spacious and comfortable, some with stone mullion windows, one with a four-poster bed. This is a non-smoking house and pre-booking is essential.
Nearby Stratford-upon-Avon; Cotswolds.

Rogers Lane, Ettington, Stratford-upon-Avon, Warwicks CV37 7SX
Tel (0789) 740216
Location in village, just off A422, 6 miles (10 km) SE of Stratford-upon-Avon; in garden with car parking
Food & drink full breakfast, dinner; full licence
Prices B&B £30-£35; dinner £16, pre-theatre supper £9

Rooms 3 double (one four-poster), one single; all with shower; all rooms have central heating, TV, radio
Facilities dining-room, sitting-room, study; croquet
Credit cards MC, V
Children accepted over 12
Disabled not suitable
Pets not accepted
Closed Dec to Jan
Proprietor Mrs Julie Graham

Town hotel, Leamington Spa

The Lansdowne

A creeper-covered Regency house in the heart of Leamington, justifiably renowned for its excellent 'British' food. David Allen (Swiss-trained chef) and his wife Gillian concentrate on quality (steak from Scotland, trout from the Cotswolds), and value. The Allens have combined home with hotel; public rooms are elegant, bedrooms cosy with stripped-pine furniture, pretty fabrics, thick carpets and all-important double-glazing to ensure an uninterrupted night's sleep. Readers have commented on the friendly atmosphere and warm welcome.
Nearby Warwick Castle, 2 miles (3 km).

Clarendon Street, Leamington Spa, Warwickshire CV32 4PF
Tel (0926) 450505
Location in middle of town near A425 Warwick road; with private car parking
Food & drink full breakfast, dinner, snacks; residential and restaurant licence
Prices B&B £19.95-£49.95; dinner from £16.95; reductions for children; 2-day breaks

Rooms 9 double, 6 with bath, 2 with shower; 5 single, 3 with shower; one family room with bath; all rooms have central heating, phone, TV, radio, tea/coffee kit, hairdrier
Facilities dining-room, sitting-room, bar **Credit cards** MC, V
Children welcome over 5
Disabled access good; 2 ground-floor bedrooms
Pets by arrangement
Closed never **Proprietors** David and Gillian Allen

Northamptonshire

Country hotel, Paulerspury

Vine House

This old farmhouse in a tiny Northamptonshire village, remains a very welcome presence in an area where good hotels are thin on the ground. It was taken over in 1991 by Julie and Marcus Springett.

The kitchen, now under the supervision of Marcus, remains at the heart of the hotel and its success. As before, everything possible is home-made, from the bread and preserves at breakfast to the petit-fours and chocolates served after dinner. There are fixed-price menus of four courses for lunch and dinner – as well as an extensive *carte*. One visitor found the cooking elaborate and highly competent but was not so impressed by the decoration of the public rooms. Another writes to commend the 'freshness and interest of the dishes'. The dining-room, with its white linen against warm Burgundy-papered walls, is a fair size – but the bar and sitting-room are rather small.

The hotel's six spotless bedrooms, all individually decorated in country style, are named after grape varieties. Back rooms overlook the walled garden and outbuildings – one of them is decidedly small, in sharp contrast to the rest. Shower rooms are also on the small side, but there is plenty of piping-hot water.
Nearby Silverstone, 5 miles (8 km); Buckingham, 9 miles (14 km).

100 High Street, Paulerspury, Towcester, Northamptonshire NN12 7NA
Tel (032733) 267 **Fax** 309
Location 3 miles (5 km) SE of Towcester, in village off A5; with ample car parking
Food & drink full breakfast, lunch, dinner; restaurant and residential licence
Prices B&B £31-£40; dinner from £19.50
Rooms 5 double, 4 with shower, one with bath; one single, with shower; all have central heating, TV, radio/alarm, phone, tea/coffee kit
Facilities sitting-room, bar, dining-room
Credit cards MC, V
Children welcome
Disabled access easy to public rooms only
Pets not in public rooms
Closed Sat, Mon and at lunch-time
Proprietors Julie and Marcus Springett

Shropshire

The Glebe Farm

'*L'endroit est ravissant et l'acceuil des plus chaleureux*', a reader of the French edition of the guide writes of this 16thC farmhouse – part timbered, part mellow stone. The Wilkeses have been farming in this pretty and peaceful spot for over 40 years, and taking in guests for at least 12 of those. They now have a faithful following of visitors who treasure the welcoming, unpretentious feel of the house and the good nature of the Wilkeses. Breakfast is served in the flagstoned dining-room and includes such treats as poached garden fruits and home-made jams and marmalades.
Nearby The White House (Munslow), 2 miles (3 km); Stokesay Castle, 7 miles (11 km); Shrewsbury, Ludlow; Wenlock Edge.

Diddlebury, Craven Arms, Shropshire SY7 9DH
Tel (058476) 221
Location in Diddlebury, just off B4368, 5 miles (8 km) NE of Craven Arms
Food & drink full breakfast; residential licence
Prices B&B £20-£25; reductions for children sharing
Rooms 5 double, 4 with bath or shower; one single; all rooms have central heating, tea/coffee kit; most rooms have TV, hairdrier
Facilities dining-room, sitting-room, bar; trout fishing on river and lake
Credit cards None
Children welcome over 8
Disabled access easy
Pets by arrangement can sleep in cars **Closed** Dec to Feb
Proprietors Michael, Eileen and Adrian Wilkes

Moat House

'A medieval experience' says the brochure, and this is no idle boast – this is a small, beautifully restored, 15thC manor house, with a water-filled moat, set in peaceful grounds full of wild flowers. Exposed beams abound and dinner (ordered in advance) is served by candlelight in the high-ceilinged hall. But there are no medieval privations: the three bedrooms are bright and pretty, the guests' parlour is cosy, with comfortable sofas before a large open fire, and the visitors' book is witness to the warmth of welcome extended by Peter and Margaret Richards since they opened their doors in 1988.
Nearby Shrewsbury, Ludlow; Shropshire Hills.

Longnor, Shrewsbury, Shropshire SY5 7PP
Tel & **fax** (0743) 718434
Location on edge of village, 8 miles (13 km) S of Shrewsbury, off A49; with water-filled moat, gardens and ample car parking
Food & drink breakfast, dinner, residential licence
Prices B&B £32; dinner £20
Rooms 3 double, 2 with bath, one with shower; all rooms have central heating, hairdrier, radio
Facilities dining-room, sitting-room
Credit cards AE, MC, V
Children not accepted
Disabled access difficult
Pets not accepted
Closed Dec to Feb
Proprietors Margaret and Peter Richards

Shropshire

Country hotel, Worfield

The Old Vicarage

When Peter Iles (an accountant) was made redundant in 1981, he and his wife Christine decided to convert this substantial red-brick vicarage into a small hotel. They have made an effort to retain the Edwardian character of the place – restoring original wood block floors, discreetly adding bathrooms to bedrooms, furnishing the rooms with handsome Victorian and Edwardian pieces, carefully converting the coach house to four 'luxury' bedrooms (one of which has been adapted for disabled guests). Readers have praised the large, comfortable bedrooms, named after Shropshire villages and decorated in subtle colours with matching bathrobes and soaps.

Attention to detail extends to the sitting-rooms (one of which is in the conservatory, with glorious views of the Worfe valley) and the three dining-rooms. Dinner (a daily changing menu with several choices) is English-based, ambitious and not cheap, served at polished tables by cheerful staff. Peter has a reasonably extensive wine cellar. The dining-room is strictly non-smoking, as are six of the bedrooms.

Nearby Severn Valley Railway, Ironbridge Museum.

Worfield, near Bridgnorth, Shropshire WV15 5JZ
Tel (07464) 497 **Fax** 552
Location in village, 3 miles (5 km) NE of Bridgnorth, N of A454; in 2-acre grounds with ample car parking
Food & drink breakfast, lunch, dinner; residential and restaurant licence
Prices B&B £42.50-£74.50; lunch £17.50, dinner £19.50-£27.50; reductions for children; leisure breaks
Rooms 14 double, 12 with bath, 2 with shower; one family room with bath; all have central heating, phone, TV, minibar, radio, hairdrier, tea/coffee kit, trouser-press
Facilities 3 dining-rooms, 2 sitting-rooms, one with bar
Credit cards AE, DC, MC, V
Children welcome; baby listening
Disabled access good; one ground-floor bedroom with special bathroom
Pets accepted, but not in public rooms **Closed** never
Proprietors Peter and Christine Iles

Staffordshire/Leicestershire

Restaurant with rooms, Waterhouses

Old Beams

The kitchen is at the heart of Old Beams. Chef and owner Nigel Wallis describes his food as 'modern English with a French classic lean' and stresses presentation and freshness – bread is baked twice a day. The lively Ann Wallis presides over the restaurant – choose between the oak-panelled dining-room in the 18thC main house and the conservatory extension, decorated with fantasy murals. Most of the compact but stylish bedrooms are in 'Les Chambres' across the road; each is named after a local pottery company and individually designed to match – complete with the appropriate china, of course.

Nearby Chatsworth House; the Potteries; Alton Towers.

Waterhouses, Staffs ST10 3HW
Tel (0538) 308254 **Fax** 308157
Location in middle of village, on A523 7 miles (11 km) NW of Ashbourne; with gardens and parking for 25 cars
Food & drink breakfast, lunch, dinner; restaurant licence
Prices B&B £38.75-£70; lunch £17.50, dinner £32; reductions for 2 nights or more, and for children sharing

Rooms 6 double, all with bath; all rooms have central heating, phone, TV, radio
Facilities dining-room, conservatory, bar area; fishing
Credit cards AE, DC, MC, V
Children accepted
Disabled access good; ground-floor rooms
Pets not accepted
Closed Jan; restaurant only Sun eve, Mon **Proprietors** Nigel and Ann Wallis

Town hotel, Uppingham

The Lake Isle

David and Claire Whitfield have gradually added more bedrooms to this rustic restaurant (once a hairdresser's) in the heart of Uppingham. The bedrooms, named after French wine regions, vary in size and style, from the bright and comfortable in a building at the rear, to the small and cosy in an adjacent cottage. There is an inviting first-floor sitting-room, with armchairs and an upright bench in front of a log fire. Lunch and dinner are served at pine tables in the original shop: delicious French food, whole loaves of home-made bread, an excellent wine list.

Nearby Rockingham Castle, 6 miles (10 km); Rutland Water.

High Street East, Uppingham, Leicestershire LE15 9PZ
Tel & Fax (0572) 822951
Location in middle of town, close to A6003 London road; with small walled garden and parking for 6 cars
Food & drink full breakfast, lunch, dinner; residential and restaurant licence
Prices B&B £31-£45; lunch £12.75, dinner £20.50-£24.50
Rooms 11 double, 9 with bath

(2 whirlpools), 2 with shower; one single with shower; all have radio, central heating, phone, TV, hairdrier
Facilities dining-room, sitting-room, bar **Credit cards** AE, DC, MC, V **Children** accepted
Disabled no special facilities
Pets well-behaved dogs in bedrooms only **Closed** never; restaurant only Mon lunch
Proprietors David and Claire Whitfield

Derbyshire

Riverside

This Georgian L-shaped house, stone-built and ivy-clad, has been a hotel since the early 1980s, when the Taylors took over. It is traditionally furnished, mostly with antiques, and an ambitious menu is served in the spacious, somewhat formal dining-room. Bedrooms vary widely in size, but are in the main richly decorated with bold floral fabrics.

Nearby Chatsworth and Haddon Hall, 4 miles (6 km).

Fennel Street, Ashford-in-the-Water, Bakewell, Derbyshire DE4 1QF
Tel (0629) 814275 **Fax** 812873
Location 2 miles (3 km) NW of Bakewell off A6, at top of village main street; in one-acre gardens, with parking for 25 cars
Food & drink full breakfast, lunch, dinner, light meals all day; full licence
Prices B&B £45-£79; dinner from £29; bargain breaks
Rooms 15 double, 13 with bath, 2 with shower (4 with four-poster beds); all rooms have central heating, TV, radio/alarm, tea/coffee kit, phone, hairdrier, trouser-press
Facilities sitting-room, bar, 2 dining-rooms, conservatory; croquet
Credit cards AE, MC, V
Children welcome, but not young babies
Disabled access easy to public rooms; 4 ground-floor bedrooms **Pets** small dogs only, by prior arrangement
Closed never **Proprietors** Roger and Sue Taylor

Wind in the Willows

The whimsical name honours not Kenneth Grahame's classic but a tree in the garden. Peter and Anne Marsh – who are brother and mother of Eric Marsh of the Cavendish at Baslow (over the page) – spent six years upgrading their Victorian guest-house before relaunching it under the new name in 1987, and an excellent job they made of it. All the bedrooms are thoroughly comfortable, but the Erika Louise room has a magnificent Victorian half tester and a splendid period-style bathroom.

Nearby Peak District.

Derbyshire Level, Glossop, Derbyshire SK13 9PT
Tel (0457) 868001 **Fax** 853354
Location 1 mile (1.5 km) E of Glossop off A57; with parking for 12 cars
Food & drink full breakfast, dinner; restaurant licence
Prices B&B £31-£70; dinner £17.50
Rooms 6 double, one with bath, 5 with shower; one family room, with shower; one suite with bath and shower; all rooms have central heating, phone, clock, radio/alarm, tea/coffee kit, hairdrier, trouser-press, TV
Facilities sitting-room/bar, study, dining-room
Credit cards AE, DC, MC, V
Children not discouraged
Disabled access difficult to bedrooms
Pets not accepted
Closed never
Proprietors Peter Marsh and Anne Marsh

Derbyshire

Country house hotel, Baslow

Cavendish

A posh, West End name and minibars in each of 24 bedrooms? The Cavendish doesn't sound like a personal small hotel. But the smart name is not mere snobbery – it is the family name of the Duke of Devonshire, on whose glorious Chatsworth estate the hotel sits (and over which the bedrooms look). And neither the hotel's size nor its equipment interferes with its essential appeal as a polished but informal and enthusiastically run hotel – strictly speaking, an inn, as Eric Marsh is careful to point out, but for practical purposes a country house.

The solid stone building is plain and unassuming. Inside, all is grace and good taste; the welcoming entrance hall sets the tone, with its paintings, striped sofas before an open fire, and elegant antique tables standing on a brick-tile floor. The whole ground floor has recently been remodelled, and a café-style conservatory added. Bedrooms are consistently attractive and comfortable, but vary in size and character – older ones are more spacious.

The elegant restaurant claims to have a 'controversial' menu; it is certainly ambitious and highly priced, but it met the approval of recent guests who described the food as 'unsurpassed – we were spoilt to death!'.

Nearby Chatsworth, 1.5 miles (2.5 km); Haddon Hall, 4 miles (6 km); Peak District.

Baslow, Derbyshire DE4 1SP
Tel (0246) 582311 **Fax** 582312
Location 10 miles (16 km) W of Chesterfield on A619; in extensive gardens with ample car parking
Food & drink breakfast, lunch, dinner; full licence
Prices B&B £44.50-£83; dinner from £22; extra bed or cot £7.50; winter weekend breaks
Rooms 24 double, all with bath and shower; all rooms have central heating, colour TV, phone, tea/coffee kit, clock radio, minibar, hairdrier
Facilities dining-room, bar, sitting-room, garden room; putting-green, fishing
Credit cards AE, DC, MC, V
Children welcome
Disabled access difficult
Pets not accepted
Closed never
Proprietor Eric Marsh

Derbyshire

Riber Hall

Twenty years ago, Alex Biggin rescued this peaceful, sturdy Elizabethan manor from the verge of dereliction, furnished it sympathetically, and opened it as a restaurant to the applause of local gourmets, who are not spoilt for choice of ambitious and competent French cooking. The bedrooms came later – created in outbuildings across an open courtyard and ranging from the merely charming and comfortable to the huge and delightful, with deep armchairs. Exposed timbers, stone walling, and antique four-posters are the norm, and all the thoughtful trimmings you could wish for are on hand.

The dining-room is elegantly traditional, and much the better for its light decoration; the small sitting-room through which it is reached is a fine place to sit before an open fire on a wild night (umbrellas are provided to get you across the courtyard), isolated from the world as well as insulated from the storm. Friendly and accommodating local staff serve meals in one and drinks in the other.

And you still have the hope that by morning the storm will have cleared, so that you can enjoy the delicious seclusion of the luxuriant walled garden.

Nearby Chatsworth House, Haddon Hall, Hardwick Hall, all 7 miles (11 km).

Matlock, Derbyshire, DE4 5JU
Tel (0629) 582795 **Fax** 580475
Location 2 miles (3 km) SE of Matlock by A615 (20 minutes from exit 28, M1); take minor road S at Tansley; in extensive grounds with adequate car parking in courtyard
Food & drink breakfast, lunch, dinner; restaurant and residential licence
Prices B&B £46-£92; dinner £26; 2-day breaks Oct-Apr
Rooms 11 double, all with bath and shower (5 with whirlpools), no twin beds, most four-posters; all rooms have central heating, minibar, colour TV, hairdrier, tea/coffee kit, trouser-press
Facilities sitting-room with bar service, conservatory, dining-room; tennis
Credit cards AE, DC, MC, V
Children not under 10
Disabled not suitable
Closed never
Proprietor Alex Biggin

Lincolnshire

Town guest-house, Lincoln

D'Isney Place

Since moving to this delightful red-brick Georgian house, on a bustling street a few yards from Lincoln cathedral, David and Judy Payne (he a property developer, she an ex-antique dealer) have been continually improving and adding to it. A year or two back they converted the former billiard room into a family suite; their next venture is to do up 5 nearby cottages for hotel guests.

For the purposes of this guide, D'Isney Place, named after its 15thC founder John D'Isney, is on the large side. And unfortunately it has no public rooms or restaurant – though there are plenty of respectable ones within walking distance. But we continue to recommend it because of the comfortable, stylish bedrooms, the well co-ordinated decorations and fabrics, the breakfast (cooked to order and served on bone china in the rooms) and, last but certainly not least, the impressive walled garden which incorporates a 700-year old tower from the old cathedral close wall.

The Paynes, who live in the middle part of the building, sandwiched between the two hotel wings, are much in evidence.
Nearby Cathedral, Bishop's Palace, Usher Gallery.

Eastgate, Lincoln, Lincolnshire LN2 4AA
Tel (0522) 538881 **Fax** 511321
Location in middle of city, just E of cathedral; with large walled garden and adequate car parking
Food & drink full breakfast, snacks at night; no licence
Prices B&B £30-£39; weekend breaks
Rooms 14 double, 12 with bath (3 with spa bath, one with Turkish steam shower), 2 with shower; 2 single, one with bath, one with shower; 2 family rooms, both with bath; all rooms have central heating, colour TV, radio, phone, tea/coffee kit; some rooms have hairdrier
Facilities none
Credit cards AE, DC, MC, V
Children welcome; cots available
Disabled access good – wheelchair ramp and wide doors; ground-floor bedrooms
Pets welcome
Closed never
Proprietors David and Judy Payne

West Essex

Manor house hotel, Broxted

Whitehall

'The Team', as the Keanes like to call themselves and their senior staff, offer a successful blend of amateur caring and professional skills. They have established such a high reputation for food and hospitality that they have been able to purchase and convert an adjoining building and more than double the number of bedrooms they offer.

It is a splendid house. The public rooms are uniform only in being thoroughly comfortable. The bar has a modern feel, decorated in grey and with abundant motor racing memorabilia. The sitting-room, decorated in pastel shades, has (like the entrance hall) comfortable, prettily covered chesterfield sofas, and pictures on the walls.

But the *pièce de résistance* is the dining-room, with its exposed oak beams and window frames, a fine view over the garden and a truly remarkable brick chimney snaking up to the vaulted ceiling. The Keanes have wisely not attempted to decorate this room in its own style, but to complement it with simple high-backed Italian chairs and peach linen. It is an appropriate setting for the stylish cooking – limited-choice menus in modern French post-nouvelle fashion.

Nearby Mole Hall wildlife park, 3 miles (5 km); Audley End House, 6 miles (10 km).

Church End, Broxted, Essex CM6 2BZ
Tel (0279) 850603 **Fax** 850385
Location 4 miles (6.5 km) SW of Thaxted on B1051; in walled garden with ample car parking
Food & drink full breakfast, lunch, dinner; restaurant licence
Prices B&B £52.50-£75; dinner £34-£37.50
Rooms 25 double, all with bath; all rooms have central heating, colour TV, phone, radio, hairdrier, trouser-press
Facilities sitting-room, bar, conference room, dining-room; outdoor heated swimming-pool, tennis
Credit cards AE, DC, MC, V
Children welcome over 5
Disabled access good to ground-floor rooms, with ramps
Pets not accepted
Closed 26-31 Dec
Proprietors Keane family

Essex

Restaurant with rooms, Harwich

The Pier at Harwich

The latest addition to Gerald Milsom's East Anglian empire, and a sharp contrast to Maison Talbooth (below) and Dedham Vale (facing page) – a seaside fish-and-chip restaurant (although naturally a relatively refined example of the breed) with a rather more ambitious seafood restaurant on the floor above (with resident pianist), and six bedrooms on the floor above that. The dining-rooms and ground-floor bar have a cheerfully nautical feel, but the rooms are more restrained, with plain colour schemes relieved by brightly floral duvet covers. What they lack in character they make up for in space, comfort and convenience. An excellent, emphatically British start or finish to a Continental expedition.

Nearby Car ferry port; Dedham Vale.

The Quay, Harwich CO12 3HH	all rooms have central heating, TV, tea/coffee kit
Tel (0255) 241212	**Facilities** 2 restaurants, bar
Location on quayside at Harwich; parking for 10 cars	**Credit cards** MC, V
Food & drink breakfast, lunch, dinner; full licence	**Children** welcome
	Disabled access possible to restaurant; only 2 small steps
Prices £31.25-£60; dinner about £30	**Pets** not accepted
	Closed never
Rooms 6 double, all with bath;	**Proprietor** Gerald Milsom

Bed and breakfast guest-house, Dedham

Maison Talbooth

For lavish comfort this rather plain-looking Victorian house is hard to beat. The bedrooms have flamboyant fabrics, luxury drapes, king-size beds, fruit and flowers; and the bathrooms have thick fluffy towels, gold taps and circular sunken baths. The French doors of an elegantly furnished sitting-room open out on to two beautiful acres of landscaped garden, and beyond that the lush pastures of Constable country. Down the road, Le Talbooth, a half-timbered weaver's cottage also under the Milsom management, provides the gastronomic highlight of the area. But a light snack will be willingly served in your room.

Nearby Castle House (in Dedham); Dedham Vale.

Stratford Road, Dedham, Colchester, Essex CO7 6HN	bath (2 with spa bath); all have central heating, TV, minibar
Tel (0206) 322367	
Location 5 miles (8 km) NE of Colchester, W of village; in 2-acre grounds with parking for 12 cars	**Facilities** sitting-room; croquet, lawn chess
	Credit cards MC, V
	Children welcome if well behaved
Food & drink breakfast and light snacks in rooms	**Disabled** easy access: 5 ground-floor rooms
Prices B&B £51.25-£107.50; dinner from £35	**Pets** not accepted
	Closed never
Rooms 10 double, all with	**Proprietor** Gerald Milsom

Essex

Country house hotel, Dedham

Dedham Vale

Dedham Vale is the youngest offspring of Gerald Milsom's family of East Anglian hotels and restaurants. The rooms are not as sumptuous as those of the Maison Talbooth, but some guests prefer the absence of the ritzy Talbooth touches. Flowing floral curtains, thick carpets and elegant painted furniture are features of all the rooms. Bathrooms are white and plain – no sunken baths or jacuzzis here. Last year we called for some refurbishment in the bedrooms, and we're pleased to hear they have been improved. Major refits, here as elsewhere, will have to await the end of the recession; meanwhile, prices have dropped.

The Edwardian house is creeper-clad and stands amid three acres of lawns and flower beds in a quiet spot in the Vale of Dedham. The theme is the outdoors – from the murals of Suffolk landscapes in the bar to the conservatory-like restaurant, where the profusion of cascading plants, the glass dome, the crisp yellow tablecloths and the white lacquered chairs create the illusion of eating alfresco. The restaurant (called the Terrace) is now closed in the evening – guests can dine at Le Talbooth, where a new, less-expensive menu has been introduced.

Nearby Castle House (in Dedham); Dedham Vale.

Stratford Road, Dedham, Colchester, Essex CO7 6HW
Tel (0206) 322273
Location 5 miles (8 km) NE of Colchester, off A12, one mile (1.5 km) W of village; in 3-acre grounds with ample car parking
Food & drink breakfast, buffet lunch (not Sat), dinner (not Sun); restaurant licence
Prices B&B £34.75-£65; dinner from £19.50
Rooms 6 double, all with bath; all rooms have central heating, radio, phone, TV
Facilities sitting-room, bar, dining-room; golf and tennis nearby
Credit cards MC, V
Children welcome
Disabled access difficult – 4 steps to restaurant and no ground floor bedrooms
Pets not accepted
Closed never
Proprietor Gerald Milsom

Country guest-house, Melbourn

Melbourn Bury

This gracious manor house, dating mainly from Victorian times although of much earlier origin, offers an intimate retreat only 20 minutes' drive from Cambridge. The whitewashed and crenellated house, with roses round the door, has a delightful setting in mature parkland with its own lake and gardens.

All the public rooms are furnished with antiques, but have just the right degree of informality to make the house feel like a lived-in home and not a museum – not surprising, when you learn that Sylvia Hopkinson's family have been here for 150 years. As well as an elegant drawing-room, there is a splendid Victorian billiards room (full-size table) incorporating a book-lined library, and a sun-trap conservatory.

The three bedrooms are spacious and comfortably furnished in harmony with the house; particularly delightful is the 'pink room' which looks out over the lake and the garden; it is a profusion of Sanderson prints and antiques, and has a large bathroom.

The Hopkinsons' dinner-party food – home-made, down to the ice-creams and sorbets – is served dinner-party-style around a large mahogany table in the dining-room.

Nearby University colleges and Fitzwilliam Museum, in Cambridge; Duxford Air Museum, 8 miles (13 km); Wimpole Hall and Audley End within reach.

Melbourn, near Royston, Hertfordshire SG8 6DE
Tel (0763) 261151 **Fax** 262375
Location 10 miles (16 km) SW of Cambridge, on S side of village off A10; in 5-acre gardens with ample car parking
Food & drink full breakfast, dinner; residential licence
Prices B&B £37.50-£50; dinner £15
Rooms 2 double, one single, all with bath or shower; all rooms have central heating, TV, clock/radio
Facilities 2 sitting-rooms, dining-room, billiard room
Credit cards AE, MC, V
Children welcome over 8
Disabled not suitable
Pets not accepted **Closed** Christmas, New Year and Easter
Proprietors Anthony and Sylvia Hopkinson

Cambridge/Suffolk

Old Ferry Boat Inn

Weekend crowds beat a path to this venerable thatched inn (another 'oldest in England') on the banks of the Great Ouse. But when day visitors leave it's a peaceful and picturesque spot. Inside are all the requisite pub trappings – log fires, oak beams, and an interesting range of good-value bar food and real ales served around the immensely curved bar. In summer families spill out to the picnic tables and lawns to let children romp unhindered. The seven bedrooms, though not large, are all attractively furnished and decorated in fresh, pretty, modern schemes. The tariff takes account of the more attractive river views.
Nearby Cambridge 12 miles (19 km).

Holywell, St Ives, Huntingdon, Cambridgeshire PE17 3TG **Tel** (0480) 463227 **Location** on banks of Ouse, signed from Holywell, 2 miles E of St Ives; with garden and car parking **Food & drink** full breakfast, lunch, dinner; full licence **Prices** B&B £25-£49.50; dinner £10-£15 **Rooms** 7 double (one twin), 4	with bath, 3 with shower; all rooms have central heating, phone, TV, tea/coffee kit **Facilities** dining room, bar **Credit Cards** MC, V **Children** welcome **Pets** not accepted **Disabled** access difficult **Closed** Christmas dinner **Proprietors** Richard and Shelley Jeffrey

The Angel Inn

The owners of this low-slung timber and brick building on a fairly busy junction rely on the time-honoured grapevine to spread the gospel about the Angel's virtues. An imaginative menu is chalked up daily on boards by the main bar, and a tall hat or two indicates the more serious food served in the dining-rooms. One of these is a lofty converted barn with an enormous brick chimney and a fern-lined brewery well-shaft (discovered during renovation and now a spotlit talking point). Above it a gallery leads to the bedroom wing, with half a dozen unevenly shaped rooms smartly kitted out in Laura Ashley wallpapers.
Nearby Constable country.

Stoke-by-Nayland, Nr Colchester, Essex CO6 4SA **Tel** (0206) 263245 **Location** on T-junction in village, 2 miles (3 km) off A134 between Colchester and Sudbury; with car parking **Food & drink** full breakfast, lunch, dinner; full licence **Prices** B&B £22.50-£42; meals £7-£20	**Rooms** 6 double (one twin), all with bath **Facilities** sitting-room, restaurant, bars **Credit Cards** AE, DC, MC, V **Children** accepted over 8 years **Pets** not accepted **Disabled** not suitable **Closed** Christmas **Proprietors** Richard Wright and Peter Smith

Suffolk

Country hotel, Long Melford

Black Lion

Long Melford is a famously attractive Suffolk village, and the Black Lion is at the heart of it, overlooking the green. It is an elegant early 19thC building, decorated and furnished with great sympathy, taste and lightness of touch. When the Erringtons took over in 1989 they brought with them their already successful Countrymen restaurant operation, which offers 'modern cuisine with a strong classical influence' and a wide-ranging wine list; with the help of Janet's parents, they can now also offer a high standard of accommodation.

Nearby Long Melford church, Melford Hall and Kentwell Hall.

The Green, Long Melford, Suffolk CO10 9DN
Tel (0787) 312356 **Fax** 74557
Location in village 3 miles (5 km) N of Sudbury, overlooking village green; with car parking
Food & drink full breakfast, lunch, dinner; full licence
Prices B&B £30-£50; dinner from £20
Rooms 7 double, one suite, one family room; all with bath; all have central heating, phone, TV, tea/ coffee kit
Facilities sitting-room, 2 dining-rooms, bar
Credit cards MC, V
Children welcome; baby-listening, highchair and cot provided
Disabled no special facilities
Pets not in public rooms
Closed Christmas
Proprietors Janet and Stephen Errington

Manor house hotel, Needham Market

Pipps Ford

A reader recommends enthusiastically this glorious half-timbered Tudor house in flowery gardens, which Raewyn Hackett-Jones has been running as a guest-house since the early 1980s. She lays great stress on the quality of her meals, producing her own bread, honey, vegetables and countless other ingredients.

   The bedrooms are delightful and full of character, with log fires burning downstairs in the winter.

Nearby Blakenham Woodland Garden, 3 miles (5 km).

Needham Market, near Ipswich, Suffolk IP6 8LJ
Tel (0449) 79208
Location in countryside one mile (1.5 km) E of Needham Market, down private road off roundabout where A140 meets A45; with car parking
Food & drink full breakfast, dinner; residential licence
Prices DB&B £47-£52; B&B by arrangement
Rooms 6 double, all with bath and shower; all rooms have central heating, tea/coffee kit, radio/alarm
Facilities 3 sitting-rooms (2 with TV), conservatory, dining-room; tennis, outdoor pool, fishing
Credit cards not accepted
Children accepted over 5
Disabled rooms and lounge in Stable Annexe on one floor
Pets not accepted in house, but can stay in car
Closed Christmas to mid-Jan; no dinner on Sun
Proprietor Raewyn Hackett-Jones

Suffolk

Twelve Angel Hill

Twelve Angel Hill occupies a house in a mellow brick terrace close to the cathedral, Georgian to the front but Tudor behind, opened as a hotel (called Kingshott's) in 1988 after thorough renovation. The spacious bedrooms are beautifully furnished, with antiques and sympathetic reproductions, bold floral decoration and fabrics – all very 'designer'. The public rooms too are warmly done out; the cocktail bar is oak-panelled. Dinner can be arranged at one of the many local restaurants.

Nearby Cathedral, Gershom-Parkington Memorial Collection.

12 Angel Hill, Bury St Edmunds, Suffolk IP33 1UZ
Tel (0284) 704088 **Fax** 725549
Location on Angel Hill, 100 metres from cathedral; with patio garden and car parking
Food & drink full breakfast; full licence
Prices B&B £32.50-£45
Rooms 5 double, 2 with bath, 3 with shower; one single with shower; all rooms have central heating, phone, TV, radio, tea/coffee kit, hairdrier, trouser-press
Facilities dining-room, sitting-room, bar, patio room
Credit cards DC, MC, V
Children accepted
Disabled access difficult
Pets dogs by arrangement
Closed never
Proprietors Bernie and John Clarke

Edgehill

Mrs Rolfe has achieved a happy combination of old and new in her handsome red-brick Georgian town house: a flagstoned hall, open fireplaces and chandeliers downstairs, bedrooms (some of which are surprisingly spacious, one with a four-poster) decorated with modern floral wall paper, matching fabrics and thick pile carpets. A fair-sized sitting-room opens on to a walled flower-garden and croquet lawn. Dinner is a cosy affair in a small but elegant room. Vegetables come straight from the kitchen garden and everything is home-made – including traditional English puddings.

Nearby Castle House, 6 miles (10 km); Dedham.

2 High Street, Hadleigh, Ipswich, Suffolk IP7 5AP
Tel (0473) 822458
Location 9 miles (14.5 km) W of Ipswich, in middle of town; with walled garden and car park at rear
Food & drink breakfast, dinner if pre-booked; residents licence
Prices B&B £21.25-£50; dinner £13.50; bargain breaks
Rooms 7 double, 3 with bath, 3 with shower; 2 single; 2 family rooms, one with bath, one with shower; all rooms have central heating, TV
Facilities sitting-room, dining-room
Credit cards not accepted
Children welcome; cot and high-chair provided
Disabled access difficult
Pets welcome
Closed one week Christmas to New Year
Proprietors Angela and Rodney Rolfe and Betty Taylor

EAST ANGLIA AND REGION

Suffolk

Restaurant with rooms, Lavenham

The Great House

The ancient timber-framed houses, the fine Perpendicular 'Wool Church' and the high street full of antiques and galleries makes Lavenham a high point of any tourist itinerary of the pretty villages of East Anglia.

The Great House in the market place was built in the heyday of the wool trade but was extensively renovated in the 18th century and looks more Georgian than Tudor – at least from the outside. It was a private house (lived in by Stephen Spender in the 1930s) until John Spice, a Texan with family roots in Suffolk, had the bright idea of turning it into a restaurant with rooms. Its food (predominantly French) is the best for miles – 'stunningly good' enthuses one visitor (a fellow hotelier) – and if you can secure one of its four bedrooms it is also a delightful place to stay. All are different, but they are all light, spacious and full of old-world charm, with beams and antiques. Each has its own fireplace and sitting-area, with sofa or upholstered chairs. The dining-room is dominated by an inglenook fireplace which formed part of the original house. In winter, log fires blaze; in summer, French doors open on to a pretty stone-paved courtyard for drinks, lunch or dinner.

Nearby Little Hall (in Lavenham); Melford Hall, 4 miles (6 km); Gainsborough's House, Sudbury, 5.5 miles (9 km).

Market Place, Lavenham, Suffolk CO10 9QZ
Tel (0787) 247431
Location 16 miles (26 km) NW of Colchester, in middle of village; garden at rear, with public car parking
Food & drink full breakfast, lunch, tea, dinner; full licence
Prices B&B £34-£75; dinner from £14.95; reduction for 2 nights or more, and for children sharing parents' room

Rooms 4 family-size suites, all with bath; all rooms have central heating, phone, colour TV, tea/coffee kit
Facilities sitting-room/bar, dining-room, patio
Credit cards MC, V
Children very welcome; cot and high chair provided, free baby-listening
Disabled access difficult
Pets welcome
Closed Jan
Chef-manager Regis Crépy

Suffolk

Otley House

Otley House has become one of the better-known examples of the 'country house party' establishment. Guests have the run of the relaxed but elegant house – 16thC but outwardly Georgian – including the grand piano in the candle-lit dining-room and the full-size table in the billiard room (where guests may smoke). Lise Hilton's Danish origins shine through in her cooking – as in her intolerance of the slightest speck of dirt. There is a licence, but no bar – 'guests are just given what they wish for'.

Nearby Woodbridge, 6 miles (10 km); Suffolk coast.

Otley, near Ipswich, Suffolk IP6 9NR
Tel (0473 890) 253
Location 7 miles (11 km) N of Ipswich on B1079; ample car parking
Food & drink full breakfast, dinner (except Sun); residential licence
Prices B&B £24-£38; dinner £15.50
Rooms 4 double, all with bath; all rooms have central heating, radio, hairdrier; 3 have TV
Facilities 2 sitting-rooms (one with TV), dining-room, billiard room, hall; croquet
Credit cards not accepted
Children welcome over 12
Disabled access not easy
Pets can be left in cars
Closed 1 Nov to 1 Mar
Proprietors L and M Hilton

The Crown

We have received conflicting reports of this refurbished inn, once the pride of Adnams – brewers to this part of the world, and wine merchants to a much wider clientele. Overall the 'ayes' have it, but only just. The hotel is a comfortably unpretentious place, with an oak-panelled bar at the back still popular with locals as well as the main bar/sitting-room, where the food served bears no resemblance to normal 'bar snacks'. In the dining-room too, the cooking is original and (usually) highly successful, with particular emphasis on fish. Bedrooms are unremarkable – small (some very small) but neat; Sunday brunch, sadly, is no more. Excellent wine list.

Nearby Suffolk Wild Life Country Park, 6 miles (10 km).

High Street, Southwold, Suffolk IP18 6DP
Tel (0502) 722275 **Fax** 724805
Location in middle of town; with ample car parking, some covered
Food & drink breakfast, lunch, dinner; full licence
Prices B&B £28-£35; dinner £16.25-£18.50
Rooms 9 double, 6 with bath, 2 with separate bath, one with shower; 2 single, both with bath; one family room with separate bath; all rooms have central heating, TV, phone
Facilities dining-room, 2 bars, function room
Credit cards AE, MC, V
Children welcome
Disabled access possible to ground floor
Pets not allowed
Closed first week in Jan
Manager Anne Simpson

Suffolk

Country hotel, Bury St Edmunds

Bradfield House

This 17thC timbered building in the countryside outside Bury had ceased to operate as a restaurant when the Ghỹbens took it over in 1988; they opened up again a few months later, and in 1989 started taking guests. It is more than a restaurant with rooms, though – there is a welcoming sitting-room equipped with books and games; the bedrooms are admirably spacious, with armchairs and ornate fireplaces; and there is a splendid, long-established garden with yew hedges. Roy is the cook, combining English and provincial French tradition in his richly satisfying dishes.

Nearby Bury St Edmunds; Long Melford, 7 miles (11 km).

Bradfield Combust, Bury St Edmunds, Suffolk IP30 0LR
Tel (0284) 386301
Location in rural setting, 4 miles (6.5 km) S of Bury St Edmunds on A134; with 2-acre gardens and parking for 14 cars
Food & drink full breakfast, dinner; full licence
Prices B&B £32.50-£50; dinner £15.50-£25
Rooms 3 double, one single, all with bath; all rooms have central heating, phone, TV, radio, tea/coffee kit
Facilities 2 dining-rooms, sitting-room, bar
Credit cards MC, V
Children welcome
Disabled no special facilities
Pets not accepted
Closed one week at Christmas; restaurant only, Sun evening
Proprietors Roy and Sally Ghỹben

Town hotel, Bury St Edmunds

Ounce House

The Pott family have lived in one half of this tall, brick-built Victorian house in central Bury St Edmunds for some time, and in the mid-1980s they bought the other half and skilfully refurbished it for guests. The six bedrooms – the best of them very spacious – are smartly done out in a restful style, with fully tiled bathrooms. Downstairs there is a palatial formal drawing-room. Dinner is a no-choice dinner-party affair, served around one table, in classic Wolsey-Lodge style – and now by prior arrangement only.

Nearby Cathedral, abbey, Gershom-Parkington collection.

Northgate Street, Bury St Edmunds, Suffolk IP33 1HP
Tel (0284) 761779
Location close to town centre; with walled garden and ample car parking
Food & drink breakfast, dinner by arrangement; residential licence
Prices B&B £32-£45; dinner £15-£20
Rooms 5 double, one single, all with bath; all have central heating, phone, TV, hairdrier, trouser-press, tea/coffee kit, phone
Facilities dining-room, 2 sitting-rooms, bar, library
Credit cards MC, V
Children tolerated; cot, highchair, baby-sitting by arrangement **Disabled** access difficult **Pets** not accepted
Closed never
Proprietors Simon and Jenny Pott

Norfolk

Country hotel, Swaffham

Strattons

Strattons epitomizes everything we are looking for in this guide. Perhaps it's because Les and Vanessa Scott are such natural hosts who love entertaining; perhaps it's because of their genuine artistic flair (they met as art students) or perhaps it's because they had a very clear vision of what they wanted to create when they bought this elegant listed villa in 1990.

Bedrooms (each in a different style) are positively luxurious. Plump cushions and pillows jostle for space on antique beds, books and magazines fill the shelves, and the same coordinated decoration continues into smart bathrooms. The two beautifully furnished sitting-rooms and newly decorated drawing room are equally impressive. Yet this isn't the kind of place where you are nervous of putting a foot wrong – it is emphatically a family home and you share it with the Scott cats and children.

The food is special, too. Strattons is creating quite a name for itself in the region – and it's easy to see why. Vanessa's daily changing menu (some choice) is inventive and appealing. It is beautifully presented and cheerfully served by Les in the cosy basement restaurant.

Nearby Norwich, 30 miles (48 km); north Norfolk coast.

Ash Close, Swaffham, Norfolk PE37 7NH
Tel (0760) 723845 **Fax** 720458
Location down narrow lane between shops on main street; with garden and ample car parking
Food & drink full breakfast, lunch, dinner; restaurant and restaurant licence
Prices B&B £35-£60; dinner £22.50
Rooms 4 double, 2 with bath, 2 with shower; 2 single, one with bath, one with shower; one family room with shower; all rooms have central heating, phone, TV, tea/coffee kit, hairdrier
Facilities 2 sitting-rooms, drawing-room, bar, dining-room
Credit cards AE, MC, V
Children welcome
Disabled access difficult
Pets welcome
Closed never
Proprietors Vanessa and Les Scott

Norfolk

Converted windmill, Cley-next-the-Sea

Cley Mill

Imagine staying in a 'real' windmill. That is the sense of adventure that Cley Mill can induce even in the most world-weary. Memories of 'Swallows and Amazons' or the 'Famous Five' crowd in as you climb higher and higher in the mill, finally mounting the ladder to the look-out room (with telescope) on the fourth floor.

The sitting-room on the ground floor of the Mill is exceptionally welcoming – it feels well used and lived-in, with plenty of books and magazines, comfortable sofas, TV and an open fire. Bedrooms in the Mill feel rather like log cabins – much wood in the furniture and fittings – and there are wide views from the little windows out across the Blakeney Marshes to the sea. They are pretty rooms, with white lace bedspreads, and bathrooms ingeniously fitted in to the most challenging nooks and crannies that the old building provides.

Jenny and Tim Mallam are a friendly couple who see the Mill primarily as a 'classy guest-house' rather than a hotel, and do not mind a bit if you simply take B&B – though they happily cook for guests who would like dinner, too. 'Good country cooking' is how they describe it, and just right, too, after a day in the fresh air. Take your own drink – no corkage charged.

Nearby Sheringham Hall, 6 miles (10 km); Cromer Lighthouse, 10 miles (16 km); Norwich within reach.

Cley-next-the-Sea, Holt, Norfolk NR25 7NN
Tel (0263) 740209
Location 7 miles (11 km) W of Sheringham on A149, on N edge of village; in garden, with ample car parking
Food & drink full breakfast; dinner on request; no licence
Prices B&B £25-£28; dinner £14.50; reductions for 3 to 7 nights
Rooms 4 double, 3 with bath,
one with shower; one single; one family room with bath
Facilities sitting-room, dining-room
Credit cards not accepted
Children welcome if well behaved
Disabled access difficult
Pets welcome if house-trained
Closed mid-Jan to end Feb
Managers Jenny and Tim Mallam

Norfolk

Country guest-house, Great Snoring

Old Rectory

Though presumably the words have a quainter etymology, Great Snoring lives up to its name. There is no shop, the last pub has closed, and it is easy to drive through the village without noticing the Old Rectory, hidden behind high stone walls beside the church. This seclusion is the pride of Rosamund Scoles, her husband and family, who have been running the red-brick parsonage – of very mixed vintage, but dating in part from the 16th century – as a hotel since 1978.

'Hotel' is scarcely the right word for this relaxed retreat. There is no reception desk, no row of keys, no signs. After early morning tea, which is brought to each of the richly and individually furnished bedrooms, you are left to your own devices in the large sitting-room with its hotch-potch of comfortable old chairs in front of an open fire.

In the dining-room, heavy velvet drapes hang at the stone mullioned windows, and fresh flowers are arranged on each of the tables. The dinner menu is traditional English in style; some may find it restricted, but guests are consulted before the one main course dish is chosen and there are plenty of mouth-watering home-made puddings to chose from.

Nearby Walsingham Abbey, 1.5 miles (2.5 km); Holkham Hall, 8 miles (13 km); Norfolk Heritage Coast; Norwich within reach.

Barsham Road, Great Snoring, Fakenham, Norfolk NR21 0HP
Tel (0328) 820597 **Fax** 820048
Location 3 miles (5 km) NE of Fakenham, in hamlet; in 1.5-acre garden with ample car parking
Food & drink full breakfast, dinner; restaurant and residential licence
Prices B&B £42-£63; dinner £20
Rooms 6 double, one single; all with bath; all rooms have central heating, colour TV, phone
Facilities sitting-room, dining-room
Credit cards AE, DC
Children accepted over 12
Disabled access difficult
Pets not accepted
Closed Christmas Day and Boxing Day
Proprietors Rosamund and William Scoles

Norfolk

Buckinghamshire Arms

This 350-year-old building is owned by the National Trust but the pub is now run by chef/proprietor, Danny Keen. Part of the appeal of the place has always been its position, next door to Blickling Hall – a superb NT pile (the grounds open year-round, house only in summer) seen to advantage from the inn. But the Arms itself is an exceptionally amiable place to stay. A choice of three real ales is served in the quaint 'snug' bar and in the larger but still rustic lounge bar. Food in the bars and in the 'Holbein' dining-room is satisfying, and there are tables in the garden.

Nearby Blickling Hall; Holt Woodlands Park, 8 miles (13 km); Felbrigg Hall (NT), 10 miles (16 km).

Blickling, near Aylsham, Norwich, Norfolk NR11 6NF
Tel (0263) 732133
Location 1.5 miles (2.5 km) NW of Aylsham on B1354; with large private car park
Food & drink breakfast, bar lunch, dinner; full licence
Prices B&B £30-£45; dinner from £12.50; reductions for children
Rooms 3 double; all rooms have four-poster bed, colour TV, tea/coffee kit
Facilities dining-room, lounge bar, smaller bar
Credit cards MC, V
Children welcome, but not allowed in bars
Disabled easy access to bars and restaurant, but not to bedrooms
Pets accepted by arrangement
Closed Christmas Day and Boxing Day
Proprietor Danny Keen

Congham Hall

Practically everything about this white 18thC Georgian house, amid 40 acres of lawns, orchards and parkland, impresses. The spacious bedrooms and public areas are luxuriously furnished, the service is solicitous and efficient, and the Forecasts themselves extend a warm welcome. Cooking (in the modern British style) is adventurous and excellent, making much use of home-grown herbs.

Nearby Sandringham, 4 miles (6 km); Norwich within reach.

Grimston, King's Lynn, Norfolk PE32 1AH
Tel (0485) 600250 **Fax** 601191
Location 6 miles (10 km) NE of King's Lynn near A148; in 40-acre grounds with parking for 50 cars
Food & drink full breakfast, lunch (except Sat), dinner; residential and restaurant licence
Prices B&B £48.50-£112.50; full breakfast £2 extra; dinner £30; weekend breaks
Rooms 11 double, all with bath; one single, with shower; 2 suites with bath; all rooms have central heating, TV, phone, radio
Facilities 2 sitting-rooms, bar, dining-room; jacuzzi, swimming-pool, tennis, croquet
Credit cards AE, DC, MC, V
Children welcome over 12
Disabled access easy to restaurant
Pets not allowed
Proprietors Christine and Trevor Forecast

Norfolk

Country guest-house, Heacham

Holly Lodge

This 16thC Elizabethan building, standing back from the road in its pretty, well-tended gardens in the unprepossessing village of Heacham, has served as a sleeping place more than once in its history. It was built as a dormitory for visiting monks, and was probably once called Holy – not Holly – Lodge. The monastic theme is echoed in some of the pictures and other treasures that decorate this lovely house, but that is where it stops. Today's overnight guests sleep in pretty, comfortable rooms, each decorated individually: some have four-poster beds; all of them have antiques, paintings and peaceful colour-schemes. Visitors dine in elegant candlelit surroundings from a menu which makes the most of local Norfolk products (asparagus, crab, duck...); they relax in small, comfortable sitting-rooms with open fires to induce post-prandial well-being.

Holly Lodge has the feel of being the home of someone who has their share of decorative taste and some beautiful possessions – and at the same time of being expertly and professionally run. Mrs Piper enjoys entertaining and puts a lot of effort into caring for her guests; she is full of information about the area and is keen to steer her guests to the best beaches and and most interesting sights.

Nearby Sandringham, 5 miles (8 km); King's Lynn, Norwich within reach.

Heacham, near King's Lynn, Norfolk PE31 7HY
Tel (0485) 70790
Location 3 miles (5 km) S of Hunstanton, off A149, on edge of village; in 1.5 acre gardens with ample car parking
Food & drink full breakfast, dinner; residential and restaurant licence
Prices B&B £42.50-£50; dinner from £22.50; 2- and

3-day bargain breaks
Rooms 6 double, 5 with bath, one with shower; all rooms have central heating
Facilities 2 sitting-rooms, dining-room
Credit cards MC, V
Children accepted
Disabled not suitable
Pets accepted by arrangement if well behaved
Closed Jan and Feb
Proprietor Lesley Piper

Lancashire *off hrf* (31)

Northcote Manor

In a part of the world where there are few satisfactory alternatives, this late-Victorian red-brick mill-owner's house stands out for a combination of good food and comfortable surroundings. The young partners, Craig Bancroft and Nigel Haworth, built up the reputation of the hotel during the early 1980s, and bought the business in 1989. Since then they have thoroughly revamped the place, making the bedrooms and public rooms a fitting match for what seems, still, to be the main attraction: Nigel's cooking – frequently changing menus of modern, ambitious and innovative dishes.

Nearby Browsholme Hall, 8 miles (13 km); Gawthorpe Hall, 8 miles (13 km).

Northcote Road, Langho, near Blackburn, Lancashire BB6 8BE
Tel (0254) 240555 **Fax** 246568
Location north of village, off A59; with ample car parking
Food & drink full breakfast, lunch, dinner; residential and restaurant licence
Prices B&B £55-£65; dinner from £25; weekend breaks
Rooms 13 double, 12 with bath, 2 with shower; one suite; all have central heating, phone, TV, radio
Facilities 2 sitting-rooms, bar, dining-room, restaurant
Credit cards AE, DC, MC, V
Children welcome
Disabled access easy
Pets not accepted
Closed 1 Jan
Proprietors Craig Bancroft and Nigel Haworth

light of 15ᵗʰ & night of 20ᵗʰ

The River House

'A rare example of old-fashioned, small-scale high quality', says a reporter of the Scotts' comfortable Victorian house on the banks of a tidal creek. The bedrooms have been redecorated over the past few years; two have priceless 19thC hooded baths. Public rooms are furnished with period pieces, paintings and bric-a-brac, and the *pièce de résistance* is the cast-iron conservatory. The food is richly international and based on excellent ingredients.

Nearby Blackpool; many golf courses.

Skippool Creek, Thornton-le-Fylde, near Blackpool, Lancashire FY5 5LF
Tel (0253) 883497 **Fax** 892083
Location one mile (1.5 km) SE of Thornton, off A585; parking for 20 cars
Food & drink full breakfast, lunch, dinner; restaurant and residential licence
Prices B&B £50-£65; dinner about £35
Rooms 3 double, with bath; one single with shower; all rooms have central heating, TV, phone, radio, tea/coffee kit, trouser-press, hairdrier
Facilities sitting-room, bar, dining-room, conservatory
Credit cards MC, V
Children welcome if well behaved
Disabled access difficult
Pets welcome if well behaved
Closed never, but booking essential; restaurant closed on Sundays
Proprietors B and C Scott

Lancashire

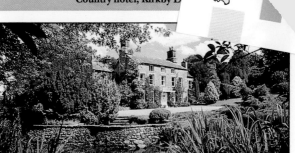

Hipping Hall

'More like staying with friends than in a hotel' is the typical reaction to a weekend at Hipping Hall. Ian Bryant and Jos Ruffle's laid-back style might come as a surprise to new guests; but, judging by the success of the hotel since opening in 1988, it is usually a pleasant one. They have adopted the house-party approach: you help yourself to drinks from the sideboard, and dinner is eaten at one table under the minstrel's gallery in the spectacular beamed Great Hall. Jos creates a daily five-course feast (no choice, but preferences taken account of) using home-grown and local produce with emphasis on 'enhancing, not drowning, natural flavours'.

Parts of the Hall date back to the 15th century when a hamlet grew up around the 'hipping' or stepping stones across the beck. It is a stone country house, set in four acres of beautiful walled gardens. After a strenuous day on the fells, you can sink into sofas in front of a wood-burning stove at the other end of the Great Hall and binge on Jos's home-made cookies. Bedrooms are spacious, comfortable and furnished with period pieces.

Although the Hall is physically as well as postally in Lancashire, it is sandwiched between Cumbria and Yorkshire.

Nearby Yorkshire Dales, Lake District; Forest of Bowland.

Cowan Bridge, Lancashire
LA6 2JJ
Tel (05242) 71187 **Fax** 72452
Location on A65, 2.5 miles (4 km) SE of Kirkby Lonsdale; in 4-acre walled gardens with ample car parking
Food & drink full breakfast, dinner; residential and restaurant licence
Prices B&B £35-£59; dinner £19.50, or £27 with wines; reductions for 3 days and over, and for children sharing
Rooms 5 double, 4 with bath, one with shower; two suites

with bath; all rooms have central heating, TV, radio, tea/coffee kit, hairdrier
Facilities dining-room, breakfast room, sitting-room, conservatory with bar; croquet, boules
Credit cards MC, V
Children welcome over 12
Disabled not suitable
Pets dogs accepted in bedrooms by arrangement
Closed mid-Nov to Jan, except for private weekend parties
Proprietors Ian Bryant and Jocelyn Ruffle

West Yorkshire

Restaurant with rooms, Otley

Pool Court

Leeds and Bradford are not over-endowed with good hotels, large or small, so a well-run restaurant with rooms a short drive from either is welcome news in any event. But this is no ordinary restaurant-with-rooms: the food has for decades been regarded as the best for miles around and has earned a Michelin star; the bedrooms, like the dining-room, are immaculately furnished with great elegance (and equipped with every imaginable extra – including a copy of the long wine-list); and the whole operation is run with admirable flair, friendliness and minute attention to detail. Though there is no separate sitting-room, there is a welcoming small bar – and most of the bedrooms are spacious. Breakfast is a magnificent meal in itself.

Nearby Harewood House and gardens, 4.5 miles (7 km); Leeds.

Pool-in-Wharfedale, West Yorkshire, LS21 1EH
Tel (0532) 842288 **Fax** 843115
Location 3 miles (5 km) W of Otley by A659, just S of Pool on A658; in extensive gardens, with ample private parking
Food & drink breakfast, lunch by arrangement, dinner Tue-Sat; full licence
Prices B&B £47.50-£95; dinner from £18
Rooms 5 double, with bath; one single with shower; all rooms have central heating,

colour TV, clock/radio, wall safe, minibar, phone, hairdrier
Facilities dining-room, bar, sitting-room
Credit cards AE, DC, MC, V
Children welcome ('often better behaved than the adults')
Disabled difficult
Pets not allowed; can be accommodated locally
Closed Sun, Mon; Christmas
Proprietors Hanni and Michael Gill

Humberside

Winteringham Fields

The name is as romantically bleak as anything conceived by the Brontë sisters, but the house is quite different: an amiable stone manor house dating from the 16th century, decoratively Victorian inside. Germain Schwab is a Swiss master chef; he and his wife Ann, who runs the front of house, have created an exceptionally alluring formula since moving here in 1988. Bedrooms are spacious and beautifully furnished; food earns high praise.

Nearby Normanby Hall, 6 miles (10 km); Thornton Abbey, 13 miles (21 km); Lincoln, 30 miles (48 km).

Winteringham, South Humberside DN15 9PF
Tel (0724) 733096 **Fax** 733898
Location in middle of village on south bank of Humber, 4 miles (6 km) W from Humber bridge on A1077; with ample car parking
Food & drink breakfast, lunch, dinner; residential and restaurant licence
Prices B&B £65-£75; lunch £14.75, dinner £34
Rooms 7 double, all with bath and shower (one four-poster, one suite); all rooms have central heating, colour TV, phone
Facilities sitting-room, 2 dining-rooms, conservatory
Credit cards MC, V
Children welcome in dining-room over age 10
Disabled access difficult
Pets arrangements can be made with local kennels
Closed Christmas and 2 weeks in Jan; 1st week Aug
Proprietors G and A Schwab

The Manor House

This late-Victorian house may not be what most people expect a manor house to be, but that can be forgiven. Under the practised eye of chef-patron Derek Baugh and his wife, it has made an exceptionally civilized hotel. The furnishings are opulent, with a sprinkling of antiques and plenty of rich fabrics in carefully harmonized colours. The original conservatory serves as a dining-room – a particular highlight. Bedrooms are notably spacious, with smart bathrooms. Food is elaborately modern.

Nearby Beverley Minster, 4 miles (6 km); Skidby Windmill Museum, 4 miles (6 km).

Northlands, Walkington, North Humberside HU17 8RT
Tel (0482) 881645 **Fax** 866501
Location on the Newbald road NW of Walkington, 4 miles (6 km) SW of Beverley
Food & drink breakfast, dinner; lunch by arrangement; residential licence
Prices B&B £37.50-£75; full breakfast £6.50, dinner from £15
Rooms 7 double, all with bath; all have central heating, TV, phone, tea/coffee kit, minibar
Facilities sitting-room, dining-room, conservatory
Credit cards MC, V
Children accepted over 12
Disabled no special facilities
Pets by arrangement
Closed Bank Holidays
Proprietors D and L Baugh

Western Dales

Amerdale House

Since they took it over in 1987, the Crappers have gradually transformed this hotel and the bedrooms have all been refurbished over the last three years. The setting is one of the most seductive in all the Dales; on the fringe of a pretty village in a lonely valley, wide meadows in front, high hills behind. Food (the owners are ex-restaurateurs) is in the modern English style and 'unbelievably good', to quote a recent visitor.

Nearby Wharfedale, Grassington, Pennine Way.

Arncliffe, Littondale, Skipton, North Yorkshire BD23 5QE
Tel (0756) 770250
Location in a rural setting; 6 miles (10 km) NW of Grassington, 3 miles (5 km) off B6160; with ample car parking
Food & drink full breakfast, dinner; residential and restaurant licence
Prices DB&B £51.50-£54.50; reductions for 7 nights or more, and for children sharing parents' room;

winter breaks
Rooms 12 double, 7 with bath, 4 with shower; all rooms have colour TV, tea/coffee kit, hairdrier
Facilities sitting-room, bar, dining-room
Credit cards MC, V
Children welcome
Disabled access easy to ground floor only
Pets not accepted
Closed Nov to Mar
Proprietors Nigel and Paula Crapper

Riverdale House

Anne Harrison's converted row of cottages on the green of this quiet little Wensleydale village is in the best tradition of the unpretentious country hotel – bedrooms freshly decorated, in simple tasteful style (those in the main building more spacious than the rather cramped ones which have been added at the back), and first-class country cooking (Anne used to be a home economics teacher) served in a tea-shop-style dining-room at polished tables. Packed lunches are available on request. We assume service remains friendly, but we lack recent reports; feedback, please.

Nearby Aysgarth Falls, 4 miles (6 km); Upper Dales Folk Museum, Hawes, 6 miles (9 km); Yorkshire Dales.

Bainbridge, Leyburn, North Yorkshire DL8 3EW
Tel (0969) 50311
Location off A684 on village green; with small garden and parking on road
Food & drink full breakfast, packed lunch, dinner
Prices B&B £18-£30; DB&B £33-£45; reductions for children
Rooms 14 double, 10 with

bath, or shower; all rooms have central heating, colour TV, tea/coffee kit
Facilities 2 sitting-rooms (one with TV), bar/dining-room
Credit cards not accepted
Children welcome
Disabled access very difficult
Pets not accepted
Closed Dec to Feb; weekends Nov to Mar
Proprietor Mrs A Harrison

Western Dales

Simonstone Hall

Although it is only a decade since the Jeffryes converted this near-derelict Georgian private house, Simonstone has something of the gentle, slightly faded feel of a much longer-established hotel, with its uncommonly large, comfortably furnished bedrooms and courteous staff dressed neatly in black and white. The panelled public rooms are painted in light colours and furnished with antiques and oil paintings, and the Jeffryes' designer daughter has been at work in the bedrooms. Dogs are welcome. Splendid views. Food aims high; there are vegetarian and 'healthy' menus.

Nearby Pennine Way, Wharfedale, Ribblesdale.

Hawes, North Yorkshire DL8 3LY
Tel (0969) 667255 **Fax** 667741
Location 1.5 miles (2.5 km) N of Hawes on Muker road; ample car parking
Food & drink breakfast, bar lunch (traditional Sunday lunch), tea, dinner; full licence
Prices B&B from £45; DB&B from £55;
Rooms 10 double, all with bath and shower; all have TV, central heating, tea/coffee kit
Facilities bar, 2 sitting-rooms, garden room
Credit cards MC, V
Children welcome
Disabled easy access to ground floor but no lift
Pets in bedrooms, extra £2.60
Closed never
Proprietors John and Sheila Jeffryes

Ashfield House

Originally three 17thC cottages, Ashfield House is now a modest hotel with a surprisingly large walled garden, tucked behind Grassington's main square, in the heart of the Dales. The rooms are all different – a white lacy duvet cover here, an antique pine wardrobe there – all simple and clean. In the 2 sitting-rooms are comfortable chairs and log fires. In the evenings guests socialize as they anticipate Linda Harrison's abundant portions of Aga cooking. This is a no-smoking house.

Nearby Skipton Castle, 7 miles (11 km); Yorkshire Dales.

Grassington, near Skipton, North Yorkshire BD23 5AE
Tel (0756) 752584
Location close to main square; parking for 7 cars
Food & drink full breakfast, dinner; residential licence
Prices DB&B £33.75-£40; half-price for children aged 5-10 sharing with an adult
Rooms 5 double, 2 twin, 6 with bath or shower; all rooms have central heating, colour TV, tea/coffee kit
Facilities 2 sitting-rooms, one with bar, dining-room
Credit cards MC, V
Children welcome over 5
Disabled not suitable
Closed Nov to Jan
Proprietors Keith and Linda Harrison

Eastern Dales

Town guest-house, Richmond

Howe Villa

This handsome Georgian house is reached by driving through an unappealing old paper mill which used to house Tom Berry's dry-cleaning works. His wife Anita has turned her natural flair as a hostess to good advantage since the children grew up. She started in 1979 offering bed-and-breakfast, soon found a demand for her honest dinners, and has since steadily acquired the skills to support more ambitious menus. The house is elegantly decorated and immaculately kept – bedrooms on the ground floor and fine public rooms on the first floor, where they enjoy a fine view of Howe Villa's beautiful grounds and across the Swale.

Nearby Richmond Castle, 1.5 miles (2.5 km); Easby Abbey, 2.5 miles (4 km); Yorkshire Dales.

Whitcliffe Mill, Richmond, North Yorkshire DL10 4TJ
Tel (0748) 850055
Location 0.75 miles (one km) W of Richmond, close to A6108; in large garden by river, with ample car parking
Food & drink full breakfast, dinner; no licence
Prices DB&B £50; reductions for 3 nights or more
Rooms 5 double, 3 with bath, 2 with shower; all rooms have central heating, colour TV, radio, tea/coffee kit, hairdrier
Facilities sitting-room, dining-room
Credit cards not accepted
Children welcome over 12
Disabled access difficult
Pets not accepted
Closed Mon; Dec to Feb
Proprietor Anita Berry

Village hotel, Middleham

The Miller's House

Something of a transformation has been wrought by Judith and Crossley Sunderland since they took over this elegant Georgian house, set back from Middleham's cobbled market square, in 1989. The public rooms have smart furniture and sumptuous drapes and the bedrooms and bathrooms are spacious and comfortable – one room has a richly festooned four-poster and a splendid Victorian bath. A professional chef produces a highly original daily menu, based on local products and home-grown herbs and vegetables, and served by candle-light.

Nearby Middleham Castle; Jervaulx Abbey, 3 miles (5 km); Wensleydale, Coverdale, Bishopsdale.

Middleham, Wensleydale, North Yorkshire DL8 4NR
Tel (0969) 22630 **Fax** 23570
Location just off market square, 2 miles (3 km) S of Leyburn; parking for 8 cars
Food & drink breakfast, picnic lunch, dinner; residential licence
Prices B&B £33.50-£42; dinner £19.50; various breaks
Rooms 6 double, all with bath; one single, with shower; all rooms have central heating, colour TV, tea/coffee kit, phone, radio/alarm
Facilities sitting-room, dining-room; croquet
Credit cards MC, V
Children welcome over 11
Disabled no special facilities
Pets not accepted **Closed** Jan
Proprietors Judith and Crossley Sunderland

Eastern Dales

Inn, Pateley Bridge

Sportsman's Arms

The perfect country inn? The Sportsman's Arms certainly comes close. The long, rather rambling building – many years ago a run-down pub – dates from the 17th century. The setting is as enchanting as the village name sounds; the river Nidd flows at the bottom of the lawn in front; Gouthwaite reservoir, a bird-watchers' haunt, is just behind; glorious dales country spreads all around. The accommodation is modest but spotlessly clean and comfortable; the bedrooms are light and fresh, and all the public rooms have recently been refurbished as well. Best of all, the staff, headed by proprietor and chef Ray Carter, are hard-working, welcoming and friendly.

And then there is the food. The Sportsman's Arms is first and foremost a restaurant, and the large dining-room is the inn's focal point, dominated by the deep pink of its table-cloths and sparkling with silver cutlery and crystal table lights. The lively menu embraces sound, traditional local fare and more adventurous dishes, with imaginative use of fruit. To back it up, there is a superb wine list – and an extremely reasonable bill.

Nearby Wharfedale, Wensleydale; Fountains Abbey, Bolton Abbey within easy reach.

Wath-in-Nidderdale, Pateley Bridge, near Harrogate, North Yorkshire HG3 5PP
Tel (0423) 711306
Location 2 miles (3 km) NW of Pateley Bridge, in hamlet; in 0.5-acre gardens, with ample car parking in front
Food & drink full breakfast, bar lunch, dinner (residents only on Sun); full licence
Prices B&B £22-£29; dinner £13-£28; reductions for more than one night
Rooms 7 double, 2 with shower; all rooms have electric heating, tea/coffee kit, TV
Facilities 3 sitting-rooms, bar, dining-room; fishing
Credit cards MC, V
Children welcome
Disabled access easy, but no ground-floor bedrooms
Pets welcome; own bedding must be provided
Closed Christmas Day and New Year's Day (though open to non-residents in the evening)
Proprietors Jane and Ray Carter

Eastern Dales

Jervaulx Hall

This low stone house sits in the grounds of the lovely flower-covered ruins of 12thC Jervaulx Abbey – an exceptionally pleasing setting for a stroll before breakfast or dinner. For serious walkers, the expanses of the Dales are just a stone's throw away.

The house is early Victorian, with spacious bedrooms and bathrooms and a comfortable lived-in feel. There is a large hall-cum-sitting-room, with a help-yourself drinks table in one corner, and an attractive drawing-room where after-dinner coffee is served. In the afternoon, tea can be taken on the front terrace overlooking the abbey.

John Sharp welcomes his guests with a hand-shake – many of them old faces returning for the umpteenth time – introduces them to one another over drinks, and presides over dinner. It is served punctually at eight and consists of a somewhat limited, straightforward menu – a cold mousse to start, perhaps, followed by a well-cooked roast or a creamy chicken dish.

Nearby Jervaulx Abbey; Middleham Castle, 3 miles (5 km); Yorkshire Dales.

Jervaulx, Ripon, North Yorkshire HG4 4PH
Tel (0677) 60235 **Fax** 60263
Location 5 miles (8 km) SE of Leyburn on A6108; in 8-acre grounds with parking for 15 cars
Food & drink full breakfast, afternoon tea, dinner; residential and restaurant licence
Prices DB&B £60-£75; reduced weekly rates; reductions Nov to Easter; reductions for children

Rooms 10 double, all with bath; all have central heating, phone, tea/coffee kit, hairdrier
Facilities 2 sitting-rooms, dining-room, croquet
Credit cards not accepted
Children welcome
Disabled access easy – no steps and one ground-floor bedroom **Pets** dogs welcome, but must not be left unattended in bedrooms
Closed Dec to Feb **Proprietor** John and Margaret Sharp

North Yorkshire

The Hawnby Hotel

After a spectacular drive through rolling valleys and the unspoilt stone village of Hawnby, the hotel may come as something of a let-down. You enter through the busy public bar, and it is not until you are ushered into the elegant sitting-room that you realize how deceptive first appearances can be.

The 'village pub' façade hides an exquisite small hotel decorated with obvious flair by the Countess of Mexborough. The hotel is part of the 13,000-acre Mexborough estate and the countess gives a lot of personal attention to it, popping in several times a week. A few years ago she entirely refurbished the six bedrooms, naming them after colour schemes (Cowslip, Coral, Jade etc) and choosing Laura Ashley wallpaper and fabrics throughout the cosy rooms and immaculate bathrooms.

The hotel does suffer slightly from a lack of space. The sitting-room is at one end of the dining-room, and although it does not feel cramped and can be curtained off at guests' request, it might be noisy and crowded at peak times. Dorothy Allanson manages the hotel and does most of the cooking. Her meals are simple and traditional, consisting of game, beef and lamb from the estate, and fresh local vegetables.

Nearby Rievaulx Abbey, 4 miles (6 km), North York Moors.

Hawnby, near Helmsley, York
Y06 5QS
Tel (04396) 202 **Fax** 417
Location at top of hill in village 7 miles (11 km) NE of Helmsley; with garden and car parking
Food & drink full breakfast, bar snacks, dinner; full licence
Prices B&B £25-£50; dinner from £12
Rooms 6 double, all with bath; all rooms have central heating, radio, TV, hairdrier, tea/coffee kit, iron
Facilities sitting-room/dining-room, bar
Credit cards MC, V
Children welcome over 10 years
Disabled access difficult
Pets not accepted
Closed Christmas; Feb
Manager Dorothy Allanson

Lastingham Grange

Lastingham Grange – a wistaria-clad former farmhouse – nestles in a delightful village on the edge of the North York Moors. Unlike many country house hotels, it manages to combine a certain sophistication – smartly decorated public rooms, friendly unobtrusive service, elegantly laid gardens – with a large dash of informality, which puts you immediately at ease. From the moment you enter, you feel as if you are staying with friends.

The main attraction is the garden. You can enjoy it from a distance – from the windows of the large L-shaped sitting-room (complete with carefully grouped sofas, antiques and a grand piano) – or, like most guests, by exploring. There is a beautifully laid rose garden, enticing bordered lawns and an extensive adventure playground for children.

In comparison, bedrooms are a little ordinary. They are perfectly comfortable, with well-equipped bathrooms, but some people may find the decoration lacking style in places. Jane cooks straightforward English meals, served at polished tables in the spacious dining-room.

Nearby North York Moors.

Lastingham, York YO6 6TH
Tel 07515 345/402
Location at top of village, 6 miles (10 km) NW of Pickering; with garden and ample car parking
Food & drink full breakfast, tea, dinner; lunches available on request; residential and restaurant licence
Prices B&B £55-£60; DB&B £70-£80 (2 nights or more)
Rooms 10 double, 2 single, all with bath; all rooms have central heating, phone, TV, radio, tea/coffee kit, hairdrier, trouser-press, baby-listening device
Facilities sitting-room, dining-room, terrace
Credit cards not accepted
Children welcome
Disabled access difficult
Pets by prior arrangement in bedrooms only
Closed Dec to Feb
Proprietors Dennis and Jane Wood

North Yorkshire

Country hotel, Hunmanby

Wrangham House

This Georgian vicarage still retains the feel of an unpretentious family-run place, with plenty of home-like touches – bookshelves line the cosy bar, ornaments and water colours decorate the public rooms, bedrooms are positively cottagey, with brass beds and lacy trimmings.

Dinner consists of simple tasty dishes, served in the elegant dining-room, by French windows that lead to the tree-lined garden. Manageress Deborah Cliff and her staff offer a warm welcome and friendly service.

Nearby beaches, walking; Scarborough Castle 9 miles (16 km).

Stonegate, Hunmanby, North Yorkshire **Tel** (0723) 891333
Location behind church in village, one mile (1.5 km) SW of Filey; with garden and ample car parking
Food & drink full breakfast, dinner; lunch on Sun; residential and restaurant licence
Prices B&B £25-£37; DB&B £38-£50; dinner £13
Rooms 11 double, 5 with bath, 6 with shower; 2 single with shower; all have central heating, hairdrier, TV, radio, tea/coffee kit
Facilities dining-room, sitting-room, bar
Credit cards AE, DC, MC, V
Children over 12 only **Pets** not accepted **Disabled** access easy; ground-floor rooms
Closed never
Manageress Deborah Cliff

Country hotel, Hutton-le-Hole

Burnley House

A German reader writes to recommend this recently opened Georgian farmhouse in a picture-postcard village on the southern flank of the North York Moors. Like its much longer-established neighbour at Lastingham (facing page), it is highly traditional in style, particularly in the cosy public rooms, both of which have open fires. Dinner (served on the stroke of 7.30) is a set, home-cooked three courses plus 'sweetmeats', normally starting with a soup. 'I never saw such a breakfast,' says our reporter – it includes a major fry-up and local honey. The Bensons manage to combine a warm welcome with immaculate housekeeping. The garden, too, is beautifully kept. No smoking is permitted.

Nearby North York Moors.

Hutton-le-Hole, North Yorkshire Y06 6UA
Tel (0751) 417548 **Fax** 417174
Location on village green 3 miles (5 km) N of A170, NE of Kirkbymoorside; in gardens, with private car parking
Food & drink full breakfast, dinner; residential licence
Prices B&B £28-£37.50; reductions for two nights or more; dinner £14.50
Rooms 7 double (2 twin), 5 with bath, 2 with shower; all rooms have central heating, hairdrier, TV, radio
Facilities sitting-room, dining-room; tennis, bowls
Credit cards not accepted
Children not accepted under 15 **Disabled** not suitable
Pets not accepted
Closed Nov to Easter
Proprietors Jean and Bryce Benson

North Yorkshire

Country hotel, Nunnington

Ryedale Lodge

This former village railway station has been transformed into a calm and well-ordered retreat. Once past the urns full of flowers either side of the door, you find yourself in the sitting-room, with its rich assortment of flowers and plants, its comfortable sofas, restful blue-and-pink colouring and pleasing tapestries. The elegant dining-room and conservatory look out over the former platform and the farmland beyond, with not another building in sight.

The bedrooms are comfortable and immaculate, each with a theme of its own. Styles vary from country cane through floral-plus-antiques to functional white melamine. All are well-equipped, with everything from TVs and flowers to trouser-presses and hairdriers – and even the occasional spa bath; it might seem carping, then, to grumble about the lack of showers (only one bedroom has one).

Janet Laird's dinner menu includes some tempting offerings, mainly in the French or international mould, and the service is friendly and willing.

Nearby Nunnington Hall; Duncombe Park, 3 miles (5 km); Rievaulx Abbey, 6 miles (10 km); Castle Howard, 8 miles (13 km).

Nunnington, near Helmsley, York, North Yorkshire YO6 5XR
Tel (04395) 246
Location 4 miles (6 km) SE of Helmsley off B1257, one mile (1.5 km) W of village; in open countryside, with large car park
Food & drink full breakfast, dinner; residential and restaurant licence
Prices B&B £41.50–£51.50; dinner from £26.75; bargain breaks
Rooms 7 double, all with bath; all rooms have central heating, colour TV, phone, radio alarm, tea/coffee kit, hairdrier, trouser-press
Facilities sitting-room, dining-room, bar servery, conservatory; fishing
Credit cards MC, V
Children welcome
Disabled access easy; one ground-floor bedroom
Pets not accepted, but may stay in cars
Closed never
Proprietors Janet and Jon Laird

North Yorkshire

Rangers House

The Butlers have adopted an unusual formula for their converted stables, built of mellow stone. Although the dining-room has elegant dark-wood tables and the lofty hall-cum-sitting-room is filled with antiques, the house has a lived-in, casual feel – some might even call it slightly tatty – which should suit families well. The Butlers are a charming, down-to-earth couple who are entirely flexible – breakfast any time you like, bring your own drinks if you prefer.

Nearby Sheriff Hutton Castle; Castle Howard, 5 miles (8 km).

The Park, Sheriff Hutton, York, North Yorkshire YO6 1RH
Tel (0347) 878397
Location 9 miles (14.5 km) N of York between B1363 and A64; in garden with ample car parking
Food & drink full breakfast, afternoon tea, dinner; restaurant and residential licence
Prices B&B £30-£32; dinner £20; DB&B £44 in spring and autumn

Rooms 4 double, one with bath, one with shower; one single with shower; one family room with bath; all rooms have central heating, tea/coffee kit, hairdrier
Facilities sitting-room, conservatory, dining-room
Credit cards not accepted
Children welcome – high tea available
Disabled access difficult
Pets dogs may sleep in cars
Closed never **Proprietors** Sid and Dorianne Butler

McCoy's

This Victorian coaching inn at the junction of two busy roads is run by three eccentric brothers and filled with an eclectic mix of antiques and junk – not everyone's cup of tea. But you may be surprised; the loud colour schemes and odd furniture somehow work, and live music drifting up from the packed basement bistro adds to the atmosphere. The roomy bedrooms have pine antiques and striking fabrics – even the showers have lace-lined curtains. But the star attraction is Tom McCoy's ambitious and excellent cooking – the best for miles.

Nearby North York Moors, Mount Grace Priory; Thirsk Museum.

The Tontine, Staddlebridge, Nr Northallerton, N Yorkshire
Tel (0609) 882671
Location in countryside, at junction of A19 and A172, 5 miles (8 km) N of Northallerton; with garden and private car parking
Food & drink breakfast, lunch, dinner; full licence
Prices B&B £50-£69; dinner £25-£30 **Rooms** 6 double, all with bath; all rooms have central heating, radio, TV, air-conditioning, phone
Facilities 2 sitting-rooms, breakfast room, bistro, restaurant, bar
Credit cards AE, DC, MC, V
Children very welcome
Pets welcome
Disabled access difficult
Closed Christmas, New Year; restaurant only, Sun & Mon
Proprietors Peter, Thomas and Eugene McCoy

North Yorkshire

Mount Royale

Comprising two William IV houses only recently joined, the Mount Royale is the Oxtobys' home. The bedrooms are spacious, each individually decorated and furnished with some splendid antiques (many four-posters and half-testers), chintz drapes and armchairs. The public areas continue the traditional decoration with some bold red colour schemes and more antiques. A modern extension provides a light and airy dining-room with views on to the neat and flowery garden. Cooking is ambitious and competent, and breakfast something of a feast.

Nearby Treasurer's House; Minster; National Railway Museum.

The Mount, York, North Yorkshire YO2 2DA
Tel (0904) 628856 **Fax** 611171
Location on A1036 near racecourse; in large garden with parking for 30 cars
Food & drink full breakfast, dinner; residential and restaurant licence
Prices B&B £37.50-£67.50; dinner from £25
Rooms 19 double, 2 single, 2 suites; all with bath and shower; all rooms have central heating, colour TV, radio, phone, tea/coffee kit, hairdrier, trouser-press
Facilities 3 sitting-rooms, dining-room, bar, snooker room, exercise room, heated outdoor swimming-pool
Credit cards AE, DC, MC, V
Children welcome
Disabled not suitable
Pets small dogs accepted, not to be left alone in bedrooms
Closed 23 to 31 Dec
Proprietors Oxtoby family

Milburn Arms

Rosedale Abbey is a favourite spot for weekend outings, and part of its appeal is this solid stone inn at the centre (physically and socially) of the small village. The bar is traditionally pub-like, but the other areas are properly hotel-like – a polished dining-room, tables laid with silver, glass and fine china, a welcoming sitting-room, and bedrooms individually decorated with some style – many of them surprisingly spacious. Cooking emphasises 'clear flavours and local produce' – which includes game in season, and fish from Whitby. Extensive wine list.

Nearby Pickering Castle, 10 miles (16 km); North York Moors.

Rosedale Abbey, nr Pickering, North Yorkshire YO18 8RA
Tel & fax (07515) 312
Location in middle of village, 10 miles (16 km) NW of Pickering; with gardens and ample car parking
Food & drink breakfast, dinner, Sun lunch, bar meals; full licence
Prices B&B £32-£44; dinner £17.50; reductions midweek and for children sharing
Rooms 9 double, 2 family rooms, all with bath; all rooms have central heating, phone, TV, radio, tea/coffee kit
Facilities dining-room, sitting-room, bar **Credit cards** DC, MC, V **Children** accepted
Disabled access fairly easy; 4 ground floor bedrooms **Pets** accepted by arrangement
Closed Christmas Day
Proprietors Terry and Joan Bentley

Southern Lakes

Country hotel, Ambleside

Kirkstone Foot

This immaculately kept white-painted 17thC house, set amid large gardens, has stuck to a comfortable traditional style – the bedrooms have been refurbished recently, but carpets continue to swirl. Housekeeping standards are beyond reproach. The kitchen is well known for its unambitious but honest and generous English country cooking, with choice of starter and main course, and an array of desserts; service is exceptionally friendly. The Bedfords know what they are doing, and do it well.

Nearby Townend, 3 miles (5 km); Lake Windermere.

Kirkstone Pass Road,
Ambleside, Cumbria
LA22 9EH
Tel (05394) 32232
Location on NE side of town, on road to Kirkstone Pass; parking for 40 cars
Food & drink full breakfast, dinner; residential licence
Prices DB&B £39.50-£58; reductions for 3 nights or more and for children under 12 sharing parents' room
Rooms 12 double, 10 with bath, 2 with shower; one single with bath; 2 family rooms, with bath; all rooms have central heating, colour TV, radio, tea/coffee kit
Facilities sitting-room, bar, dining-room
Credit cards AE, DC, MC, V
Children welcome; high tea provided
Disabled access easy to public rooms
Pets not accepted in hotel
Closed Jan except New Year
Managers Andrew and Annabel Bedford

Country house hotel, Windermere

Holbeck Ghyll

A classic Victorian lakeland house, with steep slate roofs and mullioned windows – plus oak panelling and art noveau stained glass. It enjoys a splendid position, with grand views from the immaculate gardens. The Nicholsons, professional hoteliers both, took over in 1988 and have since refurbished to very high standards in a traditional, slightly formal style – though proprietors and staff alike are friendly and relaxed. The food is a clear attraction: four inventive courses, with a good choice including a vegetarian option. No smoking in the dining-room.

Nearby Lake Windermere.

Holbeck Lane, Windermere,
Cumbria LA23 1LU
Tel (05394) 32375 **Fax** 34743
Location 3 miles (5 km) N of Windermere, E of A591; in 5-acre grounds with ample car parking
Food & drink breakfast, light lunch, dinner; residential and restaurant licence
Prices DB&B £55-£110; reductions for children and for 5 nights or more
Rooms 13 double (6 twin), one family room, all with bath; all have central heating, phone, TV, radio, hairdrier
Facilities dining-room, 2 sitting-rooms, snooker room
Credit cards AE, DC, MC, V
Children welcome; baby-listening, high tea for under 8s
Disabled access difficult
Pets in bedrooms only **Closed** never **Proprietors** David and Patricia Nicholson

Southern Lakes

Country hotel, Ambleside

Rothay Manor

This 1830s building in French colonial style seems far removed from the bustle of Ambleside. The reputation of Rothay Manor was built up over 20 years by the late Bronwen Nixon, and it is a relief (though no surprise) to report that the standards she achieved are maintained by her two sons Nigel and Stephen.

Bedrooms are neatly and subtly furnished with a full range of facilities unobtrusively accommodated, the public rooms are calm and polished, and the overall impression is one of quiet, traditional comfort.

Food remains a key part of the hotel's appeal. The basic style of cooking is unfussy and distinctly English; but other influences are not excluded, and chef Jane Binns is allowed free rein on winter Friday nights, when the dishes (and wines) of different regions are explored in special dinners. The cold buffet lunches are well known locally and offer excellent value. The afternoon teas are, if anything, even more famous – like the dinner sweet trolley, 'a dieter's nightmare'.

Nearby Townend, 1.5 miles (2.5 km); Rydal Mount, 2.5 miles (4 km); Dove Cottage, 3 miles (5 km); Lake Windermere.

Rothay Bridge, Ambleside, Cumbria LA22 0EH
Tel (05394) 33605 **Fax** 33607
Location 0.5 miles (0.75 km) S of Ambleside; in 2-acre grounds with ample car parking
Food & drink full breakfast, lunch, tea, dinner; residential and restaurant licence
Prices B&B £54-£76; dinner £21-£27; reduction for 4 nights or more; speciality winter breaks
Rooms 8 double, 2 single, 6 family rooms, 2 suites; all with bath and shower; all rooms have central heating, colour TV, phone, hairdrier
Facilities 3 sitting-rooms, dining-room; croquet
Credit cards AE, DC, MC, V
Children welcome; high tea, cots, baby-listening service
Disabled access good, with ground-floor bedrooms
Pets not accepted in hotel building
Closed Jan to early-Feb
Proprietors Nigel and Stephen Nixon

Southern Lakes

Ees Wyke

'Ees Wyke is the realisation of our dreams,' says John Williams, a catering lecturer until (in 1989) he and Margaret took over this neat and appealing house, white-and-black in the Lakeland manner. The Georgian gent who built it may have expressed similar satisfaction; he certainly picked a glorious spot – elevated above Esthwaite water, with grand views of the fells beyond. It is a home-like house – old-fashioned in the nicest sense and lovingly cared for, with light rooms (thanks to the Georgian fenestration) and modestly elegant furniture. Bedrooms are spacious and airy. John's food is traditionally based but not unadventurous, and both he and Margaret make everyone feel at home.

Nearby Hill Top – Beatrix Potter's house; Windermere.

Near Sawrey, Hawkshead, Ambleside, Cumbria LA22 0JZ
Tel (05394) 36393
Location in hamlet on B5285 2 miles (3 km) SE of Hawkshead; in garden with car parking
Food & drink breakfast, dinner; restaurant & residential licences
Prices B&B £36-£38; DB&B £48-£50

Rooms 8 double (3 twin), 3 with bath, 5 with shower; all rooms have central heating, hairdrier, TV, tea/coffee kit
Facilities 2 sitting-rooms, dining-room
Credit cards AE
Children accepted over 8
Pets allowed in bedrooms only
Disabled access difficult
Closed Jan, Feb **Proprietors** John and Margaret Williams

Crosthwaite House

Crosthwaite is a quiet village spread along a minor road at the head of the Lyth Valley, close to Windermere and within the Lakes park, but off the beaten tourist track. Crosthwaite House has a fine position at one end of the village, not far from the church and pub (which are, of course, closely adjacent). It is a handsome Georgian house, furnished and decorated with a panache that is far from universal in Lake District guest-houses – pine floors, delicate colour schemes, carefully chosen ornaments – and the Dawsons are friendly hosts. Marnie cooks excellent dinners, while Robin serves the aperitifs.

Nearby fell walking, the Lakes; Sizergh Castle 7 miles (11 km).

Crosthwaite, Nr Kendal, Cumbria LS8 8BP
Tel (05395) 68264
Location in countryside just off A5074 5 miles (8 km) W of Kendal; with garden and private car parking
Food & drink breakfast, dinner; residential licence
Prices B&B £22; DB&B £32-£34
Rooms 6 double all with

shower; all rooms have central heating, tea/coffee kit; TV on request
Facilities sitting-room, dining-room
Credit cards not accepted
Children welcome
Pets accepted
Disabled access difficult
Closed mid-Nov to end Mar
Proprietors Marnie and Robin Dawson

Southern Lakes

Country house hotel, Bowness

Miller Howe

In the late 1970s, when the idea of eating well in a British hotel was not so much novel as fantastic, the dining-room of an otherwise dreary grand hotel in Windermere started serving, at a fixed hour, a set dinner of several exquisite courses. Before long, the chef responsible set up shop on his own. The rest is common knowledge: John Tovey has become one of the few British chefs to gain an international reputation, and Miller Howe has become a place of pilgrimage.

The Tovey act is essentially unchanged – dinner still involves a lowering of lights and a marshalling of countless perfectly prepared dishes. The same care and thought that underlies the cooking goes into the hotel-keeping, and despite the rich furnishings, the atmosphere remains informal and welcoming. The public rooms, with their leather chairs, are slightly clubby; the bedrooms employ luxurious fabrics but nevertheless remain home-like.

Although the official line is that Lutyens had a hand in the design of the house, it is no beauty; but who cares, when from its windows and terrace you can gaze across sparkling Lake Windermere to the famous spiky outline of the Langdale Pikes, and dream of the days when you were fit enough to climb them?

We continue to record with despair that the hotel's tariff does not make prices as clear as it should: a 12.5 per cent service charge is added to the bill.

Nearby Windermere Steamboat museum; Lake Windermere

Rayrigg Road, Bowness-on-Windermere, Cumbria LA23 1EY
Tel (05394) 42536 **Fax** 45664
Location on A592 between Bowness and Windermere; in 4-acre landscaped garden with ample car parking
Food & drink full breakfast, picnic lunch, tea, dinner; residential and restaurant licence
Prices DB&B £79-£152; weekend breaks
Rooms 13 double, 12 with bath, one with shower; all rooms have central heating, TV, phone, radio, trouser-press, hairdrier, hi-fi
Facilities 4 sitting-rooms, dining-rooms
Credit cards AE, DC, MC, V
Children welcome over 12
Disabled access difficult
Pets accepted if well behaved, but not allowed in public rooms
Closed mid-Dec to early Mar
Proprietor John Tovey

Southern La

Uplands

'In the Miller Howe manner', declares Uplands literature at every opportunity. Tom and Diana Peter spent 13 years working for John Tovey at his renowned hotel a few miles to the north – he as one of two head chefs, she as Tovey's assistant – and the man himself is their partner in this more modest enterprise. The sitting-room is notably spacious and welcoming, the bedrooms thoroughly civilized – and Tom's set dinners (four courses, three offering a choice) do not disappoint.

Nearby Cartmel Priory, one mile (1.5 km); Lake District.

Haggs Lane, Cartmel, Cumbria LA11 6HD
Tel (05395) 36248
Location 1 mile (1.5 km) SE of Cartmel; in 2-acre garden with parking for 16 cars
Food & drink full breakfast; lunch, dinner; residential and restaurant licence
Prices DB&B £57-£75; 20% reduction for 3 nights; spring and autumn breaks; B&B by arrangement
Rooms 5 double, 2 with bath, 3 with shower; all rooms have

central heating, colour TV, phone, hairdrier
Facilities sitting-room, dining-room
Credit cards AE, MC, V
Children welcome over 8
Disabled access easy only to public rooms
Pets welcome, but not in public rooms
Closed Jan and Feb; restaurant only, Mon
Proprietors Tom and Diana Peter and John Tovey

night @ 15 ½ throo (1 night)

Lancrigg

This secluded 17thC farmhouse, much modified in Georgian and Victorian times, was opened by the Whittingtons in 1985. Their unusual emphasis on vegetarian food naturally attracts a lot of regular visitors, but an inspection visit confirms that carnivores are not made to feel uncomfortable. Some of the bedrooms are rather scruffy, but the best are eclectic and amusing. The special 'luxury' rooms include three with a spa bath. Food apart, the main attraction is the blissful setting.

Nearby Rydal Water, Lake Windermere; Langdale.

Easedale, Grasmere, Cumbria LA22 9QN
Tel (05394) 35317
Location one mile (1.5 km) NW of Grasmere off the Easedale Road; in grounds with ample car parking
Food & drink full breakfast, packed lunch, dinner; restaurant and residential licence
Prices DB&B £36-£75; reductions in winter
Rooms 13 double, 11 with

bath; one single; 2 family rooms; all rooms have TV, tea/coffee kit, hairdrier
Facilities sitting-room, dining-room; play area
Credit cards MC, V
Children welcome
Disabled access easy; 3 ground-floor bedrooms
Pets accepted in grounds and in hotel by arrangement
Closed never
Proprietors Robert and Janet Whittington

Southern Lakes

White Moss House

This fine country house, owned by the Wordsworth family until the 1930s, not only has the advantage of being close to some stunning countryside around Rydal Water, but also has an enviable reputation for the quality of its food. Peter Dixon, who cooks virtually single-handed, is considered to be in the forefront of 'modern English cooking'. The Dixons came here in 1981 to pursue full-time their long-standing love of food and wine. The main house has five comfortable bedrooms, each individually furnished, and there are two more in the secluded and peaceful cottage up the hill behind the hotel. The sitting-room is light and elegant, and the terrace overlooking the garden is pleasant. This is one of the few Lake District hotels with the genuine feel of a private house.

Nearby Rydal Mount; Dove Cottage, one mile (1.5 km); White Craggs Garden, 1.5 miles (2.5 km); Stagshaw, 1.5 miles (2.5 km); Townend, 4 miles (6.5 km).

Rydal Water, Grasmere, Cumbria LA22 9SE
Tel (05394) 35295
Location one mile (1.5 km) S of Grasmere on A591; ample car parking
Food & drink full breakfast, dinner; residential and restaurant licence
Prices DB&B £64-£87; reductions for 3 nights plus and for children in Jul/Aug
Rooms 7 double (2 part of a cottage suite), 6 with bath, one with shower; all have central heating, phone, TV, radio, hairdrier, trouser-press
Facilities sitting-room, bar, dining-room; fishing, free use of local leisure club
Credit cards MC, V
Children welcome over 10; 7-10 year olds by arrangement
Disabled access difficult
Pets not accepted in hotel; may stay in cars **Closed** Dec to Feb **Proprietors** Susan and Peter Dixon

Southern Lakes

Old Dungeon Ghyll

The Old Dungeon Ghyll is at the very heart of the Lake District –
overshadowed by the famous Langdale Pikes. The three-storey
slate-and-stone main building is in typical local style and is
flanked by a Climber's Bar. Inside the house itself, the sitting-
room is comfortably chintzy and traditional, with an open fire.
Bedrooms have a pleasant, cottagey feel, with brass and iron
bedsteads, but some are distinctly small. Food is filling and
wholesome, in enormous portions to suit walkers' appetites.
Nearby high fell walks into the heart of the Lakes.

Great Langdale, Ambleside,
Cumbria LA22 9JY
Tel & Fax (05394) 37272
Location 7 miles (11 km) NE
of Ambleside off B5343; in
countryside with ample car
parking
Food & drink breakfast,
packed lunch, dinner, bar
meals; full licence
Prices B&B £24-£30; dinner
£15.50; 4-night winter and
spring breaks (Sun to Thu);
reductions for children
sharing parents' room

Rooms 9 double, 4 with
shower; 3 single; 2 family
rooms, 3 with shower; all
rooms have central heating
Facilities sitting-room, 2 bars,
dining-room
Credit cards MC, V
Children welcome
Disabled access difficult
Pets welcome, but not allowed
in dining-room
Closed 24 to 26 Dec
Proprietors Neil and Jane
Walmsley

Mortal Man

A classic friendly Lakeland inn – white walls, slate roof, black
trimmings – off the road linking two of the loveliest lakes,
Windermere and Ullswater. The bar, too, is traditionally black-
and-white, the dining-room inoffensively neat. Bedrooms are, by
Christopher Poulsom's own admission, 'compact and functional',
but they are well equipped and most share the good views of the
Troutbeck valley. Dinners are above-average – satisfying and
mildly adventurous five-course affairs offering a reasonable
choice, always including a vegetarian option.
Nearby Windermere, 3 miles (5 km), Ullswater, 9 miles (15 km).

Troutbeck, nr Windermere,
Cumbria LA23 1PL
Tel (05394) 33193 **Fax** 31261
Location in hamlet off A592,
2.5 miles N of junction with
A591, just N of Windermere
village; with ample car parking
Food & drink breakfast, Sun
lunch, dinner; full licence
Prices DB&B £43-£52;
reductions for 3 nights or
more
Rooms 10 double (6 twin), 2

single, all with bath; all have
phone, hairdrier, TV, radio
Facilities bar, sitting-room,
dining-room
Credit cards not accepted
Children not accepted under 5
Disabled access to bedrooms
very difficult
Pets welcome
Closed mid-Nov to mid-Feb
Proprietors Christopher and
Annette Poulsom

Southern Lakes

Country hotel, Lowick Bridge

Bridgefield House

What sets Bridgefield apart from others of its ilk is the care its owners take to look after their guests without (as they put it) 'fussing' them. Two of the house's three acres form a miniature parkland of mature conifers; on the third, David Glister grows the vegetables that Rosemary later cooks with great skill and imagination. Furnishings are comfortably in sympathy with the house, and the spacious bedrooms are well equipped.

Nearby Rusland Hall, 3 miles (5 km); Coniston Water.

Lowick Bridge, Ulverston, Cumbria LA12 8DA
Tel (0229) 885239 **Fax** 885379
Location 5.5 miles (9 km) N of Ulverston, off A5084; in 3-acre grounds with parking for 10 cars
Food & drink full breakfast, dinner; residential and restaurant licence
Prices B&B £35; dinner £24; reduction for children; reductions for 3 nights or more
Rooms 5 double, all with bath; all have central heating, radio/alarm, hairdrier, phone
Facilities dining-room, bar, sitting-room
Credit cards MC, V
Children very welcome; high-chairs, cots, laundry, high tea at no extra charge
Disabled not suitable
Pets well-behaved dogs welcome, but not in public rooms
Closed never
Proprietors David and Rosemary Glister

Lakeside hotel, Ambleside

Wateredge Hotel

As its name suggests, the Wateredge is in a fine position, with its lawns leading to the very edge of Windermere; the several well-furnished sitting-rooms make the most of the exceptional views across the lake. The dining-rooms have no lake view but do share the same high standards of decoration. Dinners comprise six splendidly filling courses. Bedrooms vary in size but all are comfortable and stylishly decorated.

Nearby Stagshaw; Townend, 1.5 miles (2.5 km); Dove Cottage, 3 miles (5 km).

Borrans Road, Waterhead, Ambleside, Cumbria LA22 0EP
Tel & fax (05394) 32332
Location 1 mile (1.6 km) S of Ambleside on lakeshore, on A591; with car parking
Food & drink full breakfast, light lunch, tea, dinner; residential licence
Prices B&B £37-£58; DB&B £47-£68; reductions for 3 nights or more
Rooms 19 double, 16 with bath, 3 with shower; 3 single, one with bath, 2 with shower; one family room with bath; all rooms have central heating, TV, phone, tea/coffee kit
Facilities 3 sitting-rooms (one with TV), bar, dining-rooms; rowing-boat, private jetty
Credit cards AE, MC, V
Children welcome over 7
Disabled access difficult
Pets by arrangement, but not in public rooms
Closed Dec and Jan
Proprietors Mr and Mrs Derek Cowap

Southern Lakes

Country hotel, Witherslack

The Old Vicarage

The Old Vicarage would offer peace and seclusion even if sleepy Witherslack found itself invaded by the Lake District Bank Holiday hordes, hidden as it is in a large wooded garden. But it offers much else besides. The building is not exceptional – its Georgian vintage is scarcely evident from its proportions – but it is furnished with great care and some style, successfully combining antiques with new cane and pine to create warm and relaxing surroundings. Five of the bedrooms are in a separate building and have private terraces.

The Reeves and the Burrington-Browns, like so many of the best hotel-keepers in Britain, simply seek to provide accommodation which they would enjoy themselves. They devote equal care and enthusiasm to the meals they serve, which are justly recognized to be among the best in the area. The secret is excellent local ingredients in fresh and thoughtful combinations. Vegetarians are admirably catered for, and there is a choice of starters and puddings, which have been described by a higher authority than us as 'breathtaking'. Fortunately there are plenty of splendid local walks to mitigate the damage.

Nearby Levens Hall, 3 miles (5 km); Sizergh Castle, 5 miles (8 km); Holker Hall, 6 miles (10 km); Lake Windermere.

Church Road, Witherslack, near Grange-over-Sands, Cumbria LA11 6RS
Tel (05395) 52381 **Fax** 52373
Location 5 miles (8 km) NE of Grange off A590; in 5-acre garden and woodland with ample car parking
Food & drink full breakfast, dinner, Sun lunch; residential and restaurant licence
Prices B&B £49-£79; dinner £19.50; 2-day bargain breaks
Rooms 14 double, 10 with bath, 4 with shower; all rooms have central heating, radio/alarm, phone, colour TV,

hairdrier, tea/coffee kit
Facilities breakfast room, dining-room, 2 sitting-rooms; tennis court
Credit cards MC, V
Children welcome (high tea at 5.30pm)
Disabled not suitable
Pets dogs accepted by arrangement, but not allowed in public rooms or left unattended
Closed never
Proprietors Jill and Roger Burrington-Brown, Irene and Stanley Reeve

Southern Lakes

Farm guest-house, Blawith

Appletree Holme

The Carlsens came here in 1979 after years of running a much bigger and glossier (and in its way very successful) hotel on the shores of Ullswater – because they wanted, in Roy's words, 'to go back to looking after people again'.

The farm enjoys a lovely and totally secluded setting on the fringe of Lakeland, with nothing but fells in view. The low, stone-built house has been lovingly restored and sympathetically furnished with antiques; pictures and books abound, and open fires on stone hearths supplement the central heating. Two of the equally welcoming bedrooms have the unusual luxury of double-size whirlpool baths.

Roy believes in tailoring his menus (whether for breakfast or dinner) to suit guests' tastes and the local fruits of the land – home-grown vegetables, meat, poultry and dairy produce from neighbouring farms. And anyone whose appetite needs a lift can enlist the help of Pooch, the sheepdog, who will gladly take you for a walk over the fells.

In the interests of their guests the Carlsens discourage casual callers, so do phone ahead if you want to look around.

Nearby Rusland Hall, 4 miles (6.5 km); Coniston Water, Lake Windermere.

Blawith, near Ulverston, Cumbria LA12 8EL
Tel (0229) 885618
Location 6 miles (10 km) S of Coniston off A5084, in open countryside; in extensive grounds, with ample car parking
Food & drink full breakfast, picnic lunch on request, dinner; residential and restaurant licence
Prices DB&B £51–£70

Rooms 4 double, all with bath and shower; all rooms have central heating, phone, radio, tea/coffee kit, colour TV
Facilities 2 sitting-rooms, dining-room
Credit cards AE, MC, V
Children not suitable
Disabled access difficult
Pets not allowed in the house
Closed never
Proprietors Roy and Shirley Carlsen

Northern Lakes

Inn, Bassenthwaite Lake

Pheasant Inn

Tucked away behind trees just off the A66, the Pheasant was originally an old coaching inn, and there are many reminders of this within, particularly in the little old oak bar, which is full of dark nooks and crannies – a real piece of history, little changed from its earliest days. The building is a long, low barn-like structure that has been exceptionally well maintained, and it has a small but well-kept garden to the rear with a couple of small lawns and fine forest views.

One of the great attractions – particularly for an unpretentious roadside inn – is the generous sitting space. There are two residents' sitting-rooms to the front, both low ceilinged with small windows and plenty of small prints on the walls. A third, with easy chairs before an open log fire, juts out into the garden and has the advantage of its own serving hatch to the bar. Bedrooms are modern, light and well-equipped. The dining-room has been reorganized and refurbished to make the best of its slightly uncomfortable shape, the food – no-nonsense stuff with few concessions to modern fashions – is competently cooked, and service is outstandingly friendly.

Nearby Bassenthwaite Lake; Keswick, 5.5 miles (9 km).

Bassenthwaite Lake, near Cockermouth, Cumbria CA13 9YE
Tel (07687) 76234 **Fax** 76002
Location 5 miles (8 km) E of Cockermouth, just off A66
Food & drink breakfast, lunch, tea, dinner, bar snacks; full licence
Prices B&B £48-£55; DB&B £65.70; reduced weekly rates
Rooms 15 double, all with bath; 5 single, 3 with bath, 2 with shower; all rooms have central heating, hairdrier
Facilities bar, sitting-rooms, dining-room
Credit cards not accepted
Children welcome, but not allowed in main bar
Disabled access easy only to public rooms, and one room in bungalow annexe
Pets not allowed in bedrooms
Closed Christmas Day
Proprietor W Barrington Wilson

Northern Lakes

Country guest-house, Borrowdale

Seatoller House

It should be said at the outset that a stay at Seatoller House is something quite different from the run-of-the-mill hotel experience. You eat communally at set times, and to get the best out of the place you should take part in the social life of the house. If you do, the 'country house party' effect, much vaunted elsewhere, really does come about.

Seatoller House is over 300 years old and has been run as a guest-house for over 100 years; the first entry in the visitors' book reads 23 April 1886. The long, low house, built in traditional Lakeland style and looking like a row of cottages, is in the tiny village of Seatoller, at the head of Borrowdale and the foot of Honister Pass. Bedrooms are simple and comfortable, and all now have their own bathrooms (although some are physically separate from the bedrooms). The dining-room is in a country-kitchen style, with a delightfully informal atmosphere – one that spills over into the two sections of the low-ceilinged sitting-room. Food is excellent; and if you are thirsty, just wander to the fridge, take what you like and sign for it in the book provided.

Several times a year the house is taken over entirely by members of the Lakes Hunt, who enjoy running up and down the surrounding fells in pursuit not of foxes (the traditional quarry of local hunts), but of one another.

Nearby Derwentwater, 4 miles (6 km); Buttermere, 6 miles (10 km); Keswick, 7 miles (11 km).

Borrowdale, Keswick, Cumbria CA12 5XN
Tel (07687) 77218
Location 8 miles (13 km) S of Keswick on B5289; parking for 10 cars
Food & drink full breakfast, packed lunch, dinner (not Tue); residential licence
Prices DB&B £31-£33
Rooms 5 double, 4 family rooms; all with bath and shower, or separate bathroom; all rooms have central heating
Facilities sitting-room, library, dining-room, tea room, drying-room
Credit cards not accepted
Children welcome over 5
Disabled access easy; 2 downstairs bedrooms
Pets welcome but not in public rooms
Closed Dec to Feb
Managers Ann and David Pepper

Northern Lakes

Swinside Lodge

A reader writes in glowing terms of this typical Victorian lakeland house at the foot of Catbells – 'well maintained, tastefully decorated, with pleasant, efficient service and excellent five-course set dinners; there is a friendly and relaxed atmosphere, and the hotel is keenly priced.' Not the least of its attractions for another reporter is the position: you can enjoy excellent walks right from the door. It is carefully furnished and immaculately decorated, with a scattering of personal ornaments, books and so on. The dinners are mildly adventurous and very competently executed; take your own wine. No smoking is permitted.

Nearby Derwent Water, Bassenthwaite Lake.

Grange Road, Newlands, Keswick, Cumbria CA12 5UE
Tel (07687) 72948
Location 3 miles (5 km) SW of Keswick, 2 miles (3 km) S of A66; with garden, and parking for 10 cars
Food & drink breakfast, dinner; no licence
Prices B&B £29.50-£38; DB&B £51.50-£60; reductions for 2 nights or more

Rooms 9 double (2 twin), 8 with bath, one with shower; all have central heating, TV, radio, hairdrier, tea/coffee kit
Facilities dining-room, 2 sitting-rooms
Credit cards not accepted
Children accepted over 12
Disabled not suitable
Pets not accepted
Closed mid-Dec to mid-Feb
Proprietor Graham Taylor

The Mill

The Mill (not to be confused, as it often is, with the Mill Inn next door) is a cottagey guest-house offering good value for money and run in a quiet unassuming fashion by the Quinlan family. The main sitting-room is chintzy, relaxing and well cared for, and thirty original watercolours and oil paintings adorn the walls of the bedrooms and public rooms. The food is increasingly ambitious and generally successful, with little choice of early courses but a range of tempting puddings. Bedrooms are light and airy.

Nearby Derwentwater, Ullswater; Hadrian's Wall.

Mungrisdale, Penrith, Cumbria CA11 0XR
Tel (07687) 79659
Location 9.5 miles (15 km) W of Penrith close to A66, in village; in wooded grounds with parking for 15 cars
Food & drink breakfast, lunch, dinner; residential and restaurant licence
Prices B&B £26-£36, dinner £19.50; reductions for 5 nights or more, and for children sharing parents' room
Rooms 8 double, 5 with bath; one single; one family room; all rooms have tea/coffee kit, colour TV
Facilities sitting-room, TV room, dining-room, games room, drying-room
Credit cards not accepted
Children welcome; cots, high-chairs, laundry facilities
Disabled access difficult
Pets dogs accepted if well behaved, but not allowed in public rooms
Closed Nov to Feb **Proprietors** Richard and Eleanor Quinlan

Northern Lakes

Inn, Wasdale

Wasdale Head

The Wasdale Head is in a site unrivalled even in the consistently spectacular Lake District. It stands on the flat valley bottom between three major peaks – Pillar, Great Gable and Scafell Pike (England's highest) – and only a little way above Wastwater, England's deepest and perhaps most dramatic lake.

Over the last decade and a half the old inn has been carefully and thoughtfully modernized, adding facilities but retaining the characteristics of a traditional mountain inn. The main lounge of the hotel is comfortable and welcoming, with plenty of personal touches. The pine-panelled bedrooms are not notably spacious but are adequate, with fixtures and fittings all in good condition; one good family room has built-in bunk beds. The dining-room is heavily panelled, and decorated with willow pattern china and a pewter jug collection. Food is solid English fare, served by young, friendly staff. There are two bars. The one for residents has some magnificent wooden furniture, while tasty bar meals are served in the congenial surroundings of the public bar, much frequented by walkers and climbers.

Nearby Hardknott Castle Roman Fort, 5 miles (8 km); Ravenglass and Eskdale Railway, 5.5 miles (9 km); Wastwater; Scafell.

Wasdale Head, Gosforth, Cumbria CA20 1EX
Tel (09467) 26229 **Fax** 26334
Location 9 miles (14.5 km) NE of Gosforth at head of Wasdale; ample car parking
Food & drink full breakfast, bar and packed lunches, dinner; full licence
Prices B&B £25-£30; dinner from £16
Rooms 6 double, 5 with bath, one with shower; 2 single, one with bath, one with shower; 2 family rooms, both with bath; all rooms have central heating, tea/coffee kit, phone
Facilities sitting-room, dining-room, 2 bars
Credit cards MC, V
Children welcome, but under-8s not allowed in dining-room during dinner
Disabled access easy to ground floor, but not to bedrooms
Pets tolerated in bedrooms only
Closed mid-Nov to mid-Mar; open 2 weeks for New Year
Proprietor Edwin Hammond

Northern Lakes

Old Church

There are many hotels with spectacular settings in the Lakes but for our money there are few to match that of this whitewashed 18thC house on the very shore of Ullswater.

Since their arrival in the late 1970s, Kevin and Maureen Whitemore have developed the hotel carefully and stylishly. The three sitting-rooms, one of which is formed by the entrance hall, are all very well furnished with clever touches in their decorations that give some hint of Maureen's interior design training. They also have the natural advantage of excellent views across the lake. The bedrooms are all different in decoration but they too show a confident but harmonious use of colour. Most have lake views and are pleasantly free of modern gadgetry.

Ex-accountant Kevin does more than keep the books in order: his daily changing dinners are enterprising and expertly prepared, with a reasonable choice at each course.

'Everything one expects of a Charming Small Hotel,' says one completely satisfied visitor, 'with not a single jarring note.'

Nearby Dalemain, 3 miles (5 km); Penrith Castle, 5.5 miles (9 km); Brougham Castle, 7 miles (11 km); Ullswater.

Watermillock Penrith, Cumbria CA11 0JN
Tel (07684) 86204 **Fax** 86368
Location 5.5 miles (9 km) S of Penrith on A592; in own grounds on lakeshore with ample car parking
Food & drink breakfast, dinner; residential licence
Prices B&B £45-£75, DB&B £60-£90
Rooms 10 double, all with bath; all rooms have central heating, phone, TV
Facilities bar, 2 sitting-rooms, dining-room; boat, fishing
Credit cards MC, V
Children welcome; not allowed at dinner under 8 – cots, high-chairs, high tea available **Disabled** access difficult **Pets** not accepted
Closed Nov to Mar
Proprietors Kevin and Maureen Whitemore

Cumbria

Farlam Hall

For over eighteen years now the Quinions have been assiduously improving their solid but elegant Border country house. A reporter could find no flaw: 'charming family, quiet surroundings, excellent food, tastefully furnished bedroom'. Bedrooms vary widely and some are decidedly large and swish. Barry Quinion's dinners range from plain country dishes to mild extravagances, and there is a notable cheeseboard.

Nearby Naworth Castle, 2.5 miles (4 km); Hadrian's Wall.

Brampton, Cumbria CA8 2NG
Tel (06977) 46234 **Fax** 46683
Location 3 miles (5 km) SE of Brampton on A689, NE of Farlam village; ample car parking
Food & drink full breakfast, dinner; restaurant and residential licence
Prices DB&B £77.50-£98; winter and spring reductions
Rooms 12 double, 11 with bath, one with shower; one single, with shower; all have central heating, TV, phone, hairdrier, radio, trouser-press
Facilities 2 sitting-rooms; croquet
Credit cards AE, MC, V
Children accepted over 5
Disabled access reasonable; 2 ground-floor bedrooms
Pets welcome but not in dining-room or left alone in bedrooms
Closed Christmas week
Proprietors Quinion and Stevenson families

The Black Swan

The Stuarts offer a comfortable, relaxing and good-value home away from home, with particular emphasis on food of the first quality. The atmosphere of the Black Swan is, however, rather more formal than that of a typical country inn. There is a choice of a daily fixed five-course menu (ending with some indulgent puddings and excellent British cheeses) or a small *carte*, and a well-balanced wine-list. The dining room is appropriately polished, the sitting-room more lived-in with plenty of reading matter and an open fire. Breakfasts are a substantial home-made feast.

Nearby Brough Castle, 8 miles (13 km); Eden valley.

Ravenstonedale, Kirkby Stephen, Cumbria CA17 4NG
Tel (05396) 23204
Location 6 miles (10 km) E of M6, off A685; ample car parking
Food & drink full breakfast, lunch, dinner; full licence
Prices B&B £30-£45; dinner from £20; bargain breaks
Rooms 13 double, one single, all with bath/shower; all have central heating, tea/coffee kit, hairdrier, phone
Facilities sitting-room, lounge bar, dining-room; fishing, tennis, bowling
Credit cards AE, MC, V
Children welcome if well behaved; early tea provided
Disabled access easy to 3 ground-floor rooms
Pets welcome if well behaved, but not in public rooms
Closed never
Proprietors Gordon and Norma Stuart

Durham

Rose and Crown

Until four years ago, the Davys ran the Black Swan (facing page). Rescued from receivership and thoroughly redecorated, the Rose and Crown is thriving in their hands. The bars are typically rustic with log fires, old photographs and brass ornaments. Pub grub is served in the 'Crown room'; traditional four-course dinners in the panelled dining-room. Seven of the bedrooms (comfortable, with antique furniture) are in the main building, the rest (larger, modern) around the rear courtyard.

Nearby Barnard Castle, 6 miles (10 km).

Romaldkirk, Barnard Castle, Co. Durham DL12 9EB
Tel (0833) 50213 **Fax** 50828
Location in middle of village, on B6277, 6 miles NW of Barnard Castle; with ample car parking
Food & drink breakfast, dinner, Sun lunch; full licence
Prices B&B £37-£52; dinner £21; bargain breaks
Rooms 11 double, 8 with bath, 3 with shower; one family room with bath; all have central heating, phone, TV, radio, tea/coffee kit
Facilities dining-room, sitting-room, bar **Credit cards** MC, V
Children welcome; baby-listening **Disabled** access good; ground-floor bedroom
Pets dogs accepted in bedrooms **Closed** Christmas; restaurant only, Sun evening
Proprietors Christopher and Alison Davy

Pennine Lodge

As well as running this 16thC stone farmhouse, Yvonne Raine prides herself on doing all the cooking and baking herself. You will not be disappointed either by the food – game casseroles, home-made pies, bread straight from the oven – or by the prices. The building is long and narrow, partly covered in creeper and surrounded by lovely gardens with a waterfall (of the river Wear) behind the house. You can be assured of absolute peace here. The beamed rooms are furnished with antiques and other treasures, bedrooms are clean and comfortable with wonderful views down the valley, dotted with cottages.

Nearby Weardale, Pennine Way.

St John's Chapel, Weardale, Co. Durham DL13 1QX
Tel (0388) 537247
Location by River Wear, on A689 10 miles (16 km) W of Stanhope; in one-acre garden with parking for 20 cars
Food & drink breakfast, tea, dinner; residential licence
Prices B&B £18.50; dinner £9.50; reductions for 3 and 7 nights
Rooms 5 double, 2 with bath, 3 with shower; all rooms have central heating, hairdrier, tea/coffee kit
Facilities dining-room, sitting-room; fishing
Credit cards none
Children not accepted
Disabled access difficult
Pets well-behaved dogs accepted but not in public rooms
Closed Nov to Mar
Proprietor Mrs Y Raine

Durham

Manor house hotel, Gainford

Headlam Hall

'Extraordinary house, fine grounds, reasonable rates' was the telegraphic message that came back from one of our scouts about this mansion in a peaceful hamlet just north of the Tees. And so it is: a grand Jacobean house on three floors, its mellow stone all but hidden by creepers, with substantial Georgian additions – standing in four acres of beautiful formal gardens, with mellow stone walls, massive hedges and a canalised stream. As for the rates – although they have crept up (no doubt partly because of the new leisure facilities added in 1990), they are still reasonable. But it is equally true that Headlam is not among the best-furnished country hotels in the land – and therein lies part of its appeal, for us at least. Although there are abundant antiques alongside the reproductions (the Robinsons furnished the place from scratch after they took it over in the late 1970s) there is a comfortable ordinariness about the place which is refreshing. The Robinsons say the food is less plain than it once was.

Nearby Barnard Castle, 8 miles (13 km).

Gainford, Darlington, Durham DL2 3HA
Tel (0325) 730238
Location 7 miles (11 km) W of Darlington, off A67; in 4-acre gardens surrounded by farmland, with ample car parking
Food & drink breakfast, lunch, dinner; restaurant and residential licence
Prices B&B £35-£70; dinner £16-£19
Rooms 26 double, all with bath and shower; 2 suites; all rooms have central heating, TV, phone, tea/coffee kit
Facilities sitting-room, bar, dining-room, restaurant, snooker room; tennis, fishing, indoor swimming-pool
Credit cards AE, MC, V
Children welcome
Disabled access easy to ground floor only
Pets welcome, but dogs not allowed in bedrooms
Closed Christmas
Proprietors John Robinson, Clare Robinson

Northumberland

Country guest-house, Crookham

The Coach House

Lynne Anderson (an ex-singer, with a beautiful voice still) is a charming hostess who devotes herself to the care of guests in this group of converted farm buildings. Some bedrooms are in the old outbuildings around a sunny courtyard, others in a separate stone house. The four-course dinners (with a choice of starter and dessert) are wholesome affairs employing much local produce, as are the breakfasts.

Nearby Northumberland National Park.

Crookham, Cornhill-on-Tweed, Northumberland TD12 4TD
Tel (089082) 293
Location 4 miles (6 km) E of Cornhill-on-Tweed on A697; with ample car parking
Food & drink full breakfast, tea, dinner; residential licence
Prices B&B from £21; DB&B from £35.50; reductions for children under 10
Rooms 9 double, 7 with bath and shower; 2 singles with bath and shower; all rooms have central heating, tea/coffee kit; most rooms have fridge
Facilities sitting-room, dining-room, TV room, games room
Credit cards MC, V
Children accepted; cots and high-chairs provided
Disabled excellent facilities
Pets welcome in bedrooms but not allowed in public rooms
Closed Dec-Feb inclusive
Proprietor Lynne Anderson

Country hotel, Powburn

Breamish House

In an area where there is a dearth of characterful small hotels, it is a relief to come upon the Johnsons' establishment – originally an 18thC farmhouse, converted to a hunting lodge in the 19th century and opened as a hotel in 1982. It is a thoroughly good all-rounder, which stands comparison with many of the best hotels in parts of the country more popular with visitors – a welcoming, informal atmosphere, and solid, comfortable furniture in well-decorated bedrooms (those at the front notably spacious). The staff are charming and thoughtful, the cooking excellent.

Nearby Callaly Castle, 4 miles (6.5 km).

Powburn, Alnwick, Northumberland NE66 4LL
Tel (066578) 266 **Fax** 500
Location 7.5 miles (12 km) NW of Alnwick, in middle of village; ample car parking
Food & drink breakfast, tea, dinner, Sun lunch, residential and restaurant licence
Prices B&B £31-£48; dinner £19.95; bargain breaks
Rooms 11 double, 9 with bath, one with shower; one single with shower; all have central heating, TV, tea/coffee kit, radio
Facilities 2 sitting-rooms, dining-room
Credit cards not accepted
Children welcome over 12
Disabled access easy **Pets** by arrangement **Closed** Jan
Proprietors Alan and Doreen Johnson

Dumfries & Galloway

Inn, Canonbie

Riverside Inn

For nineteen years the Phillipses have been improving and extending this country-house-turned-inn to the point where it scores highly whether viewed as a pub, a restaurant or a hotel. We guess that motorists travelling between England and Scotland remain the mainstay of trade, despite the fact that the A7 from Carlisle to Edinburgh has been shifted westwards to by-pass Canonbie. For those who do pause there, Canonbie and the Riverside are, not surprisingly, more attractive now that very little traffic separates the Riverside from the public park it faces, and from the river Esk – offering sea trout in summer and salmon in autumn – which it overlooks fifty yards away.

Inside, the comfortable bar and cosy sitting-rooms have occasional beams and are furnished in traditional chintz, country style, while the dining-room is less pub-like. Both in the bars and dining-room, the food is way above normal pub standards, both in ambition, and execution, using fresh local produce and home-grown vegetables.

Nearby Hadrian's Wall and the Borders.

Canonbie, Dumfries and Galloway DG14 0UX
Tel (03873) 71512
Location 11 miles (18 km) N of M6 on A7, in village by river; with garden and ample car parking
Food & drink full breakfast, lunch, dinner; full licence
Prices B&B £36-£42; dinner £21; winter breaks
Rooms 6 double, 4 with bath, 2 with shower; all rooms have storage heater, tea/coffee kit,
TV
Facilities 2 sitting-rooms, bar, dining-room; fishing, tennis, green bowls
Credit cards MC, V
Children welcome
Disabled access easy – one ground-floor bedroom
Pets not accepted **Closed** Boxing Day, New Year, 2 weeks Feb and Nov
Proprietors Robert and Susan Phillips

Dumfries & Galloway

Country house hotel, Portpatrick

Knockinaam Lodge

Galloway is very much an area for escaping the hurly-burly, and Knockinaam Lodge complements it perfectly (as well as being the ideal staging post for anyone bound for the ferry to Northern Ireland). Succeeding proprietors of the Lodge have had a reputation for fine food and warm hospitality, and the tradition is thoroughly maintained with the help of an enthusiastic young staff by Marcel and Corinna Frichot – professional hotel-keepers, he of Seychellois extraction, she coming from Cheshire.

The house, a low Victorian villa, was built as a holiday home in the late 19th century and extended a few years later. Its rooms are cosy in scale and furnishings, the bedrooms varying from the stylishly simple to the quietly elegant. A key part of the appeal of the place is its complete seclusion – down a wooded glen, with lawned garden running down to a sandy beach.

Dinner is interesting and adventurous; there is a small choice of dishes at each course and the cooking is competent and stylish modern French.

Nearby Logan Botanic Gardens, 4 miles (6.5 km); Castle Kennedy Gardens, 9 miles (14.5 km); Glenluce Abbey, 11 miles (17.5 km).

Portpatrick, Wigtownshire, Dumfries and Galloway DG9 9AD
Tel (077681) 471 **Fax** 435
Location 3 miles (5 km) SE of Portpatrick, off A77; in large grounds, parking for 25 cars
Food & drink full breakfast, lunch, dinner, high tea for children; full licence
Prices B&B £50-£68; dinner £30; reductions for stays of 2 nights plus, and for children sharing parents' room; bargain breaks

Rooms 9 double with bath; one single with bath; all have central heating, TV, phone
Facilities bar, 2 sitting-rooms, dining-room; croquet; helipad
Credit cards AE, DC, MC, V
Children welcome; cots and baby-sitting available
Disabled access easy, but no ground-floor bedrooms
Pets accepted, but not in public rooms
Closed Jan to 15 Mar
Proprietors Marcel and Corinna Frichot

Lothian

Howard Hotel

The Howard consists of three houses in a Georgian terrace in the heart of Edinburgh's New Town. It has been extensively refurbished and upgraded since changing hands in 1989 and by our standards is now wildly expensive; but we have been unable to resist its elegant public rooms and large, richly furnished bedrooms. The new management have a good eye for detail – fresh fruit in all the bedrooms. There is a smart restaurant downstairs hung with modern art from an Edinburgh gallery, offering delicious-sounding menus.

Nearby Castle, Holyrood Palace; Botanic Gardens.

32-36 Great King Street, Edinburgh, Lothian EH3 6QH
Tel (031) 557 3500 **Fax** 6515
Location off Dundas St in New Town; parking for 14 cars at rear
Food & drink full breakfast, dinner; full licence
Prices B&B £90-£140; dinner £29
Rooms 10 double, 4 single, 2 suites, all with bath; all rooms have central heating, colour TV, phone, hairdrier
Facilities sitting-room, restaurant
Credit cards AE, DC, MC, V
Children welcome
Disabled some facilities
Pets accepted
Closed never
Manager Gillian Thompson

Greywalls

Greywalls is right at the top of our price-range and size-range, but we cannot resist such a distinctive place – a classic turn-of-the-century product of Sir Edwin Lutyens with a garden laid out by Gertrude Jekyll, overlooking the 9th green of the famous Muirfield golf links. The feel is still very much one of a private house, furnished largely with period pieces; the large panelled library is a particularly appealing room. The ambitious young chef uses fine local produce.

Nearby Countless golf courses; stately homes; sandy beaches.

Muirfield, Gullane, East Lothian EH31 2EG
Tel (0620) 842144 **Fax** 842241
Location 17 miles (27 km) E of Edinburgh on A198 to North Berwick; ample car parking
Food & drink breakfast, lunch, dinner; full licence
Prices B&B £70-£90; dinner £33
Rooms 18 double, all with bath and shower; 4 single, all with bath, 3 also with shower; all rooms have central heating, TV, phone, radio, hairdrier
Facilities 2 sitting-rooms, library, bar; croquet, tennis
Credit cards AE, DC, MC, V
Children welcome
Disabled access good – no steps to public rooms; a few steps to 8 ground-floor bedrooms **Pets** accepted, but not in public rooms
Closed Nov to Mar
Manager Sue Prime

Strathclyde

Town house café/pub/hotel, Glasgow

Babbity Bowster

An original name (from a rude-sounding Scottish dance) for an original little hotel, created in the shell of an 18thC mansion in Glasgow's old merchant quarter. Fraser Laurie, bearded, with eye-patch, has created a lively pub-type atmosphere and holds weekly jazz and classical concerts, regular poetry readings, and exhibitions in the first-floor Schottische restaurant/gallery. Food served in the café-bar downstairs ranges from haggis to oysters. Bedrooms are small and simple with modern pine furniture and fine prints on the walls. 'Magnificent' breakfasts.

Nearby Cathedral, Hunterian Museum and Art Gallery, Haggs castle, People's Palace.

16/18 Blackfriars St, Glasgow
G1 1PE
Tel (041) 552 5055
Location in pedestrian street, on eastern edge of city centre, near High Street station; with parking for 7 cars
Food & drink breakfast, lunch, dinner; full licence
Prices B&B £29-£40; dinner from £10.50
Rooms 5 double, one single, all with shower; all rooms have central heating
Facilities dining-room, bar/café, patio
Credit cards AE, MC, V
Children not accepted; building unsuitable
Disabled no special facilities
Pets not accepted
Closed 1 Jan
Proprietor Fraser Laurie

Manor house hotel, Kentallen

Ardsheal House

It would be hard to find a more beautiful setting for a hotel; on the edge of Loch Linnhe, surrounded by trees and rhododendrons, against a backdrop of heather. No wonder the enthusiastic Taylors fell in love with the place 17 years ago. The house is a rambling grey-and-white manor with gabled windows and a square tower. Guest rooms are individually decorated with family antiques and have wonderful views. Ambitious and highly regarded multi-course dinners (choice at all stages) are served at a fixed hour; a conservatory has recently extended the dining-room.

Nearby Glencoe 8 miles (13 km); Fort William.

Kentallen of Appin, Argyll
PA38 4BX
Tel (063174) 227 **Fax** 342
Location on shorefront off A828, 17 miles (27 km) SW of Fort William; with large grounds and car parking
Food & drink breakfast, lunch, tea, dinner; residential and restaurant licence
Prices DB&B £43.50-£90; lunch £7.50, dinner £32.50
Rooms 11 double, 9 with bath, 2 with shower; one single with shower, one family room with bath; all have radio, phone
Facilities dining-room and conservatory, 3 sitting-rooms, bar, billiards room; tennis
Credit cards MC, V
Children accepted
Disabled no special facilities
Pets dogs welcome except in restaurant **Closed** 3 weeks Jan
Proprietors Robert and Jane Taylor

Tayside

Country hotel, Cleish

Nivingston House

We have good reports of this large, amiable country house, once a restaurant with rooms, but now a full-scale hotel with a calm atmosphere, friendly service (even when confronted by patience-testing children), freshly prepared food and exemplary house-keeping. Decoration is largely in the hands of Laura Ashley and friends, except in the more formal dining-room.

Nearby Loch Leven, 3 miles (5 km); Edinburgh within reach.

Cleish, Kinross-shire, Tayside KY13 7LS
Tel (0577) 850216 **Fax** 850238
Location 4.5 miles (7 km) SW off Kinross, off B9097 (2 miles W of M90, junction 5); in 12 acres of landscaped gardens with ample car parking
Food & drink full breakfast, lunch, dinner; full licence
Prices B&B £40-£70; DB&B £54-£74; weekend breaks
Rooms 13 double, 2 single and 2 family rooms, all with bath or shower; all rooms have central heating, colour TV, phone, radio/alarm, tea/coffee kit, hairdrier
Facilities 2 sitting-rooms, bar; pitch and putt, croquet
Credit cards AE, MC, V
Children welcome
Disabled access easy, 6 ground-floor bedrooms
Pets welcome in bedrooms but must not be left unattended
Closed first 2 weeks in Jan
Proprietor Allan Deeson

Farm guest-house, Pitlochry

Auchnahyle Farmhouse

This is a small, secluded 18thC farmhouse within walking distance of the popular tourist town of Pitlochry where the How-mans have been taking guests since 1982. Game and sheep are reared on the farm and there are several family pets. Rooms in the main house are simple and comfortable – there is also a stone cottage across the courtyard suitable for families. Penny Howman's satisfying four-course dinners are served by candle-light – you are welcome to take your own wine.

Nearby Falls of Tummel, Pass of Killiecrankie; Blair Castle.

Pitlochry, Perthshire, Tayside PH16 5JA
Tel (0796) 472318 **Fax** 473657
Location on E edge of town, towards Moulin; in large gardens with ample car parking
Food & drink full breakfast, picnic lunch, dinner; no licence
Prices B&B £28-£30; dinner £18.50
Rooms 3 double, all with bath; family cottage available; all rooms have central heating, tea/coffee kit, TV
Facilities sitting-room with TV
Credit cards MC, V
Children welcome over 12
Disabled access good – one ground-floor bedroom
Pets well-behaved dogs welcome
Closed Christmas and New Year
Proprietors Alastair and Penny Howman

Inner Hebrides

Argyll Hotel

Fiona Menzies fell in love with the tiny remote island of Iona as a child and was able to take over the Argyll Hotel in 1977 – her husband runs the local pottery. The 19thC inn gained a dining-room wing in 1932 and a bedroom extension in 1971, completing the hotel as it is today. Set right on the shores of the island – its lawn runs down to the rocks and sand – the public rooms all have superb views over the Sound of Iona to Mull. Food is freshly prepared and satisfying; there is no choice, except that a vegetarian main course is always offered. Cars are left on Mull.
Nearby Beaches; abbey, Heritage Centre; Fingal's cave.

Isle of Iona, Argyll PA76 6SJ
Tel (06817) 334
Location in village street, facing Sound of Iona; reached by ferry from Mull
Food & drink breakfast, lunch, tea, dinner; residential and restaurant licence
Prices B&B £28.50-£38.50; lunch £3-£8, dinner £16.50
Rooms 7 double, 5 with bath; 10 single, 3 with bath; 2 family rooms with bath; all have tea/coffee kit, electric blankets
Facilities dining-room, 2 sitting-rooms, sun lounge
Credit cards MC, V **Children** welcome, and catered for
Disabled access difficult
Pets accepted, but not in restaurant
Closed mid-Oct to Easter
Proprietor Fiona Menzies

Ardfenaig House

Originally the Duke of Argyll's factor's house, Ardfenaig was expanded as a shooting lodge before its conversion into a hotel, in the hands of the Davidsons since 1991. The house stands at the head of a narrow sea-loch, its lawns stretching down towards the water and in the other direction leading off into splendid moorland – great for walkers. Furnishings are traditional, comfortable, without pretensions; the lighter loch-view rooms naturally have an edge. Jane cooks satisfying dinners making the best of local produce – salmon and venison, as well as home-grown vegetables. Smoking is permitted not at all in the bedrooms or dining-room, elsewhere with the consent of other guests.
Nearby walking, beaches; islands of Iona and Staffa.

By Bunessan, Isle of Mull, Argyll PA67 6DX
Tel & fax (06817) 210
Location on A849 between Bunessan and Fionnphort; with 15-acre grounds and ample car parking
Food & drink breakfast, dinner; residential and restaurant licence
Prices DB&B £78; reductions for 3 nights or more
Rooms 4 double (2 twin), one single, all with bath; all rooms have central heating
Facilities dining-room, 2 sitting-rooms; croquet
Credit cards MC, V
Children welcome, provided small children in bed by 7pm
Disabled access easy but no ground-floor bedrooms
Pets welcome but not in house
Closed Nov to Mar
Proprietors Malcolm and Jane Davidson

Inner Hebrides

Country guest-house, Mull

Tiroran House

Tiroran House is a converted shooting-lodge, backed by hills and pine forests and overlooking lawns, woodland and a loch. It is now very much a home – from the moment you arrive, there is almost nothing to indicate that you are in a hotel; no room numbers, no lift, no contrived interior decoration.

Particularly appealing are the two comfortable sitting-rooms, furnished mainly with antiques and filled with books, ornaments and family photographs; bedrooms are also comfortable and welcoming – three are in a nearby annexe. The small dining-room has a delightful conservatory extension with lovely views towards the loch. The garden and estate provide many of the ingredients for Mrs Blockey's delicious and imaginatively pre-pared meals. The elegant candlelit dinners offer a choice at beginning and end, and packed lunches are 'wonderful'. There is a wide-ranging, reasonably priced wine-list.

Fuelled by a generous breakfast, guests are encouraged to get out and about – and there is plenty of scope.
Nearby Loch Scridain; Ben More, 3,169 ft (966 m); islands of Iona and Staffa.

Isle of Mull, Argyll, Highland PA69 6ES
Tel (06815) 232
Location 23 miles (37 km) W of Craignure ferry, on W side of island, one mile (1.5 km) off B8035; in 40-acre grounds with ample car parking
Food & drink full breakfast, light or packed lunch, dinner; residential and restaurant licence
Prices DB&B £85-£125; reductions for 3 nights or more
Rooms 8 double, one single; all with bath; all rooms have central heating, tea/coffee kit, radio, hairdrier
Facilities dining-room, 2 sitting-rooms, games room; croquet
Credit cards not accepted
Children welcome over 10
Disabled access possible; one ground-floor bedroom
Pets dogs accepted by arrangement, but not allowed in public rooms
Closed early Oct to mid-May
Proprietors Sue and Robin Blockey

Inner Hebrides

Town hotel, Mull

The Tobermory Hotel

This long-established guest-house was relaunched as a hotel in 1985, and the Suttons arrived in 1990. Bedrooms and public rooms alike are light and bright; the furnishings are modern, but chosen with care to make the house pretty as well as comfortable. There is a proper emphasis on quality ingredients in the cooking (seafood is the speciality).

Nearby walking, golf; beaches.

53 Main Street, Tobermory, Isle of Mull, Argyll, Strathclyde PA75 6NT
Tel (0688) 2091 **Fax** 2140
Location on waterfront; ample car parking on street and quayside
Food & drink full breakfast, dinner; residential and restaurant licence
Prices DB&B £41-£51; weekly rates; reductions for children sharing parents' room; motorists' packages, spring/autumn breaks
Rooms 11 double, 3 with bath, 3 with shower; 4 single, one with shower; 2 family rooms with bath; all rooms have tea/coffee kit
Facilities 2 sitting-rooms (one with TV), dining-room
Credit cards MC, V
Children welcome
Disabled access easy to public rooms and 2 ground-floor bedrooms
Pets dogs welcome but not in public rooms
Closed never
Proprietors Kay and Martin Sutton

Inn, Skye

Ardvasar Hotel

The Fowlers' double act – Bill in the kitchen, Gretta managing the front of house – has proved its worth since they took over this 18thC coaching inn several years ago. With the able assistance of local ladies, they have created a warm and welcoming ambience and gained a reputation for serving good food. The house is solid and low-built, simply and cosily furnished; a log fire blazes in the sitting-room, which (like the front bedrooms) gives splendid views across the Sound of Sleat.

Nearby Clan Donald Centre, l mile (1.5 km).

Ardvasar, Sleat, Isle of Skye, Highland, IV45 8RS
Tel (04714) 223
Location in tiny village, 0.5 miles (one km) SW of Armadale ferry; on roadside, with parking for 30 cars
Food & drink breakfast bar, lunch and supper, fixed-menu dinner; bar meals; full licence
Prices B&B £29-£32; dinner from £18.50; 3-day packages available
Rooms 9 double, 7 with bath, 2 with shower; one single with shower; all rooms have tea/coffee kit
Facilities sitting-room, TV room, two bars, dining- room
Credit cards MC, V
Children welcome
Disabled access easy to public rooms but not to bedrooms
Pets well-behaved dogs accepted but not allowed in public rooms
Closed Nov to Mar
Proprietors Bill and Gretta Fowler

Inner Hebrides

Kinloch Lodge

This white-painted stone house, in an isolated position at the southern extremity of the Isle of Skye, was built as a farmhouse around 1700 and subsequently became a shooting lodge. But it escaped the baronial treatment handed out to many such houses – 'thank goodness,' says Lady Macdonald, whose style is modern interior-designer rather than dark panelling and tartan.

The Macdonalds have been running the house as a hotel and restaurant for many years; it has always had that easy-going private-house air, but it is now also their home – though they have separate quarters at one side of the house. The guests' sitting-rooms are comfortably done out in stylishly muted colours, the dining-room more elegant, with sparkling crystal and silver on polished tables at dinner. All but three of the bedrooms are undeniably on the small side, but this does not deter fans, who go here for an unaffectedly warm welcome and for the excellent food – four courses with a choice at each stage, cooked by Lady M along with Peter Macpherson. Desserts are particularly notable.

Nearby Clan Donald Centre, 6 miles (10 km).

Sleat, Isle of Skye, Highland IV43 8QY
Tel (04713) 214 **Fax** 277
Location 6 miles (10 km) S of Broadford, one mile (1.5 km) off A851; in 60-acre grounds with ample car parking
Food & drink full breakfast, lunch by arrangement, dinner; residential and restaurant licence
Prices B&B £40-£85; dinner £35
Rooms 10 double, 8 with bath; all rooms have central heating, tea/coffee kit, hairdrier
Facilities 2 sitting-rooms, dining-room; fishing
Credit cards MC, V
Children welcome if well behaved; special meals provided for those under 8
Disabled access reasonable – one ground-floor bedroom
Pets dogs accepted by arrangement but not allowed in public rooms
Proprietors Lord & Lady Macdonald

Inner Hebrides

Viewfield House

This formidable Victorian country mansion, as the name suggests, has some fine views from its elevated position. The need for costly repairs to the roof prompted Evelyn Macdonald, Hugh's grandmother, to open Viewfield to guests. The delight of it is that the distinctive character of the house was preserved; and though you will not lack for comfort or service, a stay here is likely to be a novel experience. The rooms are original, right down to the wallpaper (though all but a couple now have *en suite* bathrooms in the former dressing-rooms); there is a classic Victorian parlour and a grand dining-room.
Nearby Trotternish peninsula.

Portree, Isle of Skye, Highland IV51 9EU
Tel (0478) 612217 **Fax** 613517
Location on outskirts of town, 10 minutes walk S of centre
Food & drink full breakfast, packed lunch, dinner
Prices B&B £25-£35; DB&B £40-£50; weekly reduction
Rooms 8 double, 7 with bath; 2 single, one with bath; one family room; all rooms have central heating, tea/coffee kit
Facilities sitting-room, dining-room, TV room
Credit cards MC, V
Children welcome
Disabled access difficult
Pets welcome but not allowed in public rooms **Closed** Nov to Apr **Proprietors** Mr and Mrs Hugh Macdonald

Isle of Colonsay Hotel

Colonsay is not one of the most remote Scottish isles, but it is nevertheless a two- to three-hour steamer trip from Oban. The island's old inn is a warmly civilized place serving sophisticated fixed meals based on fresh ingredients – and the Byrnes, who have been here since 1978, are still finding ways to improve this focus of island life.
Nearby Colonsay House gardens; walking, wildlife, fishing, golf.

Scalasaig, Isle of Colonsay, Argyll, Strathclyde PA61 7YP
Tel (09512) 316 **Fax** 353
Location on E coast of island; in large gardens with car parking; car can be left at Oban
Food & drink breakfast, bar/packed lunch, high tea, dinner or bar supper; full licence
Prices DB&B £45-£70; reductions for one week or more and for children sharing parents' room
Rooms 6 double, all with shower; 3 single; 2 family rooms both with bath and shower; all rooms have central heating, tea/coffee kit; phone, TV
Facilities sitting-room, sun room, 2 bars; sea and loch fishing, golf, bicycles, sailing
Credit cards AE, DC, MC, V
Children welcome; high tea provided
Disabled access good, some ground-floor rooms
Pets dogs welcome if well behaved, but not allowed in public rooms
Closed Nov to Feb except 2 weeks at New Year
Proprietors Kevin and Christa Byrne

SCOTLAND

Highland

Inn, Arisaig

Arisaig

Not to be confused with the much grander Arisaig House nearby, this lochside inn has been meeting the needs of travellers on the road to the isles for almost 200 years. The Stewarts have given it a new lease of life. It is their hospitality that is at the heart of the hotel's appeal, but they have also invested heavily in recent improvements. Janice cooks; her dinners have a pronounced local emphasis – particularly strong on fish and seafood, which comes in by boat.

Nearby Mallaig (for ferries to Skye); white sands of Morar.

Arisaig, Inverness-shire PH39 4NH
Tel (06875) 210 **Fax** 310
Location 10 miles (16 km) S of Mallaig on A830, on edge of village; with ample car parking
Food & drink breakfast, bar lunch, dinner; full licence
Prices B&B £24-£40; dinner £11-£22
Rooms 9 double, 5 with bath; 4 family rooms, one with bath; 2 single with adjoining bath;
all rooms have radio, tea/coffee kit, phone, heater
Facilities 2 bars, sitting-room, TV area
Credit cards MC, V
Children welcome; cots and baby-listening
Disabled access easy only to public rooms
Pets dogs accepted, but not allowed in public rooms
Closed Nov to Mar
Proprietors George, Janice and Shona Stewart

Country hotel, Fort William

The Factor's House

A factor is the manager of a Scottish estate, and the estate in question here is that of the famous Inverlochy Castle hotel. This much more modest establishment is run by the son of the Inverlochy's Grete Hobbs. The turn-of-the-century house has been smartly modernized and extended, and is furnished in an informal mix of antique and modern styles, with Peter Hobbs's interest in expeditions reflected in the ornaments. Bedrooms are well-equipped, if small, and have views of Ben Nevis or the surrounding hills. A limited set-choice menu is offered, ranging from traditionally Scottish to mildly experimental in style.

Nearby Ben Nevis, the Great Glen.

Torlundy, Fort William, Inverness-shire, Highland PH33 6SN
Tel (0397) 705767 **Fax** 702953
Location 3.5 miles (5.5 km) NE of Fort William on A82; parking for 25 cars
Food & drink full breakfast, dinner; residential licence
Prices B&B £35-£50; DB&B £50-£65
Rooms 7 double, 5 with bath,
2 with shower; all rooms have central heating, colour TV, phone
Facilities 2 sitting-rooms
Credit cards AE, MC, V
Children welcome over 6
Disabled access easy – one ground-floor bedroom
Pets not accepted
Closed Nov to mid-Mar
Proprietor Peter Hobbs

194

Highland

Ceilidh Place

A 'ceilidh' (pronounced kaylee) is a sort of impromptu gathering – an evening of music, song, dance and story-telling; and the name gives a clue to the vitality of the Urquharts' 'hotel'. It started as a coffee shop in a cottage, spread into adjacent cottages to provide bedrooms, and then into other 'clubhouse' buildings nearby, where there is more basic accommodation as well as a bookshop, gallery and auditorium, and by now possibly several other things too. The essentials are all there – simple but comfortable rooms with plenty of pictures, wholesome, largely vegetarian and fish cooking, and 'no telly, no teasmaids'.

Nearby mountains; walks.

West Argyle Street, Ullapool, Wester Ross, Highland IV26 2TY
Tel (0854) 612103 **Fax** 612886
Location in middle of village; 0.5-acre garden with parking for 25 cars
Food & drink breakfast, lunch, dinner; full licence
Prices B&B £20-£45; dinner from £16; reductions for 5 nights or more
Rooms 10 double, 8 with bath; 3 single, 2 with bath; 11 family rooms (bunk beds); all rooms have central heating
Facilities sitting-room, bar, coffee shop, dining-room
Credit cards AE, DC, MC, V
Children welcome
Disabled access difficult
Pets welcome, but not in public rooms
Closed 2 weeks mid-Jan
Proprietors Jean and Robert Urquhart

Knockie Lodge

The Milwards must have had vision to see the potential in this 200-year-old shooting-lodge – then a distinctly lacklustre hotel – which they left London to take over in 1983. In less than a year they had transformed it, creating the kind of welcoming atmosphere that its romantic setting demands, and improvements continue in the same vein. Dinner is a satisfactory set meal of five 'simple but imaginative' dishes.

Nearby Loch Ness.

Whitebridge, Inverness, Highland IV1 2UP
Tel (0456) 486276 **Fax** 486389
Location 8 miles (13 km) NE of Fort Augustus on B862; in open country with ample car parking
Food & drink breakfast, bar lunch, dinner; residential licence
Prices DB&B £65-£95
Rooms 8 double, all with bath, 4 also with shower; 2 single, both with bath; all rooms have central heating
Facilities sitting-room with bar, dining-room, billiard-room; fishing
Credit cards AE, DC, MC, V
Children welcome over 10
Disabled access difficult
Pets dogs accepted, but not allowed in public rooms
Closed Nov to Apr
Proprietors Mr and Mrs Ian Milward

Highland

Bunchrew House

If you have one of the bedrooms with a sea view, you might be lucky enough to see an osprey swooping for salmon in the Beauly Firth, which laps at the garden wall of this pink sandstone turreted mansion. The setting is not the only attraction; the Dykes are said to be cheery hosts who take great pride in their 17thC home. Family photos and log fires liven up the dark wood panelled bar and sitting-room. Dinner is a candlelit affair consisting of traditional dishes – Scottish beef, venison, game, seafood – served in the rather formal dining-room. Bedrooms are large and comfortable.

Nearby fishing, shooting, golf; Cawdor Castle, 10 miles (16 km).

Bunchrew, Inverness IV3 6TA
Tel (0463) 234917 **Fax** 710620
Location in countryside, one mile (1.5 km) W of Inverness on A862; with gardens and ample car parking
Food & drink breakfast, lunch, dinner, snacks; full licence
Prices B&B £38-£78; lunch £10, dinner £20
Rooms 11 double, one family room, all with bath; all rooms have central heating, phone, hairdrier, TV, minibar
Facilities drawing room, bar; salmon fishing
Credit cards AE, MC, V
Children welcome; baby-sitting available
Pets accepted by arrangement
Disabled access easy
Closed never
Proprietors Stewart and Lesley Dykes

Ard-na-Coille

Nancy Ferrier and Barry Cottam took over this 1920s millionaire's shooting lodge, in an elevated position on the flank of Strathspey, early in 1988. They are refugees from academic life, intent upon preserving the welcoming character of the place while improving it. Pictures and books still abound; rooms are still mainly antique-furnished. Food is 'Modern British'.

Nearby Ruthven Barracks, golf, fishing; Cairngorm mountains.

Kingussie Road, Newtonmore, Inverness- shire, Highland PH20 1AY
Tel (0540) 673214
Location on N edge of town, off A86; in 2-acre grounds with ample car parking
Food & drink full breakfast, dinner; restaurant and residential licence
Prices B&B £40-£50; DB&B £47.50-£75; reductions for children under 12 sharing parents' room; winter breaks
Rooms 6 double, one single, all with bath and/or shower; all rooms have central heating, phone
Facilities 2 sitting-rooms, dining-room
Credit cards MC, V
Children very welcome if well behaved
Disabled access difficult
Pets dogs accepted by prior arrangement, but not allowed in public rooms
Proprietors Nancy Ferrier and Barry Cottam

Highland

Country hotel, Drumnadrochit

Polmaily House

Nick Parsons travelled the world for Reuters before coming to Polmaily House in 1982, while Alison honed her cooking skills by catering for embassy dinners and other formal functions. They run their tall, completely secluded Edwardian-style house almost as if it was a private home, but there is a dining-room open to non-residents. Alison's cooking, in the modern British style and making the most of highland seafood and game supplies, has won considerable acclaim, and Nick takes credit for assembling an interesting cellar. The public rooms are comfortably lived-in – particularly the sitting-room, where pre-dinner drinks are served in front of an open fire.

Nearby Urquhart Castle, 2.5 miles (4 km); Loch Ness.

Drumnadrochit, Inverness-shire, Highland, IV3 6XT
Tel (0456) 450343 **Fax** 450813
Location 2 miles (3 km) W of Drumnadrochit on A831; with ample car parking
Food & drink breakfast, dinner; residential and restaurant licence
Prices B&B £25-£50; dinner from £12; children sharing parents' room free; reductions for 3 nights or more half-board
Rooms 4 double, 2 twin, 1 family, all with bath; 2 single; all rooms have central heating, radio, phone
Facilities 2 sitting-rooms, bar, restaurant; tennis, swimming-pool, croquet
Credit cards MC, V
Children welcome
Disabled access to dining-room good, but not to bedrooms
Pets not accepted
Closed never
Proprietors Alison and Nick Parsons

Highland

Summer Isles

Mark and Geraldine Irvine run this very remote, cottagey hotel which has belonged to the family since the 1960s. The decorations and furnishings remain simple but satisfactory, the food wholesome and interesting (a different five-course set dinner is served each night), the views across Loch Broom and the Summer Isles themselves riveting. The emphasis is on eating well, sleeping well and relaxing in beautiful surroundings – 'there is a marvellous amount of nothing to do'.

Nearby walking, beaches, boat cruises.

Achiltibuie, by Ullapool, Ross-shire, Highland IV26 2YG
Tel (085482) 282
Location close to village post office; car parking
Food & drink full breakfast, lunch, dinner; full licence
Prices B&B £31-£59; dinner £30; reductions for 6 nights or more
Rooms 12 double, 9 with bath, one with shower; one single; one family room with bath; all rooms have central heating
Facilities dining-room, sitting-room, 2 bars, sun room; fishing
Credit cards not accepted
Children welcome over 8
Pets dogs allowed, but not in dining- or sitting-rooms
Closed mid-Oct to Easter
Proprietors Mark and Geraldine Irvine

Osprey

This modest hotel without any grounds stands on a corner of the village street at a distance from the main road to Aviemore, so it is not too noisy. The sitting-room is small but welcoming, the bedrooms clean and cosy, decorated with light floral wallpapers and furnished in various styles. The Burrows took over in October 1990; like so many 'amateur' hoteliers in these pages, they have succeeded in offering a warm informal welcome combined with excellent home-cooked meals – using fresh local produce and including vegetarian alternatives – served in the tiny dining-room.

Nearby Highland Folk Museum (in Kingussie).

Ruthven Road, Kingussie, Inverness-shire, Highland PH21 1EN
Tel (0540) 661510
Location in middle of village on A86; herb garden and parking for 10 cars
Food & drink breakfast, packed lunch, dinner; residential and restaurant licence
Prices B&B £22-£36; DB&B £39-£54
Rooms 7 double, one with bath, 6 with shower; one single; all have central heating
Facilities sitting-room, TV room, dining-room
Credit cards MC, V
Children welcome **Disabled** wheelchair access difficult; one ground-floor room **Pets** dogs accepted by arrangement
Closed first 2 weeks Nov
Proprietor Robert and Aileen Burrow

Highland

Town hotel, Nairn

Clifton

It is not unusual to come upon small hotels with a theatrical touch, but the Clifton is in a different league; it actually is a theatre, staging plays and recitals in the dining-room during the winter months, to the delight of locals and visitors alike. The hotel has been run by Gordon Macintyre for 40 years and his hotel-keeping act is by now thoroughly polished.

The Victorian house is richly furnished to ensure not only the comfort but also the amusement of guests; paintings fill the walls (which are themselves works of art), flowers fill antique vases, books fill shelves, knick-knacks fill every other nook and cranny, and a welcoming calm fills the air. Whatever your mood, one of the several public rooms should suit. The bedrooms are individually decorated and furnished in what Gordon (with characteristic modesty and humour) calls 'a mixture of good antiques and painted junk'.

The cooking, supervised by Mr Macintyre, imposes French provincial techniques on the best local produce – particularly seafood, upon which lunch in the smaller Green Room is largely based – with huge success, and there is a fine, long wine-list. Typically, breakfast is served without time limit.

Nearby Cawdor Castle, 5 miles (8 km); Brodie Castle, 5 miles (8 km); Fort George, 8 miles (13 km); Inverness within reach

Nairn, Highland IV12 4HW
Tel (0667) 53119 **Fax** 52836
Location on sea-front in middle of town, close to A96; with own parking
Food & drink full breakfast, lunch, dinner; full licence
Prices B&B £44-£54; dinner £17-£25
Rooms 8 double, 4 single, all with bath; all rooms have heating
Facilities 2 sitting-rooms,

TV room, 2 dining-rooms
Credit cards AE, DC, MC, V
Children welcome, but no special facilities
Disabled access difficult – no ground-floor bedrooms
Pets well behaved dogs accepted but not allowed in restaurant
Closed Dec to early Feb
Proprietor J Gordon Macintyre

Highland

Country hotel, Ullapool

Altnaharrie Inn

There are good hotels in many unlikely-sounding places in Britain, but this one takes first prize. Ullapool itself is pretty remote, but to get to Altnaharrie you have to make a 10-minute crossing of Loch Broom in the inn's private ferry – or tackle it from Little Loch Broom and hike 2 miles over the mountains.

Such complete seclusion has a powerful appeal in itself; at least to some, there can hardly be a better way to appreciate the wild grandeur of this north-western extremity of the British mainland than to explore it on foot from this remote spot. But the really remarkable thing about staying here is that it involves no compromises whatever. The inn is as welcoming a house as you will find anywhere; what is more, the food is widely acknowledged to be stunningly good.

Gunn does the cooking and brings to it the same originality she employs in painting and weaving. Fresh local ingredients – including superb seafood and game in season – form the basis of her set menus, which defy classification but have achieved wide acclaim. There are no better restaurants in the Highlands, and few in the whole of Britain.

The centuries-old white-painted stone house, only a stone's throw from the loch, is warmly and prettily decorated with woven wall-hangings, Middle Eastern rugs and a sprinkling of antiques. Note that prices are among the highest in these pages.

Nearby walking, birdwatching; Loch Broom Highland Museum, Ullapool; Inverewe gardens.

Ullapool, Highland IV26 2SS
Tel (085483) 230
Location SW of Ullapool across Loch Broom – reached by private launch; private car park in Ullapool
Food & drink full breakfast, light lunch (residents only), dinner; residential and restaurant licence
Prices DB&B £100-£140
Rooms 8 double, 7 with bath, one with shower

Facilities 2 sitting-rooms, dining-room
Credit cards not accepted
Children welcome if well behaved, but not suitable for small children
Disabled access difficult
Pets dogs may be accepted by prior arrangement
Closed part of winter
Proprietors Fred Brown and Gunn Eriksen

Outer Hebrides

Country guest-house, Harris

Scarista House

Harris has little in the way of hotels, but Scarista would stand out even among the country houses of the Cotswolds. It is not uncommon to discover that several of the guests at Scarista have re-arranged their holiday itineraries to be sure of a stay.

The converted Georgian manse stands alone on a windswept slope overlooking a wide stretch of tidal sands on Harris's western shore. The decoration is quite formal, with antiques throughout, but the atmosphere is relaxed, and by the open peat fires, conversation replaces television. The bedrooms, all with private bathrooms, have selected teas, fresh coffee, and home-made biscuits. Five of them are in a new single-storey building; the three in the house itself are non-smoking.

The Callaghans quit banking and antiques to take over at the beginning of 1990 and have since refurbished the public areas and most of the bedrooms. They aim to be welcoming and efficient, but never intrusive, and to preserve that precious private home atmosphere.

One of Scarista's greatest attractions, particularly rewarding after a long walk over the sands, is the meals. The imaginatively prepared fresh local and garden produce and an impressive wine list ensure a memorable dinner in the candle-lit dining-room.

Nearby swimming, walking, bird-watching, diving, boat trips.

Harris, Western Isles
PA85 3HX
Tel (0859) 550238 **Fax** 550277
Location 15 miles (24 km) SW of Tarbert on A859, overlooking sea; in 2-acre garden, with ample car parking
Food & drink full breakfast, packed/snack lunch, dinner; residential licence
Prices B&B £42-£57; dinner £25.00

Rooms 8 double, all with bath; all rooms have central heating, tea/coffee kit
Facilities library, sitting-room, dining-room
Credit cards not accepted
Children welcome over 8
Disabled access easy, but no ground-floor toilets
Pets welcome if well behaved
Closed mid-Oct to mid-Apr
Proprietors Ian and Jane Callaghan

Outer Hebrides/Shetland

Country guest-house, Lewis

Baile-na-Cille

Discovered in a ruinous state by the Gollins, this beautifully set 18thC manse has been lovingly restored, and the adjacent stables converted into light, pretty rooms. Many discarded antiques were restored and given new life in this friendly, relaxed guest-house. The home-cooked meals, which include freshly baked bread, are served around communal tables in a lofty dining-room. It is essential to book well ahead.

Nearby walking, climbing, birdwatching, sailing, fishing.

Timsgarry, Uig, Isle of Lewis, Outer Hebrides PA86 9JD
Tel (085175) 242 **Fax** 241
Location 32 miles (51 km) W of Stornaway, close to end of B8011, in countryside, with ample car parking
Food & drink full breakfast, dinner, packed lunch; residential licence
Prices B&B £22-£32; dinner £20; children in bunk bed £12 inc. supper
Rooms 9 double, 7 with bath; 3 single; 2 family rooms; all rooms have storage heater or radiator
Facilities 3 sitting-rooms, dining-room, TV room; dinghy, wind-surfing, boat trips
Credit cards not accepted
Children welcome; climbing frames/playroom
Disabled unsuitable
Pets welcome
Closed Nov to late Mar
Proprietors Richard and Joanna Gollin

Country guest-house, Shetland

Burrastow House

If remoteness appeals, Burrastow makes the ideal goal – a calm solid stone house, romantically isolated on a rocky shore, reached down a long single-track road. Plans are afoot to build an extension in place of the old barn, but we are confident that the three new rooms, restaurant and conservatory will be in keeping with the honest character and simple style of the place. Bo Simmons cooks enthusiastically.

Nearby walking, swimming, boating, bird-watching, fishing.

Walls, Shetland Islands ZE2 9PD
Tel (059571) 307
Location 3 miles (5 km) W of Walls; in spacious grounds with ample car park
Food & drink breakfast, dinner, high tea; residential and restaurant licence
Prices DB&B £56-£61; reduction for 4 nights or more; spring weekend breaks; big reductions for children
Rooms one double, one family suite of 2 rooms with lobby and bath; all rooms have central heating, hairdrier, tea/coffee kit; TV on request
Facilities dining-room, 2 sitting-rooms; dinghy, fishing
Credit cards not accepted
Children welcome
Disabled access easy to barn extension
Pets dogs accepted, but not in public rooms
Closed Nov to Mar except Christmas
Proprietor Bo Simmons

Kerry

Doyle's Seafood Restaurant

The visitor's book of this delightful small hotel in the middle of a quaint fishing village on the Dingle Peninsula perches on an antique writing-desk in the elegant sitting-room; it drips with superlatives, and rightly so. John and Stella Doyle escaped the Dublin rat-race over two decades ago, moving to this wild and lovely corner of Kerry for John to set up as a fisherman. Soon afterwards, Stella opened the restaurant and John gave up his trawler to help run their increasingly popular seafood bar.

In 1987 the next-door house came on the market and the couple were able to add eight spacious bedrooms and a sitting-room. The bedrooms are all beautifully decorated with floral fabrics, stripped wood furniture and wonderful antiques (Stella is quite a collector). The four back rooms have balconies looking over the tiny garden, and the two downstairs rooms (suitable for disabled guests) open on to it. Fresh flowers and potted plants abound throughout.

The restaurant is as popular and cosmopolitan as ever, and it is easy to see why. The menu is mainly, but not exclusively, fishy, and changes with the seasons.

Nearby Dingle Peninsula, Ring of Kerry (beaches, historical sites, coastal walks).

John St, Dingle, Co Kerry
Tel (066) 51174 **Fax** 51816
Location just off main street of town; with small garden and on-street parking
Food & drink breakfast, lunch, dinner; full licence
Prices B&B IR£31-IR£39; dinner IR£19
Rooms 8 double, all with bath; all rooms have central heating, phone, TV, hairdrier, radio
Facilities dining-room, sitting-room
Credit cards DC, MC, V
Children welcome; babysitting by arrangement
Disabled 2 ground-floor bedrooms
Pets not accepted
Closed mid-Nov to mid-Mar
Proprietors John and Stella Doyle

Kerry

Country hotel, Caragh Lake

Caragh Lodge

A hundred-year-old house furnished with antiques and log fires, a 300-yard lake frontage, nine acres of parkland with a fine planting of rare and sub-tropical shrubs, views of some of Ireland's highest mountains, abundant facilities for relaxation, quick access to the sea and glorious sandy beaches: Caragh Lodge offers a heady combination attractive to a great many holidaymakers. Golf is a favourite pastime, with an excellent local course and four championship courses nearby.

In mid-1989 Caragh Lodge was taken over by Mary Gaunt, an ex-Aer Lingus stewardess who spent her childhood holidays on the far side of the lake. She immediately set about a thorough redecoration of the public rooms, bedrooms and the previously rather drab annexe rooms, and has achieved some impressive results. As a result, the hotel is now a happy combination of elegance and informality. Mary's satisfying cooking – featuring seafood, wild salmon and local lamb – has earned high praise from recent visitors.

Nearby Killarney, 15 miles (24 km); Ring of Kerry.

Caragh Lake, Co Kerry
Tel (066) 69115 **Fax** 69316
Location 22 miles (35 km) NW of Killarney, one mile (1.5 km) off Ring of Kerry road, W of Killorglin; in 9-acre gardens and parkland, with ample car parking
Food & drink full breakfast, dinner; restaurant licence
Prices B&B IR£50-IR£82.50; dinner IR£26.50
Rooms 8 double, 2 family rooms (mainly in annexes); all with bath; all rooms have central heating
Facilities 2 sitting-rooms, dining-room; table tennis, tennis, swimming in lake, fishing, boating, sauna, bicycles **Credit cards** AE, MC, V **Children** welcome
Disabled access easy – some ground-floor bedrooms
Pets not accepted
Closed mid-Oct to Easter
Proprietor Mary Gaunt

Cork

Assolas Country House

This historic, mellow country house, in a fairy-tale setting of award-winning gardens beside a slow-flowing river, has been in the Bourke family since the early years of this century. The familiar story of escalating maintenance costs and dwindling bank balances led to their taking in guests in 1966, and since then they have never looked back. Assolas is still their family home, and the business of sharing it has obviously turned out to be a pleasure.

The house was built around 1590, and had unusual circular extensions added at two corners in Queen Anne's time; beyond the expanses of lawn are mature woods, and then hills and farmland. Inside, the public rooms are richly decorated and elegantly furnished, almost entirely with antiques, and immaculately kept. The bedrooms are notably spacious and many have large luxury bathrooms – the 'circular' rooms at the corners of the house are particularly impressive. Three of the rooms are in a renovated stone building in the courtyard.

The food, prepared by Hazel Bourke, is in what might be called modern Irish style – country cooking of fresh ingredients (many home-grown) with progressive overtones.

Nearby Killarney (Ring of Kerry), Limerick, Blarney.

Kanturk, Co Cork
Tel (029) 50015 **Fax** 50795
Location 12 miles (19 km) W of Mallow, NE of Kanturk, signposted from N72; in extensive gardens with ample car parking
Food & drink full breakfast, light or packed lunch, dinner; full licence
Prices B&B IR£40-IR£70; dinner £26; reductions for children under 12 sharing
Rooms 9 double/family rooms, all with bath and shower; all rooms have central heating, phone
Facilities sitting-room, dining-room; fishing, tennis, boating, croquet
Credit cards AE, DC, MC, V
Children welcome
Disabled access fair
Pets welcome, but must stay in stables
Closed Nov to Mar
Proprietors Bourke family

Cork

Town hotel, Cork

Arbutus Lodge

Arbutus Lodge is a substantial suburban house, well known for its food and for its terraced gardens planted with rare trees and shrubs, including an arbutus tree. Superb shellfish, fish and game are the specialities of the suitably grand restaurant – and there is a top-notch wine list. A reporter confirms that the public rooms have been pleasantly redecorated, and that there have been major improvements to several bedrooms; though those in the main house have more character than the ones in the modern extension.

Nearby Blarney Castle, 6 miles (10 km).

Middle Glanmire Road, Montenotte, Cork, Co Cork
Tel (021) 501237
Location 0.25 miles (0.4 km) NE of middle of Cork; with garden and ample car parking
Food & drink breakfast, lunch, dinner; full licence
Prices B&B IR£34-IR£85; dinner IR£21-IR£25; weekend breaks
Rooms 12 double, all with bath, 4 also with shower; 8 single, 4 with bath, 4 with shower; all rooms have central heating, TV, phone, radio, minibar
Facilities sitting-room, bar, dining-room
Credit cards AE, DC, MC, V
Children welcome if well behaved **Disabled** access difficult – 5 steps at entrance
Pets not accepted
Closed 24 to 30 Dec; restaurant only Sun (limited bar menu for residents)
Proprietors Ryan family

Country house hotel, Mallow

Longueville House

The O'Callaghans' imposing pink Georgian country house is full of beautifully ornate plastered ceilings, elaborately framed ancestral oils and graceful period furniture. But the house is not the stiff place it might be in Britain. Equally important, it does excellent food (particularly local lamb and fish), served in the marvellous Victorian conservatory in summer.

Nearby fishing, walks; Blarney castle, 12 miles (19 km).

Longueville, Mallow, Co Cork
Tel (022) 47156 **Fax** 47459
Location 4 miles (6 km) W of Mallow on Killarney road; on 500-acre wooded estate with ample car parking
Food & drink full breakfast, lunch, dinner; full licence
Prices B&B IR£55-IR£75; dinner IR£25
Rooms 12 double, 4 single, all with bath or shower; all rooms have central heating, TV, radio, phone, hairdrier
Facilities sitting-room, drawing-room, bar, 2 dining-rooms, conference room, billiards, table tennis; fishing
Credit cards AE, DC, MC, V
Children welcome over 10
Disabled access easy to public rooms only
Closed Christmas to 10 Mar
Proprietors the O'Callaghan family

Cork

Country house hotel, Shanagarry

Ballymaloe House

Thirty bedrooms would rule out any normally attractive hotel, but we can not resist this amiable, rambling, creeper-clad house – largely Georgian in appearance but incorporating the remains of a 14thC castle keep – set in rolling green countryside.

The Allens have been farming here for 40 years, opened as a restaurant in 1964, started offering rooms three years later, and since then have added more facilities and more rooms – those in the main house now outnumbered by those in extensions and converted out-buildings. Despite quite elegant and sophisticated furnishings, the Allens have always managed to preserve intact the warmth and naturalness of a much-loved family home. But not all visitors agree: one reporter judged that Ballymaloe was becoming rather commercialized – he was particularly unimpressed by an impersonal reception and by under-trained dining-room staff.

Even that reporter, however, was impressed by the food, created by Myrtle Allen – a self-taught cook whose genius has gained a high international reputation. Classic French and Irish dishes are prepared alongside original dishes, all based on home produce and fish fresh from the local quays. (Sunday dinner is always a buffet.) Just as much care is lavished on breakfast, and the famous children's high tea. More reports welcome.

Nearby Beaches, cliff walks, fishing, golf.

Shanagarry, Midleton, Co Cork
Tel (021) 652531 **Fax** 652021
Location 20 miles (32 km) E of Cork, 2 miles (3 km) E of Cloyne on the Ballycotton road, L35
Food & drink breakfast, lunch, dinner; full licence
Prices B&B IR£55-IR£77; dinner IR£30; reductions for children, bargain breaks Nov to Mar **Rooms** 27 double, 25 with bath, 2 with shower; 3 single, one with bath; one family room; all have central heating, phone
Facilities 3 sitting-rooms, conference/TV room, conservatory, library; tennis, golf, heated outdoor swimming-pool (summer)
Credit cards AE, DC, MC, V
Children welcome; high tea provided **Disabled** access easy; some rooms built for wheelchairs **Pets** tolerated – not in bedrooms/public rooms **Closed** over Christmas
Proprietors I and M Allen

Cork

Country hotel, Innishannon

Innishannon House

Conal O'Sullivan returned to his Irish roots in 1989 when he and his wife Vera moved to this attractive, imposing 18thC house on the banks of the Bandon river. The couple are seasoned hoteliers and travellers, having run hotels all over the world (their last stop the Carribean) but they are particularly excited at this latest challenge.

The hotel has already become a welcoming haven, its comfortable, attractive rooms hung with the O'Sullivans' extensive collection of modern art (including two possible Gauguins in the dining-room). Vera has a great eye for interior design, and has redecorated all the bedrooms with infinite care and flair – number 16 is a cosy attic room with an antique bedspread, number 14 a fascinating circular room with small round windows and a huge curtained bed – and the latest addition to the antiques around the hotel is Winston Churchill's bath.

Conal's enthusiasm for the food and drink he serves is catching. We were treated to one of his bar 'snacks', and if this is anything to go by, dinner in the lovely pink dining-room must be a gastronomic delight. Pre-dinner drinks are served outside in summer, or in the airy lounge, or cosy bar – full of photos of Conal's car rallying days.

Innishannon is not the last word in seclusion or intimacy; there are facilities for conferences and wedding receptions.
Nearby Kinsale, 7 miles (11 km); Cork, 15 miles (24 km).

Innishannon, Cork
Tel (021) 775121 **Fax** 775609
Location on banks of river, near village; with gardens and car parking
Food & drink breakfast, lunch, dinner, snacks
Prices B&B IR£32.50-IR£62.50; dinner from IR£18.50; weekly reductions
Rooms 14 double, all with bath; all rooms have central heating, phone, TV, hairdrier
Facilities dining-room, sitting-room, bar, terrace; fishing, boating
Credit cards AE, DC, MC, V
Children welcome
Disabled no special facilities
Pets accepted in bedrooms only
Closed never
Proprietors Conal and Vera O'Sullivan

Cork

Sea View House

Kathleen O'Sullivan grew up in this white Victorian house a stone's throw from Ballylickey bay. In 1978 she turned it into a successful small hotel. For years she has been planning an extension to give double the number of rooms, and this was finally realised in 1990 – although it would take a sharp-eyed visitor to distinguish the new wing from the old.

The new bedrooms are all similar in style, beautifully decorated in pastel colours and floral fabrics with stunning antique furniture – especially the bed-heads and wardrobes, and matching 3-piece suites, collected or inherited from around the Cork area. The rooms in the old part of the house are more irregular and individual. All front rooms have large bay windows and views of the garden and sea (through the trees). The 'Garden Suite' downstairs is especially adapted for wheelchairs.

There are two sitting-rooms – a cosy front room adjoining the bar and a large family room at the back. The dining-room has also been extended (though many regular guests do not believe it). The menu changes daily, and Kathleen is forever experimenting with new dishes – roast smoked pheasant on the day we visited. The staff, some of whom have worked here since Kathleen set up the hotel, live locally and greet regular guests as old friends.

Nearby Bantry, 6 miles (10 km); Beira Peninsula; Ring of Kerry.

Ballylickey, Bantry, Co Cork
Tel (027) 50073 **Fax** 51555
Location in countryside, just off N71, 3 miles (5 km) N of Bantry; in large grounds with ample car parking
Food & drink breakfast, lunch (Sun only), dinner; full licence
Prices B&B IR£30-IR£50; dinner IR£22; reductions for children sharing, and for stays of 3 or 7 days
Rooms 12 double, 11 with bath, one with shower; 7 family rooms, 5 with bath, 2 with shower; all rooms have central heating, phone, TV, hairdrier
Facilities 2 dining-rooms, sitting-room, TV room, bar
Credit cards AE, MC, V
Children welcome; baby-sitting
Disabled access easy – one ground-floor adapted room
Pets dogs accepted in bedrooms only
Closed Nov to Mar
Proprietor Kathleen O'Sullivan

Tipperary

Country house hotel, Ballinderry

Gurthalougha House

By the time you reach the end of the mile-long drive which twists and turns through the forest on the way to this hotel beside Lough Derg, it is easy to believe you have travelled back to an altogether more peaceful and graceful era.

Michael and Bessie Wilkinson have, since they arrived in 1981, managed to create an atmosphere as civilized and serene as the hotel's setting. The spacious high-ceilinged public rooms have plenty of pictures and antiques, but the search for style has not got in the way of comfort. The long, well-lit sitting-room, with its two open fireplaces and big cosy armchairs, is notably relaxed, while the enormous panelled library has a substantial collection of books about the locality. This restraint continues into the bedrooms, which are spacious and carefully (though fairly sparsely) furnished, with no modern trimmings.

Bessie, who has long experience of the hotel business, looks after the front of house, while Michael does the cooking, producing a smallish *'table d'hôte'* menu each evening, which may include locally-caught pike and smoked eel.

Nearby Birr Castle gardens, 12 miles (19 km); Limerick.

Ballinderry, Nenagh, Co Tipperary
Tel (067) 22080 **Fax** 22154
Location just W of village, 10 miles (16 km) N of Nenagh off L152; in 100- acre woodland on lakeside, with ample car parking
Food & drink full breakfast, dinner, snack (or packed) lunch; wine licence (though other drinks available)
Prices B&B IR£34-IR£40; dinner IR£22; bargain breaks
Rooms 8 double, 6 with bath, 2 with shower; all rooms have central heating, phone
Facilities dining-room, sitting-room, library; rowing-boats, table tennis, croquet, fishing, tennis
Credit cards AE, MC, V
Children accepted, if well behaved; high tea available
Disabled access not easy – 2 sets of steps on ground floor
Pets accepted if well behaved
Closed Christmas, Feb
Proprietors Michael and Bessie Wilkinson

Clare/Laois

Gregans Castle

Peter and Moira Haden have created a hotel that is impeccably civilized throughout, with rich and harmonious colour schemes. Bedrooms range from relatively simple to distinctly sumptuous, with lots of space and fine views of the Burren mountains and Galway bay. Pictures of local flora adorn the walls of the cosy, book-filled sitting-room; arm-chairs, antiques and an open fire-place grace the central hall. The dining-room has been elegantly and subtly extended; the food is adventurous and satisfying.

Nearby The Burren; Cliffs of Moher, 14 miles (22 km).

Ballyvaughan, Co Clare
Tel (065) 77005 **Fax** 77111
Location 3.5 miles (5.5 km of Ballyvaughan, on N67, in open countryside; in large gardens, with ample car parking
Food & drink full breakfast, lunch, dinner; full licence
Prices B&B IR£55- IR£95.50; DB&B IR£86-IR£126; reduced rates for longer stays
Rooms 18 double, all with bath; 4 suites with bath and sitting-room; all rooms have central heating, hairdrier
Facilities 2 sitting-rooms (one with TV), bar, dining- room
Credit cards MC, V
Children accepted
Disabled access easy – 7 ground-floor rooms
Pets not accepted
Closed Nov to Feb
Proprietors Peter, Moira and Simon-Peter Haden

Roundwood House

It is now more than a decade since ex-IBM analyst Frank Kennan and his wife Rosemarie took over this perfectly proportioned Palladian mansion, set in acres of lime, beech and chestnut woodland. They have wholeheartedly continued the work of the Irish Georgian Society, who rescued the house from near-ruin in the 1970s. All the Georgian trappings remain – bold paintwork, shutters instead of curtains, rugs instead of fitted carpets, and emphatically no TV. The Kennans believe in their guests mixing – either around the dining-room table during Rosemarie's plentiful four-course meals, or over coffee and drinks by the open fire in the drawing room. Children welcome (the Kennans have six).

Nearby walking, horse-riding, fishing; Slieve Bloom mountains.

Mountrath, Co Laois
Tel (0502) 32120 **Fax** 32711
Location in countryside, 3 miles (5 km) N of Mountrath on Kinnitty road; with gardens and ample car parking
Food & drink full breakfast, dinner, lunch on Sunday only; wine licence
Prices B&B IR£32-IR£38; dinner IR£19; Sunday lunch IR£12
Rooms 6 double (2 twin), 2 family rooms, all with bath; all rooms have central heating
Facilities sitting-room, study, dining-room, hall; croquet
Credit Cards AE, DC, MC, V
Children very welcome
Pets accepted by arrangement
Disabled not suitable
Closed Christmas Day
Proprietors Frank and Rosemarie Kennan

Connemara

Country guest-house, Moyard

Crocnaraw

A long, low, white-painted Georgian building on a small hilltop, Crocnaraw has won prizes for its lush, well-tended gardens sloping down to the main coast road; nevertheless it is the simple, elegant modernity of the interior that is its most striking feature. Plain white walls, bright rugs and stylish modern furniture predominate – the large light drawing-room on the corner of the house is almost austere. The same can hardly be said of the food, which is adventurous and often includes local seafood, and vegetables and fruit from the garden.

Nearby Kylemore Abbey, 5 miles (8 km); Joyce Country.

Moyard, Connemara, Co Galway
Tel (095) 41068
Location 6 miles (10 km) N of Clifden, on shores of Ballinakill Bay; in 20-acre grounds, with ample car parking
Food & drink full breakfast, lunch, dinner; full licence
Prices B&B IR£25-IR£40; dinner IR£20; reduced DB&B rates for 3 or 7 nights
Rooms 6 double with bath, one also with shower; 2 single; all rooms have central heating
Facilities 2 sitting-rooms, dining-room; fishing, riding and golf nearby
Credit cards AE, DC, MC, V
Children accepted by arrangement
Disabled access easy to one ground-floor bedroom
Pets dogs welcome except in dining-room
Closed Nov to Apr
Proprietor Lucy Fretwell

Country house hotel, Oughterard

Currarevagh House

This solid country house on the quiet, leafy shores of Lough Corrib has been in the Hodgson family for five generations and its sense of traditional styles and standards meticulously preserved is quite overpowering. Many of the guests come back again and again for the fishing on the lough and, not surprisingly, fish often crops up on the simple but carefully chosen menus. Afternoon tea in the airy, spacious sitting-room is quite a ritual, as are the 'Edwardian' breakfasts. Rooms vary but all are spotless.

Nearby Connemara; Joyce Country; Aran Islands; The Burren.

Oughterard, Connemara, Co. Galway
Tel (091) 82312 **Fax** 82731
Location 4 miles (6 km) NW of Oughterard; in 150-acre woodlands beside Lough Corrib, with ample car parking
Food & drink breakfast, picnic-lunch, tea, dinner; licence
Prices B&B IR£45-IR£60; dinner IR£20; reductions for 3 nights or more
Rooms 12 double, 10 with bath, 2 with shower; 2 single, one with bath; one family room, with bath
Facilities 3 sitting-rooms (one with TV), bar, dining-room; tennis, boats, croquet, fishing
Credit cards not accepted
Children accepted
Disabled not ideal
Pets accepted **Closed** Nov to Mar **Proprietors** Harry and June Hodgson

Connemara

Country house hotel, Cashel

Cashel House

Despite its size, this immaculate white-painted Victorian establishment, set in luxuriant and exotic gardens on the southern finger of Connemara, has the feel of a comfortable and relaxed country house. The antique-laden sitting-rooms are notably cosy, the greatly extended dining-room has been redecorated and the bar is entirely done out in leather. Some of the bedrooms are quite palatial.

Nearby Kylemore Abbey, 21 miles (35 km); Clifden, 12 miles (19 km); Lough Corrib; Connemara National Park.

Cashel, Connemara, Co Galway
Tel (095) 31001 **Fax** 31077
Location 42 miles (67 km) NW of Galway, 3 miles (5 km) S off N59; on seashore with ample car parking
Food & drink full breakfast, snack lunch, dinner; full licence
Prices B&B IR£46-IR£60; dinner IR£26-IR£28
Rooms 16 double, 3 single, 13 mini-suites; all with bath and shower; all have central heating, phone, hairdrier, TV
Facilities 2 sitting-rooms, TV room, library, bar, dining-room; tennis, private beach, boat, horse-riding
Credit cards AE, MC, V
Children accepted over 5
Disabled access easy; several ground-floor bedrooms
Pets not accepted in public rooms **Closed** never
Proprietors Dermot and Kay McEvilly

Country house hotel, Letterfrack

Rosleague Manor

The Georgian builder who erected this fine square house had a superb eye for scenery. But the brother-and-sister Foyles have just as good an eye for what makes a hotel. Paddy supervises the kichen, which specializes in Connemara lamb and seafood, and makes much use of home-grown fruit and vegetables. Anne takes charge of the front of house, including the large, elegant dining-room decked out with antiques and chandeliers. Some of the bedrooms are equally sumptuous.

Nearby Connemara National Park; Joyce Country.

Letterfrack, Connemara, Co Galway
Tel (095) 41101 **Fax** 41168
Location one mile (1.5 km) W of Letterfrack, on shores of Ballinakill Bay; in 30-acre grounds with ample car parking
Food & drink breakfast, light lunch, tea, dinner; full licence
Prices B&B IR£35-IR£55; dinner from IR£24
Rooms 22 double (5 suites), all with bath; all rooms have central heating, phone
Facilities 3 sitting-rooms, bar, dining-room, conservatory, billiard room
Credit cards AE, MC, V
Children accepted, but not specially catered for
Disabled ramp to public rooms and access at rear to ground-floor bedroom
Pets dogs accepted in bedrooms by arrangement
Closed Nov to Easter
Proprietors Patrick and Ann Foyle

Mayo

Country hotel, Crossmolina

Enniscoe House

Susan Kellett's family home, opened to guests since 1982, is a Georgian country house, set in wooded parkland on the shores of Lough Conn. The public rooms, with their open fires and family portraits, are lived-in and welcoming. There are canopy and four-poster beds in four of the period-style bedrooms. For those who prefer to cook for themselves there are sympathetically converted units around the old courtyard. Susan Kellett produces fine, unfussy Irish country house food (including Irish cheeses). There are good trout and salmon fishing facilities.

Nearby Moyne Abbey, 10 miles (16 km); Lough Conn.

Castlehill, near Crossmolina, Ballina, Co Mayo
Tel (096) 31112 **Fax** 31773
Location 12 miles (19 km) SW of Ballina, 2 miles (3 km) S of Crossmolina on Castlebar road; in parkland on 300-acre estate, with ample car parking
Food & drink breakfast, dinner; wine licence
Prices B&B IR£38-IR£60; DB&B IR£56-IR£72; reduced weekly, weekend and family rates
Rooms 3 double, 3 family rooms, all with bath; all rooms have central heating
Facilities sitting-room, dining-room; boating, fishing
Credit cards AE, MC, V
Children welcome
Disabled not suitable
Pets accepted only by special arrangement
Closed Oct to Mar
Proprietor Susan Kellett

Country house hotel, Newport

Newport House

Fishing is the preoccupation of most visitors to Newport House, though it is by no means the only attraction. The Georgian house is gracious and elegant, but the Thompsons encourage a caring, friendly attitude rather than super-slick professionalism in their staff. The bedrooms are spacious and individually decorated. Simplicity is the hallmark of the food, making full use of local Clew Bay seafood – and the kitchen does its own butchering as well as baking. Wines are Kieran's hobby.

Nearby Lough Conn; Joyce Country.

Newport, Co Mayo
Tel (098) 41222 **Fax** 41613
Location on edge of town, overlooking Newport river; ample car parking
Food & drink breakfast, light lunch, dinner; full licence
Prices B&B IR£44-IR£60; dinner IR£28
Rooms 14 double, 2 single, 2 four-poster bedrooms, all with bath; some rooms in annexes adjacent to main house; all rooms have phone
Facilities 2 sitting-rooms, bar, dining-room; fishing
Credit cards AE, DC, MC, V
Children accepted
Disabled access possible – some ground-floor bedrooms
Pets accepted, but not in main house or public rooms
Closed Oct to mid-Mar
Proprietors Kieran and Thelma Thompson

Sligo

Country house hotel, Riverstown

Coopershill

Anyone who worried that Brian O'Hara would have trouble following his mother Joan's act in running this delightful country house can relax. In the seven years since he took over with his wife Lindy, the style of the place has been subtly improved without interfering with its essential appeal.

The house, though not a pretty one by Georgian standards, has splendidly large rooms (including the bedrooms, most of which have four-poster or canopy beds), and is furnished virtually throughout with antiques; but it is emphatically a home, with no hotel-like formality – and there is the unusual bonus of a table-tennis room to keep children amused. The grounds are big enough not only to afford complete seclusion, but also to accommodate a river on which there is boating, coarse and game fishing.

Lindy cooks honest country dinners based on English and Irish dishes, entirely in harmony with the nature of the place, while Brian knowledgeably organizes the cellar.

Nearby Sligo, 10 miles (16 km); Lough Arrow, Lough Gara.

Riverstown, Co Sligo
Tel (071) 65108 **Fax** 65466
Location 1 mile (1.5 km) W of Riverstown, off N4 Dublin-Sligo road; in large garden on 500-acre estate, with ample car parking
Food & drink full breakfast, dinner, light or packed lunch; restaurant licence
Prices B&B IR£40-IR£42; dinner IR£21; reductions for 3 or more nights; 50% reduction for children under 12 sharing with parents
Rooms 7 double, 5 with bath, one with separate bath, one with shower; one family room with bath; all rooms have tea/coffee kit
Facilities sitting-room, dining-room; boating, fishing
Credit cards DC, MC, V
Children welcome if well behaved
Disabled no access
Pets welcome if well behaved, but not allowed in public rooms or bedrooms
Closed Nov to mid-Mar
Proprietors Brian and Lindy O'Hara

Reporting to the guides

Please write and tell us about your experiences of small hotels, guest-houses and inns, whether good or bad, whether listed in this edition or not. As well as hotels in Britain and Ireland, we are interested in hotels in France, Italy, Spain, Austria, Germany and Switzerland. We assume that reporters have no objections to our publishing their views unpaid, either verbatim or in edited form.

Readers whose reports prove particularly helpful may be invited to join our Reporters' Register; this means that you receive a free copy of the new edition of the guide in the winter, preceded by a newsletter in the autumn and followed by another in the spring. In return, we hope to receive further reports.

Register members who report regularly and reliably may be invited to join our Travellers' Panel. Members give us notice of their own travel plans; we suggest hotels that they might inspect, and contribute to the cost of accommodation.

The address to write to is:

Chris Gill,
Editor, *Charming Small Hotel Guides*,
The Old Forge,
Norton St Philip,
Bath, BA3 6LW,
England.

Checklist
Please use a separate sheet of paper for each report; include your name and address on each report.

Your reports will be received with particular pleasure if they are typed, and if they are organized under the following headings:

Name of establishment
Town or village it is in, or nearest
Full address, including post code
Date and duration of visit
The building and setting
The public rooms
The bedrooms and bathrooms
Comfort (chairs, beds, heat, light, hot water)
Standards of maintenance and housekeeping
Atmosphere, welcome and service
Food
Value for money

Index of hotel names

In this index, hotels are arranged in order of the most distinctive part of their name; other parts of the name are also given, except that very common prefixes such as 'Hotel' and 'The' are omitted.

Index of hotel names

Index of hotel names

Index of hotel locations

In this index, hotels are arranged by the name of the city, town or village they are in or near. Where a hotel is located in a very small place, it may be under a larger nearby place.

Index of hotel locations

Index of hotel locations